Memory**Fitness**

A GUIDE FOR SUCCESSFUL AGING

Gilles O. Einstein and Mark A. McDaniel

Yale University Press   New Haven and London

Designed by Sonia Shannon.
Set in Adobe Garamond and Gill Sans types by The Composing
Room of Michigan, Inc.
Printed in the United States of America by R. R. Donnelley &
Sons.

Library of Congress Cataloging-in-Publication Data

Einstein, Gilles O., 1950–
    Memory fitness : a guide for successful aging / Gilles O.
Einstein and Mark A. McDaniel.
        p.   cm.
    Includes bibliographical references and index.
    ISBN 0-300-10023-X (cloth : alk. paper) —
ISBN 0-300-10570-3 (pbk. : alk. paper)
    1. Memory disorders in old age—Prevention—Popular
works.   2. Memory—Popular works.   3. Brain—Aging—
Popular works.   I. McDaniel, Mark A.   II. Title.
RC394.M46E36 2004
618.97'684—dc22

                                        2004000254

A catalogue record for this book is available from the British
Library.

The paper in this book meets the guidelines for permanence and
durability of the Committee on Production Guidelines for Book
Longevity of the Council on Library Resources.

10 9 8 7 6 5 4 3 2

We thank our parents, Charline and Ernst Einstein and Thelma and Ernest McDaniel, who taught us the value of determination and the rewards of learning. We also warmly thank Patty, Julie, and Alex and Lynn, Austin, Jesse, Leda, Grant, and Tyler, who keep teaching us the importance of love and family. They continually help us balance the seriousness of our work with the humor of life.

Contents

Preface

Slowly but surely the world is experiencing a demographic shift, with older adults constituting the most rapidly growing segment of the population. The importance and consequences of this demographic shift were captured in the 1992 Human Capital Initiative, a document written by representatives from nearly seventy psychological organizations and sponsored in part by the National Institutes of Health for the purpose of developing this nation's behavioral science agenda. One of the six target areas is the aging society, and the initiative sounded a clarion call for more research into how to make the older years productive. This proposed scientific agenda sparked an explosion of research on cognitive functioning and memory that bears directly on concerns of aging and older adults. The past ten years have witnessed exciting discoveries documenting the positive effects of physical exercise, mental exercise, and nutritional brain supplements on memory performance, and the research on Alzheimer's disease is expanding dramatically. The results appear in scientific journals but are not quickly and comprehensively accessible to the general public. Our understanding of how to make the older years more fruitful is rapidly developing. We believe this important information can be useful for helping to stem and possibly even reverse the declines in memory that most people experience as they get older.

Over the past several years, through lectures to groups and classes for older adults, as well as discussions with our research participants, we discovered that many middle-aged and older adults are eager to learn more about how aging affects memory. They are also eager to find out what they can do to prevent and control memory loss. We wrote this book in response to frequent requests for resources on this topic.

Many popular books on this subject provide simplistic and speculative prescriptions for improving memory. Some of them offer bold advice based on modest scientific evidence or, in some cases, no evidence at all. For instance, one book encourages readers to modify habits—such as wearing your watch upside down or brushing your teeth with your nondominant hand—to increase their ability to solve problems and sharpen thinking (*Brain Fitness*, p. 36). To the authors' knowledge, however, no published studies support a causal connection of this sort. Another book, *The Memory Cure*, claims that taking phosphatidylserine (PS) can cure age-related memory impairment. Examination of the scientific evidence (see Chapter 12) shows that PS can produce a modest increase on some memory tests for some people. But, in the authors' opinion, the scientific evidence falls far short of supporting PS as a memory cure. In some cases, books offer advice that runs counter to the scientific evidence. A common claim is that repeating information over to yourself is useful for remembering information. This common recommendation is not supported by an extensive experimental literature, which has demonstrated that rote rehearsal is not very effective for embedding information into long-term memory (see Chapter 6). In general, we were worried that some popular books were creating misleading impressions of the potential remedies for memory declines associated with aging.

It is very difficult today to discriminate fluff from substance when it comes to claims about various memory boosters and cures. For example, one infomercial has claimed that a nutritional substance improves not only concentration, learning, and memory but also your moods and marriage! These advertisements are often presented in a superficially compelling fashion, featuring emotional testimonials from enthusiastic and satisfied users. The problem is that these accounts are virtually useless in evaluating the effectiveness of any kind of treatment. Even if one assumes that these are honest testimonials, the scientific truth is that people's subjective impressions of treatments are highly influenced by their expectations. Indeed, studies commonly show that users rate placebos as highly effective in treating disorders even though they have absolutely no biological effects. If, for example, you put tiny bits of cat food in capsules and advertised them as memory boosters, a surprisingly large number of users would come to believe that these capsules were very effective in producing their advertised effects. Clearly, the only proper way to evaluate the effectiveness of supplements is with scientifically controlled experiments that include proper control groups (see Chapter 12). One of the goals of this book is to help you develop a more discerning approach to evaluating the claims you hear.

Our coverage of the effects of aging on memory and our recommendations for improving memory are grounded in accepted scientific evidence. Indeed, we have not let our eyeballs stray from the data! Our goal has been to translate the latest findings into an understandable and usable book. Based on questions audiences posed at our community talks and those generated from surveys we conducted with middle-aged and older adults, we developed four main areas that people identified as relevant and important to their understanding of memory. Our book explores each of those areas.

The first five chapters of this book address the fact that many adults have an incomplete or inaccurate understanding of memory. These chapters provide not only an overview of how memory works and how memory processes change with age but also important recommendations for improving memory. We believe that once you understand the basic principles of memory functioning, creating solutions to memory challenges is often a matter of common sense.

Chapters 6 through 8 present techniques and strategies for improving memory in frequently encountered and often challenging situations. If you have difficulty remembering names, remembering what you've read in the newspaper, or remembering to take medications, turn to these three chapters for help.

Chapters 9 through 12 suggest lifestyle adjustments to improve

your mental powers and memory. These chapters offer recommendations regarding physical and mental exercise, and we discuss the negative effects of stress and anxiety on memory. We also comprehensively review and evaluate the scientific evidence regarding the effects
of so-called brain nutrients on memory.

Finally, Chapter 13 explores Alzheimer's disease and its devastating consequences. People are often overly fearful that the decline in
memory that normally accompanies age is a sign of Alzheimer's disease. This last chapter provides an up-to-date description of the
symptoms of the disease and the diagnostic procedures for identifying it. We also discuss possible causes of Alzheimer's and current recommendations for treatment.

Someday, it is hoped, science will reveal simple "cures" for the
memory problems that nearly everyone experiences with advancing
age. Indeed, many assume that scientists will come up with the "Via-
gra" for memory problems. We believe this is an unreasonable expectation. Because memory is a complex system, remedies for the negative effects of aging cannot be reduced to a single, or even several,
simple solutions. This book provides a complete approach to understanding the different facets of aging and memory. The good news is
that individuals can choose from a rich array of approaches and techniques—which includes recognizing situations in which memory is
likely to fail, using effective memory strategies, and making lifestyle
adjustments—to ameliorate the normal memory loss that occurs
with age. We encourage you to make the effort to translate the general
principles in this book into specific techniques that work for you.

Acknowledgments

A project of this scope owes much to many. From helping us develop our initial ideas for the book to the production of the final manuscript, we benefited from the wise and generous help of a multitude of colleagues and friends. Stacey Burr, Karen Dean, Patty Einstein, Jody Gatten, Judy Grisel, Kathie Insel, Carol Kooistra, Ernest McDaniel, Keith McDaniel, Lynn McDaniel, Thelma McDaniel, Ray Moss, Lib Nanney, Frank Powell, Steve Richardson, Peggy Sauvain, and David Spear read and commented on earlier drafts of this book and alerted us to interesting material and stories. Nancy Chavez, Donna Greene, Dave Hochstein, and Karissa King helped us immensely in putting together the final version of the manuscript. We thank Tim Salthouse and Chris Hertzog for their insightful and constructive comments on the entire book. We also owe a deep debt of gratitude to Susan Arrellano and David Myers, who, early on, gave us guidance and encouraged us to pursue this project. From Erin Carter, who guided us through the entire process, to Nancy Moore, who gently but expertly improved the crispness and felicity of our writing, we deeply appreciate the help of everyone at Yale University Press. This work would not have been possible without substantial support from our colleges, Furman University and the University of New Mexico, and we thank them for granting us sabbaticals that were instrumental in the writing of this book.

Although the final responsibility for the clarity and wisdom of our writing is ours, we owe much to our teachers. We especially thank Bill Battig, Lyle Bourne, Burt Cohen, Norm Henderson, Steve Maier, and Peter Polson, who introduced us to the excitement of science, the mysteries of memory, and the importance and art of communicating applications of scientific discoveries to the general public.

Most of all we thank those older people we have met through our research projects, talks, and friendships for showing us that grace, beauty, inquisitiveness, and lifelong learning are realistic expectations of older adulthood.

CHAPTER ONE

Thanks for the Memories

AGING AND REMEMBERING

The sign in St. James Pharmacy, appropriately located on St. James Place, promised "prescription services, reliability, Breyer's ice cream, and prompt delivery." But owner "Doc" James Schimmenti gave much more than the advertisement promised. Fastidiously dressed in a white jacket with a white-sleeved dress shirt, bow tie, and dark pants, Doc was neighborhood nurse and doctor combined. If one of us scraped a knee, he would bandage the cut. If someone got a splinter, he would extract it. When he printed prescription labels, he put his home number on the front so that his customers could call at any hour if they had a question or needed a refill. He was known to deliver as far away as Garden City and as late as 3 a.m. Even on holidays, he was always available. He was so beloved in our neighborhood that we affectionately joked that the store was named for him—St. James—rather than the street on which it stood.

—Doris Kearns Goodwin, *Wait Till Next Year: A Memoir*

I t is likely that Doris Kearns Goodwin had many poignant moments as she thought about the people and events that shaped her early life. Recounting her younger years stimulated her to remember her past, which is something we all do quite often. In addition to being powerful and incredibly important for functioning every day, memory adds a great deal of pleasure to our lives. We spend a good bit of time just sitting around and remembering. When we get together with family and friends, we often have enjoyable times discussing past reunions and vacations, touching moments, stupid things we did, interesting movies, old jokes, and so on. Whenever the authors of this book get together, we have many laughs discussing some of the crazy things we have done over the twenty-nine years that we've known each other. We also experience a good deal of joy and other emotions from retrieving memories when we are alone. It's fun for people to reminisce and think about their first kiss, their first day of school, their last kiss, and so on. Memories bring a large measure of warmth and happiness to our lives.

The Importance of Memory

If we think about it even minimally, it is obvious that memory is one of our most important capacities. Just think of what your life would be like without it. You wouldn't know how to prepare a meal, how to shop for food, or, for that matter, how to get to the grocery store. Without the ability to retain vocabulary and the rules of grammar, you couldn't communicate with others. Life as we know it would be impossible without memory. Indeed, every day would be a *completely* new day.

Unfortunately, an estimated four million Americans do know what life is like without memory. They have Alzheimer's disease, the fourth leading cause of death in older adults (after heart disease, cancer, and stroke).[1] The onset of this pernicious disease is marked by the minor memory lapses all of us experience, such as problems remembering the plot of a movie or remembering an appointment. Eventually, however, individuals with Alzheimer's are unable to store new information in memory. Ultimately, they can't retain or recall long-standing and cherished information such as who their children are. This disease also affects personality and, in the later stages, the ability to function independently. The final chapter of this book discusses Alzheimer's disease in great detail.

People, especially older people, tend to be critical of their own ability to remember. They view memory as weak and fragile. The fact that we forget things annoys us, but we rarely acknowledge the vast archive of information we have successfully stored and can recall. Think of your knowledge of the town where you live; your mental maps enable you to easily get where you want to go. Think of all the faces you recognize daily, including those of your family, your friends, actors, and politicians. Think of your vocabulary—the thousands of words you are able to use. Think of all the odors and tastes you can identify. Now try remembering the number of windows that were on the front of the house you lived in when you were a child. Most people can do this, by generating a mental image of the house and then actually counting the number of windows in that image. Memory is remarkable, enabling us to store both important information and trivial facts. For example, many of you probably remember the name of Roy Rogers' horse. If you didn't remember it outright, you would probably be able to pick it from among the following five possibilities: Bullet, Trigger, Henry, Dale, and Fury. (For those of you who weren't fans of Roy Rogers, the answer is "Trigger.")

Unfortunately, as we age, this remarkable ability tends to decline. This chapter presents an overview of how aging affects memory as well as two very different views on what causes the memory losses typically observed with advancing age.

How Does Aging Affect Memory?

This question is becoming ever more important as the demographics of the United States and, indeed, the world are changing. The fastest growing segment of the world's population is older adults, especially those over 80. In 1850, for example, there were over four times as

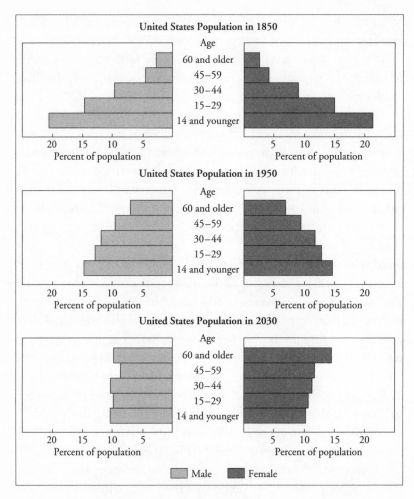

Figure 1.1 Demographic changes in the U.S. population for 1850, 1950, and 2030.

many people under 14 as there were people over 60 (Figure 1.1).[2] The pendulum has gradually swung in the other direction, however, and it is predicted that by the year 2030 there will be more people over age 60 than under age 14. These proportions reflect the fact that people are now living longer and having fewer children.

This chapter provides a general answer to the question of how aging affects memory, and Chapter 2 presents a more complete explanation. The broad answer is that many types of memories show some

level of age-related decline. A typical procedure that is used to study
the effects of aging on memory is shown below.

Learn Pairs of Words
dog—table
grass—wall
    .
    .

Delay Interval
Test Memory

    .
    .

dog—
grass—

In this procedure, people of various ages are brought to a laboratory
and asked to learn a list of word pairs. There might be twenty or thirty
word pairs in a list, and each pair might be presented for about five
seconds. After a delay of a minute or so, memory is tested by presenting the participants with the first member of the pair and asking them
to recall the second member. The results of six studies that have used
this basic procedure consistently demonstrate age-related declines on
this kind of memory task (Figure 1.2), suggesting that people in their
60s and 70s remember around 65 to 75 percent of what most 20-
year-olds remember on this kind of task.[3]

It is important to know that several factors qualify the relation between aging and memory. First, as mentioned earlier, the degree to
which age-related declines are evident depends on the kind of memory task. As discussed in Chapter 2, on some memory tasks older people actually have better memory than younger people. Second, when
comparing younger and older people, the distributions of scores for
these two populations tend to overlap. That is, some older subjects
score better than many younger subjects on these memory tasks.
Third, there is great variability in how aging affects memory. Some
people show only small changes in memory as they get older, whereas
others show more pronounced effects.[4]

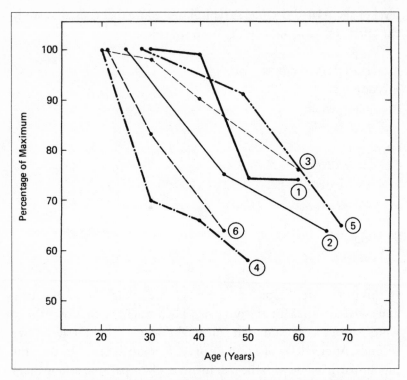

Figure 1.2 Age-related declines as measured in 6 studies. *Note:* Each line (and circled number) represents a different experiment conducted by different researchers. The scores for each experiment are expressed as a percentage of the recall obtained by the youngest group. Thus, for example, 70-year-old participants remembered about 65 percent or so of what the 20-year-old participants remembered. *Source:* Adapted from Salthouse (1982).

What Produces Age-Related Memory Declines?

A conversation with an older friend a while back revealed that he had "given up" when it came to trying to learn anything because "old people simply can't learn and remember things." Underlying his thinking is the assumption that aging leads to fundamental biological deterioration and this interferes with the storage and retrieval of memories. But it is also important to note that his negative attitude about the effects of aging, which is common in our culture, led him to abandon active learning strategies—this alone can cause major problems in remembering.

Perhaps the most central question in the area of aging and memory is what produces age-related declines in memory. Among the many individual theories, two general classes of answers can be identified and explored. One class of theories assumes that age-related memory deficits are related to declines associated with the nervous system. That is, that the age-related changes in memory are an inevitable result of biological aging. Another class focuses on social or cultural factors that might lead older adults to engage in poor learning strategies.

Biological Explanation

The brain is made up of neurons that conduct electrical signals; these neurons process information. The actions of these neurons regulate our breathing; create our vivid perceptual experiences; enable us to have emotions, memories, and thoughts; and, in short, create who we are. We are born with perhaps as many as 100 billion neurons, a number that declines with age as neurons die. Interestingly, more neurons are lost during fetal and neonatal development than at any other period of life. Until recently, the belief was that large-scale and global loss of neurons occur with normal aging. Indeed, microscopic examinations of older brains often revealed accumulations of amyloid plaques (also called neuritic or senile plaques), which are clumps of dead neurons clustered around molecules of amyloid protein. Today, researchers believe that these earlier pronouncements overestimated the neuronal loss that occurs with *normal* aging. The earlier studies tended to use less precise measurement techniques and often included diseased brains (i.e., those with Alzheimer's disease), factors that surely affected cell counts. Indeed, today's thinking is that amyloid plaques are highly prevalent in the brains of people with Alzheimer's but are not generally characteristic of people who are aging normally. In addition, it is now thought that typical age-related declines in brain weight and volume are relatively moderate in nature. The best estimates are that we lose about 2 percent of our brain weight and volume each decade of our lives.[5]

More pronounced changes, however, do occur in the brain as we get older. The belief today is that aging causes structural and functional changes in neurons rather than widespread neuronal loss, and that these changes compromise the efficacy of neuronal functioning and hence mental processing. These alterations in the brain include: general shrinkage of neurons; losses in myelination (fatty cells that surround many neurons), which slow the speed of neural impulses; reduction in the number of connections among neurons, which is thought to be important for learning and memory; decreased availability of certain neurotransmitters (these allow communication among neurons) in brain circuits involved in learning and memory; and reduced blood flow in the brain.[6]

These age-related changes in neurons do not occur uniformly throughout the brain. Rather, some areas are affected more than others. For example, aging seems to have little effect on the hypothalamus, the center that controls hunger and thirst, but it has large effects on the prefrontal cortex. The prefrontal area is thought to be involved in attention and in maintaining the activation of representations in consciousness (e.g., in keeping the thought to take your medication activated in consciousness while carrying on a conversation). This is the area of the brain that is destroyed in a prefrontal lobotomy, a fairly popular procedure in the 1940s and 1950s that was used to control aggression and other unmanageable behaviors. Of course, loss of function in the prefrontal areas can noticeably affect the performance of the memory system.[7]

This rather pessimistic analysis of aging suggests that memory declines are an inevitable result of the deterioration of the brain. Before you get too depressed, however, you should realize that many studies have *not* shown a clear relationship between measures of age-related brain pathology and intellectual functioning. In fact, research shows that some people with rather small brains (owing to injury or disease) are capable of remarkable intellectual feats. One of the long-held principles of neuroscience was that mammalian brains cannot generate new neurons. There is now some evidence, however, that the brain can grow new neurons, even in older adulthood. Also, some researchers have found some growth of connections among neurons in people in their early 70s. But it is not clear at this point the extent to which these generative processes can mitigate some of the neuronal damage that occurs with age.[8]

Social Cognitive Explanation

A very different explanation for age-related memory declines is that the changes one sees are the result of expectations concerning the effects of aging. A very strong assumption in American society is that memory suffers with age. Surveys show that older people overestimate their memory problems and clearly see their memories as not as good as they once were. Indeed, the view that older adults are forgetful is so widespread and accepted that it is the basis of many jokes. Consider, for example, the following funny story:

Two friends were talking at one end of the dinner table while their wives were talking at the other end.

The first man said to the other, "I attended a wonderful memory clinic last week. The professor was energetic. And, we learned the latest memory techniques for how to remember names, appointments, telephone numbers, and a variety of other difficult things. It was terrific!"

His friend was intrigued and responded, "That sounds great. What was the name of the clinic?"

The first man replied, "The name? Huh." He stammered a while and then asked, "What is the name of that flower? It has long prickly stems and we give bouquets of them to our wives on special occasions."

The friend answered, "A rose?"

The first man then responded, "Yeah, a rose." He then turned to his wife and asked, "Rose, what was the name of that memory clinic?"

This social cognitive theory of aging, then, posits that the stereotypes of aging create expectations of poor memory in older adults (Figure 1.3). In turn, these expectations encourage older adults not to

> Negative stereotypes of aging
> Expectations of poorer memory
> Decreased use of active strategies
> Poorer recall

Figure 1.3 Levy and Langer's view of how negative stereotypes about aging can affect memory.

actively process information (i.e., to use passive and poor encoding strategies), a passive approach to learning that inevitably leads to poor memory. In essence, the view here is that self-fulfilling prophecies lead older adults to "give up" and "not put forth the effort" in a learning situation, and it is the failure to actively process information (as opposed to a biological decline in the ability to store new information) that causes the decline in memory.[9] If you think back to your high school and/or college days, you will remember that you studied when you wanted to remember information for a test. That is, rather than quickly reading an article, you reread it, highlighted it or took notes on it, and practiced recalling it. Thus, what seems today to be a loss of memory may actually be the failure or refusal to "study" the relevant material.

A study by Levy and Langer provides strong support for this view. They examined the relation between aging and memory in three different cultures. The authors assumed that in contrast to the negative stereotypes about aging in the American hearing culture, there are very different attitudes about aging among the American deaf population and among people from Mainland China. Specifically, in these latter two cultures, older adults are seen as wise and intelligent role models. Levy and Langer figured that if our attitudes about aging affect how we process and study information (and ultimately memory), then different relationships between aging and memory would be reflected across these three cultures.[10]

In the course of their experiment, Levy and Langer measured attitudes toward aging. One method of doing this was to ask partici-

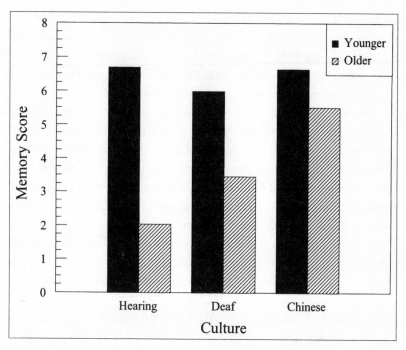

Figure 1.4 Memory scores from the Levy and Langer research—the higher the score, the better the memory.

pants to list five descriptions of older adults. As expected, they found more positive attitudes about aging in the Chinese and deaf cultures than in the American hearing culture. That is, when describing older adults, Chinese and deaf participants were more likely to use positive words (e.g., "friendly," "kind," "wise") than were American hearing participants, who tended to use more negative words (e.g., "slow," "forgetful," "frail"). Interestingly, the attitudes of older hearing Americans were almost as negative as those of younger Americans. During the course of their experiment, the authors also measured memory on four different tests. A composite memory score representing performance across all four memory tests is shown in Figure 1.4 (a constant was added to each score in order to more easily interpret the means). The interesting comparison is between the younger and older subjects in each culture. Higher scores indicate better memory. The results clearly show a large memory difference between younger and older participants in the hearing culture. The difference in memory performance between younger and older subjects was small in the deaf culture and almost nonexistent in the Chinese culture.

These intriguing results suggest that in the United States, part of the age-related differences in memory correlate with our attitudes about aging—at least in the hearing population. It should be noted that very little research has examined age differences across cultures. One paper, comparing memory performance across younger and older Anglophone and Chinese Canadians, does question the extent to which cultural biases can explain age-related memory differences. Other results, however, are consistent with the more general point that negative attitudes and expectations about the effects of aging on memory can affect memory performance in older adults. Rahal, Hasher, and Colcombe, for example, presented younger and older participants with a set of rather obscure trivia items (e.g., "It takes six hours to boil an ostrich egg"). After they presented each item, they told the participants whether it was true. Following the presentation of the entire set, they presented the items once again and then asked the participants to indicate which were true and which were false. Because this type of memory task typically demonstrates large age-related differences, these researchers wondered whether they could affect the results by varying the instructional emphasis. So, half the participants were repeatedly told that the purpose of the research was to test their memory ability (strong memory instructions) and the other half were more subtly informed that the research was designed to assess their ability to learn trivia items (weak memory instructions).[11]

By now, you might be able to guess their results. Across several experiments using the strong memory instructions, the younger participants showed substantially better memory than the older participants. With the weak memory instructions, no age-related differences were evident. One interpretation of these results is that strong memory instructions are threatening to older people, who in our culture believe that aging destroys the ability to remember and hence "shut down" or "give up" in terms of trying to use active learning strategies. When this threat isn't present, however, most older individuals are perfectly capable of actively processing material—successfully learning it and retaining it. Because most studies of memory use strong memory instructions, then, the results are skewed in that they tend to overestimate age-related differences in memory.

If we take these studies together, they suggest that memory loss that typically occurs with age is not an inevitable consequence of biological decline. Older adults with a pessimistic view of aging may be less likely to make the effort to process information, virtually ensuring poor memory.

Conclusion

Which of these views best explains the memory declines that accompany aging? Is this decline an inescapable result of losses in the nervous system or is it related to our attitudes about aging? At this point, it is impossible to fully answer this question—we need much more research on the topic. The answer isn't a simple one, and most likely both factors contribute to age-related memory declines. The evidence strongly indicates that biological changes in the brain accompany the aging process. But you can take steps to reduce or slow down these changes. Chapters 9 through 12 of this book provide you with information about these steps: as you will see, there is good evidence that mental activity and physical exercise can help. The second factor, negative attitudes about aging and memory, not only lowers expectations among the younger population but also undermines performance among the older population. What's more, research results make it abundantly clear that good learning strategies can improve memory—at any age! So, even if some decline in memory is caused by the aging of your biological system, be assured that you can take steps to improve your memory. Chapters 3 through 8 present strategies, techniques, and mental processes that will help you.

CHAPTER TWO

Overview of Memory Systems and Processes

THE EFFECTS OF AGING

A s a psychologist who studies memory, I am often struck by the variety of reactions my research elicits in people of different ages. When I am introduced at parties or gatherings as a memory psychologist, younger people typically respond with mild interest. In contrast, middle-aged and older people respond with keen interest. The same reaction occurs when I lecture to different age groups: younger people show some academic interest in the topic, whereas people over age 30 tend to show a much deeper and more personal interest.

Today's media are saturated with articles and news clips about how our ability to learn and remember declines with age. We are also bombarded with advertisements and infomercials touting the virtues of various kinds of memory cures. One result is that there is now a pervasive stereotype in our culture, among people of all ages, of older adults as forgetful. As we hear the jokes about aging and as we begin to notice our own occasional memory lapses, perhaps with increasing frequency, many of us start to develop the gnawing fear that we are starting to lose our memory.

With all that we hear today, it is very important to examine the facts about how aging affects memory. Based on a torrent of research on this topic over the past twenty years, this chapter presents an up-to-date and realistic view of how aging affects memory. It focuses on the aging process in healthy people, not in those who have suffered strokes or other kinds of diseases that affect memory (see Chapter 13, on Alzheimer's disease). An introduction to the basic theoretical underpinnings of memory, this chapter serves as a foundation for appreciating the complexities of aging and memory. However, if you are in a hurry to learn about strategies and lifestyle adjustments for improving memory, feel free to go directly to the later chapters.

Knowledge is power. You will find it reassuring to know that certain kinds of memory loss are normal with age. You will also be reassured to learn that only some kinds of memory capacities and processes are markedly affected by age. By understanding how your memory works and what abilities are most affected by age, you can develop strategies and alter your lifestyle and environment to minimize or avoid memory loss.

Understanding the basic processes of memory will also help those of you who do not have concerns about memory loss at this point. College-aged students, for example, quickly realize that they can improve their memory after understanding some basic principles and processes of memory. Because memory challenges are present for everyone, this understanding can help people of all ages improve memory.

An Analysis of Memory

Before the 1960s, when psychologists thought about memory they tended to think about a single memory store. Today, they think in terms of information being processed by different kinds of memory stores or systems. This chapter presents a current view of memory (Figure 2.1), giving you a basic understanding of these memory stores

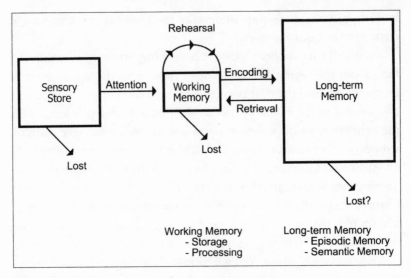

Figure 2.1 Overview of important memory stores and processes.

as well as highlighting important processes such as attention, rehearsal, and retrieval.[1] Also, current research results are provided to indicate how aging affects the processing of information through this system and the consequences of these effects for memory.

Sensory Information Stores

As Figure 2.1 shows, information first enters our system via one of the sensory information stores. There is a sensory information store for every sensory system that we have. That is, there is a visual sensory information store (also known as iconic memory), an auditory sensory information store (echoic memory), one for taste, one for touch, and so on. These stores have a very large capacity, holding everything that strikes our receptors with sufficient intensity. Imagine yourself at a cocktail party. All the people you can see in your peripheral vision would be stored in your visual sensory information store, and all the conversations (that are loud enough to activate your auditory receptors) would be stored in your auditory sensory information store. These memory stores are preattentive stores, which means that information is registered in these memory stores whether or not you are paying attention. Thus, whether or not you are really paying attention to this page, the words here are entering your visual sensory information store.

Teachers console themselves on their worst days by telling themselves that at least their lectures went as far as the sensory information store of their students. Even if students are daydreaming about their last meal or their weekend plans, the sight of teachers with their mouths moving enters into students' visual sensory information store, and the sounds of the words enter their auditory sensory information store. The only way students can keep teachers out of their sensory information store is by closing their eyes and putting their hands over their ears. Thankfully, most students are too polite to do this. The good news about sensory information stores is that they have a large capacity, but the bad news is that they have a fairly rapid decay rate. Information is held only briefly and is lost within about a half second to seconds.

Because we are rarely conscious of our sensory information stores, it is difficult to appreciate them without some further thought. To sensitize you to your visual sensory information store (called iconic memory because it holds icons or images), take a pencil and hold it between your forefinger and thumb and flip it up and down rapidly. You should see at least two blurred images of the pencil, giving it the illusion of a bendable rubber object. This demonstrates how your mind is able to take an image of one pencil and hold it in memory for a short amount of time while processing another image of the pencil. In order to have this visual experience, one image must last for a short time—evidence of brief visual memory. We are made aware of our auditory sensory information store (called echoic memory because it holds echoes) when someone says something to us when we are not paying attention. In these situations, most of us have had the experience of responding with a "What?" But before the person can repeat the message, we are able to retrieve the earlier statement and respond. In these situations, we are retrieving information from our auditory sensory information store.

Psychologists have developed sophisticated techniques for measuring the capacity and duration of sensory information stores, methods that are outside the scope of this book. What can be noted here, however, is that experiments using these methods have shown no or only small changes in the sensory information stores as a result of aging.[2]

Selective Attention

Another memory store in the system is working memory. Working memory is described in greater detail in the next section, but for now you can think of it as the memory store that includes the conscious portion of your mind and the part of your mind that actively processes information. One of the striking features of working memory is that it has a very small storage capacity. It holds between five and nine items; the average person can hold about seven items. Before you go on, you should try Demonstration 2.1, which illustrates the digit span task. The demonstration not only gives you an idea of the storage capacity of your working memory but also helps sensitize you to the nature of working memory.

Because sensory information stores have a large capacity and the storage capacity of working memory is small, we must select a portion of the information from the sensory information stores for further processing. In other words, it is impossible to process all the information that gets registered in these sensory information stores. That which is selected goes to working memory, and the nonselected information is lost from memory. Our ability to selectively attend to some sources of information and to ignore others is really quite remarkable. If you think of this in the context of a party, you will realize that you have an amazing ability to tune into one conversation and to tune the others out. As long as that one conversation is interesting, you will continue to focus in on it and to "hear" it. If the conversation gets boring, however, or you hear your name mentioned in another part of the room, you are able to tune into another discussion and to ignore the conversation in front of you. The information you select will be further processed in working memory, whereas the information you

Demonstration 2.1

Starting with the first set of numbers and then working your way down, read each set of numbers and then look away and try to repeat them out loud. Try to recall them in order, and keep going until you can no longer recall a set of items. The last set of numbers that you can correctly recall in order is a measure of the storage capacity of your working memory. In the laboratory, many different trials would be used to estimate an individual's working memory storage capacity.

Digit Span Capacity	Number Set
4	9264
5	43721
6	580426
7	2734981
8	83061425
9	395286740
10	6047326380

do not select receives only minimal processing and you will retain very little of it.

There is reliable evidence that older adults are *not as good* as younger adults at selectively attending to information. That is, they have a bit more difficulty in choosing an external signal and ignoring irrelevant information. For example, if older adults were asked to sort cards according to the number of the card, they would do this more slowly than would younger subjects. If you added irrelevant information to the cards (such as colors, symbols, etc.), this task would become proportionately more difficult for older adults. What the research suggests is that age attenuates our ability to focus our mental energy on one source of information while ignoring others, and that this is particularly true in complex situations—that is, ones in which a lot of irrelevant information is competing for our attention (e.g., having a conversation with other discussions going on in the background or reading a book while the television is on). One obvious solution to this problem is to remove potential distractions.[3]

Selective attention applies to distraction that comes from both external and internal events. For example, while reading a book, our minds often wander. Instead of thinking about the book, we are thinking about our last trip to the museum, how we might have been able to pay a little less for the car we just bought, or how we are looking forward to a social engagement. An important theory suggests that aging affects our sensitivity to internal as well as external distraction. According to this theory, aging disrupts an inhibitory mechanism that normally serves to block thoughts unrelated to the task at hand from occupying our attention or working memory. For example, while reading a book, you might find yourself thinking about the leaves on your lawn and how badly you need to rake it. Naturally, attention to your thoughts about raking the lawn will detract from your processing of the book and hence reduce your memory of the book. According to the theory, our inhibitory mechanism that normally serves to dampen or inhibit these off-task thoughts (e.g., raking the leaves) becomes less efficient with age. The consequence is that older adults have increased "off-task thoughts,"—their minds wander. This problem is thought to account for a wide variety of memory difficulties; the inability to concentrate interferes greatly with memory. This problem and some strategies for coping with it are covered in more detail in Chapter 4.[4]

Although a great deal of evidence indicates that older adults have difficulty ignoring irrelevant external information, some research suggests that they do not experience this problem in all situations. With the surge of research in recent years, there are inevitably contradictory views. Further research will yield a more refined understanding of this problem. Currently, however, most of the research supports the view that aging compromises our ability to filter out irrelevant distraction.[5]

Working Memory

As mentioned earlier, working memory includes the conscious aspects of your mind. This is where you rehearse and "work" on information in an effort to transfer that information into long-term memory. The idea is that by using active, deep, and elaborate processing strategies, you are more likely to be able to store information in long-term memory. Thinking deeply about the meaning of information, organizing information, and imaging information require a great deal of effort, but these efforts yield great benefits in making memories more durable. Chapter 6 talks much more extensively about how to use good processing strategies.

When testing your working memory capacity earlier, using Demonstration 2.1, you probably discovered that you could store between five and nine items. The average person is able to hold about seven items in working memory—it is no coincidence that telephone numbers consist of seven numbers. Information that enters working memory and that is not rehearsed will be retained there for under fifteen seconds. This is a very basic limitation of working memory that we have all experienced. Not long ago, I was in the kitchen looking up a number in the telephone directory. After finding it, I started to walk toward the telephone. At that point, my youngest daughter asked me a question about her homework. After answering it for her (at least to my satisfaction), I picked up the phone receiver and started to dial the number. I realized that I had forgotten it and had to look it up again. Another example is when we are introduced to someone but do not rehearse the person's name as we begin a conversation. Very shortly thereafter we realize that we can no longer remember the person's name, even though it has been a matter of seconds since we were introduced (see Chapter 7).

We can, however, maintain information in working memory for long periods of time by repeating or refreshing the information (by continually thinking about it). Of course, we are not able to continue rehearsing indefinitely, which leads to one very common problem with using memory. When information is maintained in working memory, we assume that we are retaining it. This is a natural assumption, because the information seems so clear and available at the time. But unless we keep refreshing (rehearsing) that information in working memory, it is likely to vanish. Memory plays a rather nasty trick on us. Rote rehearsal maintains information in working memory but is *not* effective for embedding information in long-term memory. This is a centrally important point and one for which there is much misunderstanding.

Aging and the Storage Capacity of Working Memory

Working memory is the active area of memory involved in holding current thoughts, evaluating them, and deciding on courses of action. In developing an accurate picture of the functioning of working memory and possible age differences in working memory, it is important to make a distinction between its storage capacity and its overall capacity. The storage capacity in working memory is measured by techniques such as the digit span task presented in Demonstration 2.1. Most research shows no or only small age differences in storage capacity, and also in the rate at which information is forgotten. Thus, it seems that younger and older people can hold about the same amount of information in working memory, and that information is forgotten at about the same rate.

Aging and the Overall Capacity of Working Memory

The overall capacity of working memory refers to how well or how quickly information can be manipulated within working memory while maintaining information in memory. We draw on this capacity quite often. For example, think of a complex reasoning task that requires you to hold several items of information while processing other sources of information and then requires combining both sources of information in order to come up with a conclusion (like solving a complex multiplication problem in your head). Think about what you have to do in planning or organizing your activities on any given day. These kinds of problems require you to maintain items in memory while evaluating them in the service of structuring a solution. In other words, they require you keep track of ideas and to juggle them rapidly. Our capacity to do this, as it turns out, is significantly affected by age.

One way to measure your overall capacity of working memory is by using Salthouse and Babcock's computation span task, shown below, which requires you to solve math problems while simultaneously remembering the last digit in each problem.

For this task, you need to perform arithmetic operations while holding the second number of each problem in memory. So, for the following example problem, read the equation out loud, note the second number, say the answer, and then move on to the next problem. When you are finished, try to recall the second number from each problem.

Example:
$4 + 2 = ?$
$5 - 3 = ?$
$9 - 6 = ?$
Recall the second number of each problem
2, 3, 6

Now try the problems in Demonstration 2.2.

In one study, fifty people from each of seven age groups were tested on four measures of working memory capacity (one of which was the computation span task in Demonstration 2.2). Figure 2.2 shows the results of this study. As you can see, working memory capacity is at its peak in our twenties and declines afterward.[6]

Working memory, when measured in this way, turns out to be a very important concept for psychologists. Performance on this type of measure correlates significantly with reading comprehension, learning how to spell, following directions, vocabulary learning, the quality of note taking, writing, reasoning, and complex learning (e.g., how much someone can learn from a typical course of study).[7] All these tasks seem to rely on working memory capacity.

Demonstration 2.2

As you go through the problems, use a piece of paper or card to block out each problem (line) after you have read it.
Problem 1
　　$2 + 7 =$
　　$8 + 1 =$
Recall the second numbers.

Problem 2
　　$3 + 4 =$
　　$6 - 3 =$
　　$1 + 8 =$
Recall the second numbers.

Problem 3
　　$6 + 2 =$
　　$4 + 5 =$
　　$7 - 4 =$
　　$2 - 1 =$
Recall the second numbers.

Many people believe that working memory capacity is highly dependent on the speed of one's mental operations. In fact, there is increasing evidence that cognitive slowing occurs, which is the slowing of the speed of mental operations with age. The idea is that our mental processing operations (such as adding two numbers, comparing one thing to another, making a decision) slow down as we get older and that this cognitive slowing naturally creates difficulties on tasks that measure overall working memory capacity. Try Demonstration 2.3. This pattern comparison test, developed by Salthouse and his colleagues, is thought to measure the basic speed of your mental operations. As can be seen in Figure 2.3, mental or processing speed (as

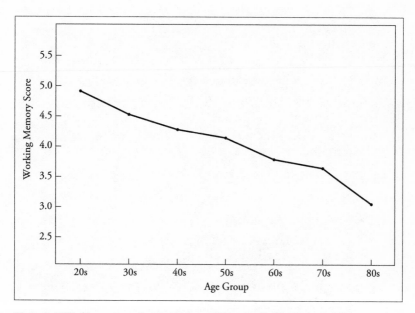

Figure 2.2 Working memory capacity measured across the life span.

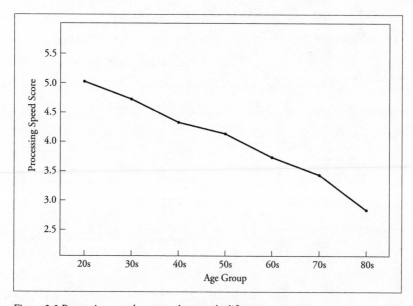

Figure 2.3 Processing speed measured across the life span.

Demonstration 2.3

In this test you will be asked to determine whether two patterns of lines are the same or different. If the two patterns are the *same*, write an S on the line between them. If they are *different*, write a D on the line. Try the following examples.

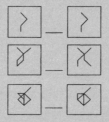

Now get someone to time you and see how many you can do in 10 seconds. This exercise should give you a good idea of how processing speed is measured. Do the left column and then the right.

measured by several tests including the pattern comparison test) slows down across the life span. Salthouse and his colleagues have shown that when people are tested for overall working memory capacity (Demonstration 2.2) and for processing speed (Demonstration 2.3), there is a strong correlation between these two measures. This result supports the idea that changes in processing speed may underlie the declines we tend to find in working memory capacity.[8]

Throughout this book the implications of cognitive slowing are discussed. For now, you should realize that good, active processing of information (done with working memory) is critical for good memory. As you get older, this processing takes more time, and it is more difficult to juggle a lot of information. Thus, as you age, you should give yourself more time for learning and take more notes when necessary.

Long-Term Memory

Information that is processed well will be transferred to long-term memory, where it may last a lifetime. As far as we know, long-term memory has unlimited capacity, and our heads do not "fill up." In fact, contrary to our experiences in school when we sometimes felt that our heads were full, the current view of memory is that the more you learn, the more you can learn. You can appreciate this by thinking about the difficulty of learning something that is completely new compared with the relative ease of learning something related to what you already know. When you have a good store of general background knowledge in an area, learning is relatively easy, which suggests that the more knowledge you have, the better you learn. Memory researchers make a distinction between two kinds of long-term memory: episodic memory and semantic memory.

Episodic Memory

Episodic memory is memory for personally experienced events, such as what you had for breakfast this morning or the contents of last

---

Phase 1: Learn a list of words
        dog, table, shoe, . . .

Phase 2: Test memory
        Free Recall—"Recall"
        Recognition—"Circle the old items"
                cat
                table
                dog
                chair
                milk
                dress
                show
                . . .
                . . .
                etc.

Figure 2.4 Recall versus recognition.

night's evening news or the gossip you heard yesterday. It is measured in the laboratory by having participants memorize something such as a list of words or a paragraph or a series of pictures. Figure 2.4 shows examples of episodic memory tasks. Note that the participants in this task do not learn anything new; they are already familiar with the words and the meaning of these words. Instead, this experiment requires them to learn an episode—to learn that these words are presented for study in this particular experiment. Once the words have been studied, memory can be tested in a variety of ways, two of which—recall and recognition—are shown in the figure. Notice that on the recall task, participants are given very few cues for retrieval except the general cue to begin attempting recall. With the recognition test, on the other hand, participants are given great cues for retrieval (the items themselves) and are asked simply to circle the old items from a list of items containing both old and new items. It turns out

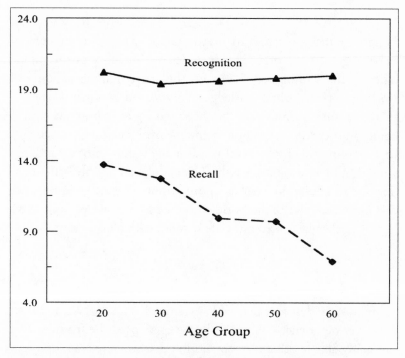

Figure 2.5 Memory performance for different age groups on recall and recognition tests.

age-related differences in performance depend critically on the specific memory test given. As Figure 2.5 shows, no or minimal age differences are observed on recognition tests, whereas fairly large age differences can be found on recall tests. The explanation that most people have for these kinds of results is that aging disrupts the ability to retrieve information from memory on one's own. Thus, as we get older, we need more and more help in finding information that is stored in memory. Chapter 5 provides guidelines for how to do this. The good news is that given the right kind of cues, older participants tend to perform as well as younger ones on these kinds of memory tests.[9]

Semantic Memory

Long-term memory also contains what is called semantic memory, or knowledge of the world. This includes our memory of the capital cities of the United States, our vocabulary, our understanding of world geography, our knowledge of facts, and so forth. Logically, then, semantic memory can be measured by testing knowledge. A common measure of semantic memory involves asking participants to determine which of several words is the synonym of a particular word. On these vocabulary tasks, older adults do reliably better than do younger adults. So, on a very positive note, there is good evidence that our knowledge of the world continues to increase as we age. Perhaps this is why we often associate wisdom with older age.

Forgetting

It would seem desirable to be able to remember all the events that we have ever experienced. All of us have experienced the frustration of not being able to remember something that we have read for a test, not being able to remember someone's name as we are making introductions, or not being able to remember the words to a song that we once knew. Although these lapses are annoying, it is probably the case that forgetting is adaptive. Imagine, for example, what life would be like if we did not forget. We would remember every meal that we have ever had, every conversation, every detail of every trip we have ever taken, all the television commercials we have ever watched. If that doesn't boggle the imagination, think of what the mind of a short-order cook, a waiter, or a telephone operator would be like! Although the capacity of long-term memory is thought to be unlimited, at some level it must, of necessity, be finite. Surely, remembering *all* the events of our lives (large and small) would tax our capacity. Even if we could store everything in memory, we probably would have difficulty accessing and prioritizing that information. For example, when we tried to retrieve our phone number, perhaps all our past phone numbers would come to mind. Even worse, when retrieving the name of our current lover, all our past lovers would come to mind. So a memory system that forgets is an adaptive mechanism—for the most part, it stores the more important events in our lives and allows the currently important information in our lives (our current phone number and lover) to be most accessible. Despite the initial appeal of being able to remember absolutely everything all the time, then, there would be costs. (Chapter 3 provides a fuller exploration of the nature of forgetting.)

Today, psychologists believe that forgetfulness is in large part the result of retrieval failure. That is, our inability to remember certain things is probably *not* due to the fact that information is no longer available in our long-term memory; rather, it is likely due to problems we have in accessing information that continues to reside in our long-term memory. For example, you might forget having attended a party, then remembered after someone else, say, a spouse or a friend, reminded you about the outfit you wore or the people who were there. By providing you with retrieval cues, your spouse or friend helped you to access this memory. Have you ever walked into the kitchen and forgotten your reason for going in there? Often, you can recover your memory by walking back to where you were before you walked into the kitchen. These examples illustrate the important point that retrieval cues are very helpful in recovering memories. This is central in overcoming age-related memory losses because older adults are thought to have particular difficulty retrieving information on their own.[10]

Conclusions

This chapter is an overview of how people process information and how aging affects the processing of information. Notice that the news is not all bad. As can be seen in Table 2.1, age differences are fairly large on some kinds of tasks but small or minimal on others, and often actual improvements with age occur in knowledge or semantic memory. In addition, even on the tasks in which normal aging tends to have negative effects, those effects are not dramatically large. Even on tests of episodic memory, which tend to show large age differ-

Table 2.1 Summary of Age Differences

Memory Store or Process	Age Effects
Sensory store	Small (if any)
Selective attention	Some age differences
Working memory	
Storage capacity	Small (if any)
Overall capacity	Fairly large
Long-term memory	
Episodic memory	Fairly large
Semantic memory	Older adults score better
Retrieval from long-term memory	Fairly large with no retrieval cues
	Small with retrieval cues

ences, older adults in their 60s and 70s typically remember about 70 percent of what 20-year-olds can remember. Also, as mentioned earlier, research clearly shows that older adults can benefit and improve their memory from the use of good, active processing strategies.

Finally, keep in mind that while it is clear that aging does affect memory, normal aging tends not to have catastrophic effects. We may become increasingly irritated by not being able to remember the specifics of the magazine article we read a week ago or whether or not we turned off the oven (and thus we might have to check it more often than we would like), but we tend not to forget the really important things in our lives, such as who our families are, our love for our families, and who we are.

CHAPTER THREE

Forgetting and Distorting Are Normal—At All Ages!

One of my friends, a professor, recently visited his under-graduate college for his twenty-fifth reunion. His alma mater is a relatively small liberal arts college in the Midwest. It is the kind of school that has small classes and where professors get to know their students and especially their majors. Professors at this college are very likely to talk about and take pride in their students who go on to graduate school and later become professors. At the reunion, my friend attended a department reception where he had the opportunity to talk with three faculty members who were teaching when he was a student. One professor had been his teacher for two courses, and this professor remembered him fondly and in fact recalled a good bit of information about him. Interestingly, the second professor, whom he had had for two classes, did not remember him at all. Perhaps even more interesting, the other professor, with whom he had taken no classes, remembered my friend but in addition "misremembered" that he had taken a course with him. This was not a vague or faint recollection that my friend had been in his class; this professor thought he remembered where my friend sat in the classroom, that he asked good questions, and that he was a good writer! Thus, one professor remembered him and did so accurately, one professor forgot him entirely, and the other appropriated one of the department's success stories as his own.

The collective memories of these three professors realistically capture the possible fates of our memories for events over time. Very often we correctly remember events as they occurred, but we often forget events or may distort them. True, the professors in this story happened to be a bit older and we are judging their memories for events that occurred twenty-five years earlier; however, these kinds of errors occur in younger people and with much shorter retention intervals as well—and in general they are symptomatic of how our memory system works.

Challenging the Videotape Recorder View of Memory

The goal of this chapter is to help you realize that memories are rarely, if ever, perfect and thus to give you an idea of what you can or should expect from your memory system. Because we forget so often, we tend to be harsh critics of our memory and to believe that we forget more often than others do. Perhaps we have these thoughts because we have an unrealistic expectation of memory. Many of us have the *videotape recorder view* of memory, believing that all events we experience are indelibly etched in memory exactly as they occurred. Several surveys have shown that the large majority of people, even highly educated people, believe that our detailed experiences are faithfully recorded in memory, that they are maintained there over time without distortion, and that when something is difficult to remember, only special retrieval techniques like hypnosis can be used to recover them.[1] For example, you might believe that your mind holds a record of the objects you passed on the drive you took through town this morning, even though you may feel you have very little recollection of it. Further, you might believe that with hypnosis you could "replay the tape" and even focus in with telescopic clarity on details like the license plate number of the car in front of you.

Current research makes it clear that this view is no longer tenable. The phenomenon of photographic memory, if it occurs at all, is extremely rare. In the few cases of adults who seem to have it, it takes a great deal of attention to form an image and the stored images are ephemeral. Research also argues against the view that we store photographically detailed images and can focus in on them with extraordinary retrieval techniques like hypnosis. Hypnosis tends to lower the inhibitions that prevent people from reporting events, so that under hypnosis they recall more events, including events that did not occur. So, if you subtract the false memories from the accurate ones, hypnotized people do no better and quite often worse than nonhypnotized people on recall tasks. Thus, instead of aiding memory, hypnosis simply makes people more willing to guess about what they might have experienced.[2]

Memories are not literal representations of events as they occurred. Our mind retains information in a fairly literal state for at most two seconds. We don't encode an event or store it for conscious access nearly as effectively as researchers once thought. Moreover, what is stored is subject to omissions, distortions, and additions. Just because an event is remembered, this does not mean that it is remembered accurately. Memories are dynamic entities that are susceptible not only to forgetting over time but also to bias and interference from information that occurs both before and after the event. In the words of two leading researchers in the area, "The metaphor of memory as the theater of the past implies that memory is not so much a vehicle for accessing static snapshots of the past as it truly 'was,' so much as it is a dynamic medium of experience imbued with drama and feeling and invigorated by the inherently human capacity for narrative creation. As a dynamic medium of experiencing the past, memory may be imperfect, reconstructive, and shaped by present expectancies, needs, and beliefs."[3]

The literature also clearly shows that these problems are somewhat more pronounced in older individuals. There is evidence that older adults have more difficulty retaining memories in general, encoding and remembering specific details (as opposed to the gist of an event), binding the event with the appropriate context (remembering where and when the event occurred), and remembering the source of an event (remembering who said what). Also, as we age we become more susceptible to the interfering influences of information from other sources. Whereas older adults do appear to be more susceptible to these kinds of errors, it is important to realize that it is difficult for *people of all ages* to accurately remember the details of events. Thus, after long delays between the occurrence of an event and recall, the memories of people in general should be regarded with caution.

So, what does this mean in terms of the likelihood that we will be able to remember the details of this weekend's dinner at our favorite restaurant two weeks from now? It means that we may end up forgetting or misremembering some of the conversation or forgetting or misremembering the entrée that we ordered. The constructive lesson to learn, then, about how memory works is that memory is not highly accurate after long delays. Thus, *if it is important to remember the details of an event,* you should take notes on that event as soon as you can. By being aware of the fragility of memory, you will have a better idea of what you can and cannot expect from it.

Information Is Forgotten Over Time

A fundamental feature of memory is that forgetting occurs over delay intervals. Although this point is obvious, it is worth illustrating with a typical example used to study memory. Assume that a group of participants is brought in to study a list of word pairs (e.g., dog—table, grass—wall). There might be twenty or thirty word pairs in a list, and each pair might be presented for about five seconds. After delays of various intervals, memory is tested by presenting participants with the first member of the pair and asking them to recall the second member. If memory is tested immediately after each individual pair is presented, then memory is virtually perfect. However, as the delay increases (from no delay to one minute to one hour to one day to one week), participants recall less and less information. The rate of forgetting depends on many variables but is thought to be steepest during the first twenty-four hours.

If people of different ages were brought into the laboratory and compared on the above task, age-related declines in memory would emerge. Both younger and older adults (65 years of age and older) would perform at 100 percent if they were tested immediately after presentation of each individual pair. On memory tests administered a minute or so after the entire list was presented, however, older adults would remember less than younger adults. Under these general conditions, 70-year-old adults are likely to remember about two-thirds of what 20-year-old adults remember (see Figure 1.2, in Chapter 1).[4]

Please note that when younger and older adults are compared in this book, averages are used. So, when groups of older and younger adults are tested, the average of the younger group is likely to be higher than the average of the older group. But it is important to remember that there will be overlap between the two distributions such that some of the older adults will remember more than some in the younger group.

We Do Not Encode All the Details of Events

An interesting and somewhat surprising feature of memory is that we typically do not encode (i.e., embed in memory) all the features of events. For example, even though we have seen a penny thousands of times, the average person has difficulty remembering the figures and words on a penny and their proper locations. You can check this for yourself by trying to select the correct penny in Demonstration 3.1.[5] If you are like most people, this will not be easy. (The answer is provided near the end of this section.)

The fact that identifying the correct penny is difficult for most of us suggests that our visual system does not faithfully create a detailed videotape representation of the world; rather, it seems that we encode features that are in some sense relevant to us at the time. Processing that a penny is copper, that it has a certain shape and size, and that it has a portrait of Lincoln on one side (or a picture of the Lincoln Memorial on the other side) is usually sufficient to identify a penny when counting change. In fact, in most cases it is unlikely that we would encode the images on the penny, and it would probably be fairly easy to slip someone a counterfeit penny as long as it had the

Demonstration 3.1

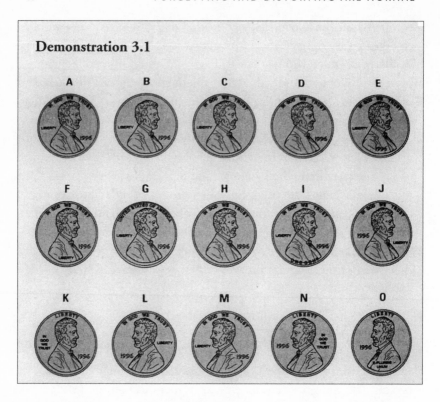

correct color, size, and shape. Rather than interpreting this as a short-coming of your processing system, you should see it as an adaptive way to deal with the multitude and complexity of information you are constantly exposed to.

Consistent with this phenomenon, Simons and Levin have found that people tend to have surprisingly little memory for the details of an event immediately after it occurs.[6] As shown in the panels of Figure 3.1, they had an experimenter approach an unsuspecting person on a college campus and ask him/her directions to another part of the campus. While they were talking, two confederates of the experimenter rudely interrupted the conversation by walking between the experimenter and the participant while carrying a large door. The interesting manipulation was that while they did this, the experimenter switched places with one of the people carrying the door. After the interruption, the new person took the place of the pre-

Figure 3.1 Scenes showing the participant giving directions to the original experimenter (panel a); the two confederates rudely interrupting (panel b); and the participant giving directions to the replacement experimenter (panel c); panel d shows the two experimenters who switched places.

vious experimenter and continued to ask about directions. Despite the fact that the original experimenter and the replacement experimenter did not look much alike (see panel d in Figure 3.1), fewer than half of the participants noticed the switch. On the basis of these results and others, Simons and Levin argue that unless there is a specific reason for precise encoding, people typically encode the general features of events. This is not to say that we do not ever encode the specific features of a person's face. If you were in an amorous mood and you were struck by the beauty of someone who happened to ask you directions, it is likely that you would encode and remember the person's facial features.

This tendency to encode the general features or gist of events is even more pronounced in older adults. Studies show that older adults are especially likely to falsely remember information that was not presented but that was consistent with a theme of an event. In addition, even when an event is presented several times, older adults are more likely to recall the implied (but not presented) item. With each new exposure younger adults reduce their false recall whereas older adults do not. This difficulty in noticing the details of an event and using them to update one's recall suggests an overreliance on encoding the gist (at the expense of the details) of an event. Perhaps this is a natural consequence of the slowing of cognitive processes that occurs with aging; given that encoding the details of a situation takes time as we get older, we may rely increasingly on shortcuts in appraising a situation.[7] (The correct penny is the first one.)

At this point in your reading, take a break and perform Demonstration 3.2 (adapted from research conducted by Roediger and McDermott).[8] It will not make a great deal of sense at this point; its purpose is explained at the end of the chapter.

Memories Are Constructions

A fundamental characteristic of memory that should be fairly obvious by now is that what is stored in memory is a representation of the event that occurred. It is not a literal copy, and the representation is affected by our knowledge of the world, our biases, and any inferences that we might make when we experience an event. Thus, quite often distortions in memory occur that reflect information supplied by the learner and not information from the event itself. These are called constructive processes, reflecting the idea that we construct a representation rather than copy information directly into memory.

In constructing representations we often rely on schemas. These are organized concepts that we have about the world. Thus, you probably have a schema for dogs (e.g., you know that most dogs have four legs, bark, walk, wag their tails, like to fetch sticks, and become endearing to their owners), and you use this knowledge to process or interpret events related to dogs. If you were reading a story about a dog owner taking her dog to a field with a stick in her hand, you would probably generate some expectations about what they were going to do in the park (e.g., that they were going to play a game in which she

Demonstration 3.2

Please go through the following phases *exactly* as instructed.

Phase 1. Read each of the following words to yourself. Think about each word for about 2 seconds and then go on to the next one. (*Actually, this works better if you can get someone to read them to you at the rate of one word every 2 seconds—so try that if you can.*) After reading the words, cover them up with a piece of paper, and keep them covered until you get to the last phase.

Slumber, tired, rest, night, dark, comfort, sound, eat, bed snore, dream, awake, drowsy

Phase 2. Do not look back at the words above, and solve the following arithmatic problems as quickly as possible. You can use a scrap piece of paper or write in the margins.

$48 + 37 =$ _____ $98 - 37 =$ _____
$36 + 24 =$ _____ $29 \times 3 =$ _____
$11 \times 12 =$ _____ $55 - 28 =$ _____

Phase 3. Now, try to recall as many words as you can from the list of words.

_____   _____
_____   _____
_____   _____
_____   _____
_____   _____
_____   _____
_____   _____

Phase 4. Now, go back circle the words you are positive that you read.

Phase 5. Compare your recall with the words in Phase 1 to see how many you recalled and whether you recalled any words that were *not* presented. Please return to reading the chapter. This demonstration is explained later in this chapter.

throws the stick and the dog retrieves it). These expectations could influence your processing and memory of the story.

As a consequence of living in this world, we have developed schemas for a variety of concepts and situations. For example, we have a restaurant schema that consists of events that typically occur when we go to a restaurant (initial greeting, seating, reading the menu and discussing the choices, ordering, eating, paying the bill, and leaving). You are also likely to have a fast-food restaurant schema that consists of a very different set of elements. Some people have developed a romance novel schema (boy meets girl, the couple goes through a blissful period, conflict arises, they stop talking, they work through the conflict, they live happily ever after). Schemas are very useful to us. They enable us to quickly process, organize, and anticipate situations that are familiar to us. But schemas can have a cost. Sometimes we overschematize, failing to differentiate between what we have inferred from our schema and what actually happened. The following two examples illustrate this point.

Baggett presented participants with several photographs to view.[9] Figure 3.2 shows simple line drawings of these photographs, which include: (1) a long-haired person walking to the barbershop, (2) a long-haired person entering the barbershop, (3) a long-haired person sitting in the barber's chair, and (4) a short-haired person walking out of the barbershop. Baggett never presented a picture of the barber cutting the person's hair, yet this is something that nearly all the participants thought about during the presentation of the pictures. Baggett was interested in whether participants would erroneously remember a picture of the barber cutting the hair of this person. The participants who were tested immediately were very adept at indicating that they had not seen that specific image. The majority of the other participants, who were tested after a one-week delay, falsely thought they had seen a picture of the barber cutting the person's hair. Baggett's interpretation is that immediately after an event, people are very good at distinguishing between what actually occurred and inferences they made while processing the event. After a delay, however, inferences become part of the memory representation, and it is very

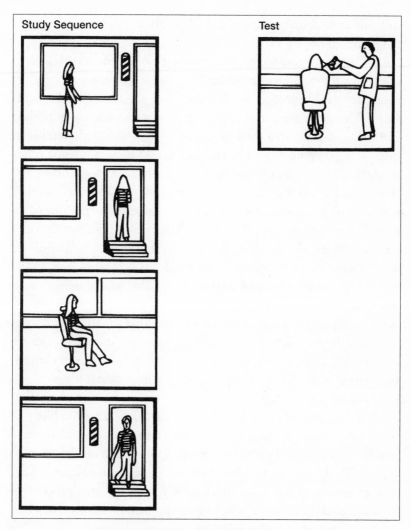

Figure 3.2 Pictures used by Baggett to test whether people can distinguish between what they see and what they infer. *Source:* Adapted from Schmolck, Buffalo, and Squire (2000).

difficult to distinguish what was thought about from what was actually seen.

This type of recall error is not always caused by long delays. In one study, for example, Brewer and Treyens asked people to wait in a room that had been decorated to look like a graduate student's office.[10] The room contained a typewriter (this research was published in 1981), a table with a coffeepot, a desk along with desk items, and other things. Some items not typically found in an academic office were there (e.g., a skull) and some that are typically found were *not* there (e.g., books). Participants were left in the room for about thirty-five seconds and asked to wait while the experimenter performed an errand. Participants were then immediately taken to another room and asked to recall everything they could about the room. The results were interesting: participants often recalled objects that were in the room, but nearly one-third incorrectly recalled seeing books there. So, even after being in the room only a minute earlier, many participants confused what they expected to see in that situation with what they actually saw. Results like these suggest that our memories are constructions based not only on what occurs, but also on our conceptual understanding of what typically occurs in certain settings.

Because older adults remember less in general and remember fewer details in particular, it is thought that they are more likely to rely on their knowledge, biases, and perhaps even wishes in remembering. This may also occur because of acuity problems that tend to occur with age. As we get older, for example, it becomes more difficult to hear, and we may therefore rely more on our preexisting knowledge to fill in the gaps.[11] In general, then, it is likely that older adults are more susceptible to overreliance on schemas.

Binding the Context with the Event: Remembering the Source of a Memory

An important function of memory is to bind or associate events that are experienced with the context in which they occur. In many cases it is important to remember not only what we heard but also who said it and when and where it was heard. For example, we may hear that a particular investment is sound, but it is critical that we also remember who made the recommendation (was it a stockbroker or was it our neighbor?).

Studies clearly show that older adults have greater difficulty remembering the source of acquired information.[12] For example, if people are presented with a set of words to learn and half of the words are spoken by a male and half by a female, older adults will have more difficulty remembering who said which word, even when they remember what was said.

In addition to being less likely to accurately report who presented information, older adults have more difficulty remembering where and at what time the information was given. In one study by McIntyre and Craik, for example, younger and older participants were taught "made-up facts" about public personalities (e.g., "Bob Hope's father was a fireman"). A week later, the participants were given a general knowledge test and asked questions like "What did Bob Hope's father do for a living?" and when and where they had first learned the information. Interestingly, the researchers found that older adults were likely to remember the "fact" from the previous week but were especially likely (relative to younger adults) to misattribute the source of that information. That is, older adults were very likely to believe that Bob Hope's father was a fireman but to forget that they had learned that during the previous week's session and instead misattribute their knowledge to the newspaper, television, or some other source outside the experiment. Other studies have found similar results.[13]

On an encouraging note, research does show that older adults can remember the source of information if they attend to it at the time they've learned it. Naveh-Benjamin and Craik, for example, found that when older adults knew that the source of information would be needed on a later memory test, they focused on it and remembered it well—in some cases as well as younger adults.[14] Importantly, then, if you need to remember the source of information, pay special attention to where it came from or who said it. If it is critically important to remember the source of a message, then, write it down.

Memories Are Highly Susceptible to Interference from Other Information

Researchers have learned in recent years that memory is very susceptible to misinformation from outside sources. Thus, after an event occurs, related events that we see or hear about can modify the memory of the original event. As an example, consider an experiment by Belli in which participants were shown a series of slides of a staged car accident where a Toyota came to a corner with a stop sign, turned, and hit a pedestrian. After a delay, participants were asked questions about the accident and some were exposed to false information about the accident. Specifically, participants in the experimental group were asked whether or not another car had passed the Toyota when it was at the yield sign. The attempt here was to see whether the presentation of false information (a yield sign instead of a stop sign) in the post-event questioning could alter memory of the original event. After another delay, participants were tested for memory about whether the original traffic marker was a stop or a yield sign. Depending on the experiment, the participants who were exposed to misinformation were 20 to 40 percent more likely to falsely remember that it was a yield sign. It appears that when memories become somewhat fuzzy after a delay, we are very willing to accept other information and create a blended memory, a mix of what was originally experienced as well as what was seen and heard after the event.[15]

Zaragoza and Mitchell have reported similar results. They found that many participants very confidently remembered witnessing *suggested* events after having watched a video of a burglary. Interestingly, the researchers also found that this misinformation effect was especially pronounced after repeated exposure to the misleading suggestions. These results are alarming because witnesses to dramatic events are sometimes questioned repeatedly about those events later on. These interrogations provide numerous opportunities for implanting new, and possibly false, information in memory. Thus, after a sufficient amount of time has passed, it is very difficult to evaluate the accuracy of a memory. It is not surprising that the National Institute of Justice, in a set of guidelines published in 1999, encourages witnesses to "avoid contact with the media or exposure to media accounts" and to "instruct the witness to avoid discussing details of the incident with other potential witnesses" in order to obtain more accurate information. Given the age-related declines in linking events with their contexts, it should not be surprising that older adults are more susceptible to accepting misinformation than are younger adults.[16]

Our memories are also very susceptible to interference from internal sources. After experiencing a fairly important event, we are likely later to think again about that event, and research clearly shows that we are susceptible to confusion between our thoughts and actual events. Consider, for example, Demonstration 3.2, shown earlier in this chapter. The demonstration is adapted from the research of Roediger and McDermott in which they presented participants with special lists of items. The lists consisted of words that were all associated with a particular target word that was *not* presented. For example, the words that participants read included "slumber, tired, rest, night, dark," but they were never presented the highly associated word "sleep." After being presented with these words, participants were given a five-minute delay and then asked to recall as many items as they could and to indicate the confidence in their memory. The experimenters found that people were very likely to falsely recall, with good confidence, the word "sleep" even though it had not been presented. Now, look back at your recall in Demonstration 3.2 and see whether or not you falsely recalled the word "sleep." A popular interpretation of these results is that people think "sleep" when they see "tired." Even after short delays (five minutes), they confuse their thoughts of the word "sleep" for the originally presented items. Consistent with the general problem of remembering the context and source of events, older adults have been shown to be especially susceptible to this type of false memory.[17]

A Real-World Example of False Memory: Repressed Childhood Sexual Abuse

As should be apparent by now, the fallibility of human memory can lead to mistaken recollections. This section explores the interesting possibility that false memories could underlie at least some of the reports of repressed childhood sexual abuse. These are cases in which adults suddenly remember being abused as children, even though they had no recollection of it over the intervening years. Over the past decade, reports of this type of crime have occurred with alarming frequency. These accounts seem highly credible because they are in many cases very detailed and put forth with a great deal of emotion. What is responsible for these reports? One possibility is that there was indeed childhood sexual abuse but that the memory was repressed (made unconscious) at some point because of its highly traumatic nature. Sometime, later in life, the victim sees a therapist and the therapist is able to elicit the repressed memory. The basis of much of Freud's theorizing is that we repress anxiety-provoking events and banish them to the unconscious. Even though they are repressed, these memories fuel certain symptoms and healing does not occur until the repressed memories are released from the unconscious. So, this possibility is consistent with Freudian or psychoanalytic interpretations of mental dynamics.

A very different possibility, however, is that there was *no* childhood sexual abuse and that the memory of such events is actually a false memory that was suggested by an overly directive therapist. How could a person come to believe that something this traumatic and devastating occurred when in fact it did not? One theory is that therapists can unwittingly implant this idea in a vulnerable patient. Although by no means typical, there are quite a few therapists today who believe that childhood sexual abuse and incest are rampant and contribute to a wide range of adult problems. Loftus and Ketcham have documented some of the behavioral characteristics that these therapists believe are symptoms of adult victims of childhood sexual abuse.[18] In addition to anxiety, panic attacks, depression, and sexual dysfunction, these symptoms include being afraid to try new experiences, wearing a lot of clothing, having an aversion to noise, having nightmares, having difficulty falling asleep, doing things to excess, being easily startled, spacing out or daydreaming, and so on. Who does not have at least one of these symptoms!

So, imagine that you are an adult who is having some problems (let's say, feeling anxious) and you happen to see a therapist who has this particular orientation. After talking to the therapist about your symptoms (and perhaps admitting that sometimes you are afraid to try new situations, sometimes you are easily startled, and sometimes you daydream), the therapist might tell you that you show the classic symptoms of childhood sexual abuse. Remember, some therapists believe that childhood sexual abuse occurs at epidemic levels and that the above symptoms are convincing signs of repressed sexual abuse. When you say that you don't remember having ever been abused as a child, the therapist might say that that is very common also.

Then the therapist might ask you to try harder to remember. When you protest that you cannot remember and that the whole idea is ridiculous, she or he may remind you that you exhibit the classic signs of childhood sexual abuse and that you should try even harder to remember—because these kinds of memories can be deeply repressed. The therapist might even suggest that you try special retrieval techniques such as imagining yourself sitting on your parent's lap when you were five years old and remembering the caresses your parent gave you. You might even try to dream about having sex with your parent in order to help reawaken the memory. Perhaps images eventually become more and more familiar to the point that they now seem real. All of this is likely to take place over several weeks. During this period, patients are often medicated, often vulnerable, and after trying all these retrieval techniques, some of them begin to remember. Although it may be possible for a person to recover a repressed memory, Loftus and Ketcham argue that in many cases the memory that emerges is a false memory—one that was implanted by the therapist.[19]

In these cases, it is very difficult to know who the victim is—is it the child or the parents, or are the child and the parents all victims of the therapist? This discussion doesn't deny the existence of actual abuse, and it doesn't invalidate accurate memories of abuse; rather, it emphasizes the difficulty in determining the "truth" in any given situation of a "recovered" memory. Research shows that in a substantial number of cases, what initially seemed to be repressed childhood sexual abuse turned out not to be possible. Also, as Loftus and her colleagues have shown, it is relatively easy to implant the idea that fairly dramatic events (like getting lost in a shopping center as a child) did occur in a person's past. A fascinating exploration of this topic is Loftus and Ketcham's book, *The Myth of Repressed Memories.*[20]

The Compelling Nature of False Memories

An important feature of false memories is that they very often seem just as real and clear as accurate memories. Apart from the work of Loftus and Ketcham mentioned above, Ceci and his colleagues have shown that after exposure to misinformation, children recall such false events with a great deal of confidence, detail, and elaboration. Witnesses to an event, whether they are right or wrong, have roughly similar levels of confidence in their memories. Thus, your conviction about the accuracy of a memory is a poor measure of its actual accuracy. False memories can feel powerfully real.[21]

A striking example of the compelling nature of false memories can be found in the research of Neisser and Harsch.[22] Previously, researchers had found highly detailed and accurate memory for special and emotional events (such as what we were doing when we heard that President Kennedy was shot), yet these same researchers did not think to or were not able to check the faithfulness of these kinds of memories. Neisser and Harsch were able to do this by taking advantage of the space shuttle *Challenger* tragedy. They interviewed people within twenty-four hours of the incident and asked them what they were doing at the time they heard about the tragedy, where they were, and whom they were with. They then contacted these same people two and a half years later and asked them again about the details of what they were doing when they heard about the accident. Interestingly, they found that over one-third of the participants had very inaccurate memories, even though they had complete confidence in their accounts. Indeed, some participants were so sure of their current memories that they told the experimenter they must have been wrong the first time they were interviewed!

The results of a study by Schmolck, Buffalo, and Squire in which people were asked to recall where they were when they heard the O. J. Simpson trial verdict confirm that distortions of this type are com-

No distortion: Subject K. V.
Recollection 1 (3 days)
Leaving a 10:00 a.m. psych(ology) class, my roommate and I heard someone commenting on it, so we asked him the verdict.
Recollection 2 (15 months)
I first heard the verdict coming out of a lecture with my roommate. The verdict was to be read in the morning and we had psych(ology) during that time. As we left the lecture hall, I heard someone tell a girl next to me that he was found guilty. I was stunned and asked him to repeat himself and tell me about the verdict.

Minor distortion: Subject P. H.
Recollection 1: (3 days)
I awoke to screaming outside my apartment window, so I looked at the clock (10:05) and realized the verdict had just been announced. I stayed in bed and reached for the stereo remote and turned the radio to 100.7 and listed to the verdict replayed.
Recollection 2 (15 months)
I knew what time the verdict would be read, so I set my stereo to wake me up so I could hear it. I was sitting in bed and listening to the radio and the screams from the other apartments outside.

Major distortion: Subject M. G.
Recollection 1: (3 days)
I was in the Commuter Lounge at Revelle (College) and saw it on TV. As 10:00 approached, more and more people came into the room. We kept having to turn up the volume, but it was kind of cool. Everyone was talking.
Recollection 2 (32 months)
I first heard it while I was watching TV. At home in my living room. My sister and father were with me. Doing nothing in particuar, eating and watching how the news station was covering different groups of viewers waiting to hear the verdict. I think that the focus was mostly on law students and their reactions to the verdict.

Figure 3.3 Examples of the recollections of participants 15 and 32 months after the O. J. Simpson verdict. *Source:* Schmolck, Buffalo, and Squire (2000).

mon. Participants were asked three days after the verdict and then again either fifteen months or thirty-two months later. As you might be able to guess, the researchers found that memory distortions were greater after longer intervals. Over 40 percent of the participants had distortions that were classified as "major," and, as Figure 3.3 shows, these were often presented in great detail. An important additional finding was that these distortions were in most cases presented with a great degree of confidence.[23]

Conclusions

Contrary to what most people believe, our memories do not faithfully and indelibly capture the details of our lives. In most cases we encode the gist or general features of episodes. Especially in the case of older adults, what we do initially store in memory is not only susceptible to forgetting over time but also vulnerable to bias from our schemas and other sources such as misleading information and our own thoughts. Some have made the claim that memories are always distorted and cannot be trusted. Some have even claimed that memories are so malleable that any memory, under the right conditions, can be modified. Yet these views are as untenable as the videotape recorder view of memory; memories are not entirely distorted, just as they are not entirely reproductions of episodes. Indeed, in many cases individuals probably remember events fairly accurately. Nevertheless, it is worthwhile recognizing that memories can be forgotten and/or distorted. Being aware of the limits and malleability of memory should help us exercise caution when interpreting the recollections of people in general and older people in particular.

The other general advice is rather obvious, but it is something that people rarely do. When it is important to remember an event accurately, make an external record of it. How many of you would be able to make a list of the furniture, rugs, artwork, and other valuables in your house from memory? This is important information that becomes essential after a catastrophe such as a fire. Given the nature of memory, it would be worthwhile to videotape the contents of your house and make a list of the manufacturer, cost, and so on of each article. You should also take detailed notes as soon as you can when you have an important conversation and especially when you believe that the contents or nature of the conversation might be discussed or disputed. What seems exceedingly vivid at the moment will not be so clear several months from now—and you or others might distort the memory. To find out more about the different ways in which we forget and the underlying reasons, read Schachter's *The Seven Sins of Memory*.[24]

CHAPTER FOUR

Working Memory and Avoiding Distractions

THE RIGHT TIME FOR THE RIGHT TASK

On a recent flight, I began a conversation with an older businesswoman who was sitting in the next seat. After finding out about my research background in the area of aging and memory, she offered that she felt mentally alert in the morning and got progressively more sluggish as the day progressed. As a result, she tried to accomplish all her important and cognitively demanding work (like report preparation and creative thinking) in the morning and saved her routine work for later in the day. She wondered whether there is any support for her intuition that she is mentally at her peak in the mornings.

There is strong evidence for the idea that our peak cognitive powers vary through the day. But while the optimal time of day for most older adults is in the morning, it varies from individual to individual. Also, being at your peak mental capability affects performance only on some tasks. This chapter discusses the very important topic of working memory, its susceptibility to distraction, how its efficiency is affected by time of day, and steps to take to overcome these limitations.

The Nature and Importance of Working Memory

As mentioned in Chapter 2, working memory capacity is critical for good learning, remembering, and problem solving. Working memory refers to the mental resources we use for manipulating, storing, and evaluating the current contents of consciousness. These resources enable us to keep information activated in memory (i.e., in consciousness or easily accessible to consciousness) while considering other information. Working memory resources are necessary for intelligent behaviors such as reading a book, listening to a conversation, trying to remember someone's name whom you have just met, and attempting to solve a simple or complex problem. As a specific example, consider language comprehension. When listening to language, we constantly need to maintain ideas in memory while we process new speech, develop relations among ideas, determine the referents of pronouns, and so on.

Think about the activities you have planned for today or tomorrow. Perhaps you are planning to withdraw money from the bank, wash the car, take clothes to the laundry, and finish reading this chapter. As you mull over your planned activities and when you want to accomplish each one, you are likely to simultaneously consider the constraints associated with each one (e.g., you may need to get money before you wash your car), as well as the most efficient means for carrying out all the tasks (e.g., you may want to couple the bank and car washing tasks because they are near each other). While your knowledge of banks, laundries, car washes, and so on is stored in long-term memory, effectively planning your day requires that you consciously consider and assess the various facets of these activities. This is done in working memory, and it involves activating this knowledge and evaluating it. In general, then, working memory is critical for the effective and deliberate use of our knowledge.

The ability to keep information accessible while simultaneously processing new information is also useful when mentally solving problems. Consider, for example, the problem of mentally multiplying 14 times 19. One way to solve this would be to first multiply 4 times 19, for a total of 76. Then, while holding 76 in memory (specifically in working memory), you would multiply 10 times 19 and come up with the total of 190. Next, you would add 76 to 190 in order to produce the sum of 266. Thus, in solving this kind of problem, you are continuously performing mental operations (multiplying 4 times 19, multiplying 10 times 19, and adding 76 to 190) in working memory and temporarily storing the products of these operations (76 and 190). It is thought that these kinds of calculations are accomplished with working memory resources.

As illustrated above, working memory involves using our mental resources to both process and store information. Perhaps the clearest way to understand working memory is to consider the way it is measured. Tests of working memory typically involve asking people to perform mental operations and examining whether they are able to keep information sufficiently activated in order to recall it. One way to measure working memory was presented in Chapter 2 (Demonstration 2.2); a slightly different measure, developed by Turner and Engle in 1989, is presented below.[1] (You may want to compare and contrast these two measures—as this is mental activity that also draws heavily on working memory resources.)

Is $(9/3) - 2 = 6$?   _____   table
Is $(3 \times 5) - 7 = 8$?   _____   grass
Is $(8/4) - 3 = 5$?   _____   paint

In this task, the participant is asked to read the problem out loud, answer the problem (in this case, the answer is no, because 9 divided by 3 minus 2 is equal to 1), and then say the word "table" out loud. Once this is done, the experimenter presses a key that replaces the first line with the second line. Then, the participant reads the next problem out loud, answers it, and reads the word out loud. The experimenter then presses a key that replaces the second line with the third line. After all three lines have been read, the participant is given a recall signal

Demonstration 4.1

To do this correctly, go through each problem and word quickly and do not look back. Better yet, see if you can get someone to read these to you.

Is $(4 \times 4) + 1 = 17$? _____ fish
Is $(9 \times 3) - 2 = 25$? _____ hole

Recall_____

Is $(9/1) - 5 = 4$? _____ bush
Is $(9 \times 1) + 9 = 1$? _____ jar
Is $(10/1) + 3 = 13$? _____ beans

Recall_____

Is $(10/5) + 4 = 6$? _____ wax
Is $(2 \times 3) + 1 = 4$? _____ bear
Is $(8/2) + 4 = 2$? _____ cone
Is $(6 \times 1) - 2 = 2$? _____ ground
Is $(9 \times 3) - 3 = 24$? _____ dad
Is $(9/1) + 8 = 18$? _____ flame

Recall_____

that is his or her cue to recall the three target words in order. Working memory is scored as correct if all three words are recalled in order. Inherent in this task is the ability to maintain the activation of ideas (table, grass, paint) while performing the arithmetic tabulations. Now test your working memory in Demonstration 4.1.

The ability to hold information in the mind while actively performing other mental activities is critically important. Performance on this task is related to performance on a wide variety of intellectual endeavors. Working memory capacity, as measured by a task like this, has been shown to be highly related to reading comprehension, language comprehension, learning to spell, vocabulary learning, the quality of notes that people take, quality of writing, and reasoning ability. Working memory scores also predict academic performance—for example, test scores in a weeklong course on computer programming. Interestingly, working memory, not math or science ability, was the best predictor of performance in this course. It is no wonder, then, that working memory ability correlates with a fluid intelligence, which is a general intelligence factor that represents the ability to acquire new information, grasp relationships, and solve abstract problems.[2]

Aging and Working Memory Capacity

Our basic working memory capacity is probably to a large extent genetically determined, and unfortunately this capacity tends to decline with age (see Figure 2.2, in Chapter 2).[3] Thus, as we get older, recently processed information is likely to become less accessible, and we become less able to manage several thoughts simultaneously.

Working memory also comes into play when we are required to listen to a question that contains several response alternatives. When the question and alternatives are presented auditorily, working memory resources are maximally taxed, because we must keep the possible answers activated in order to review and compare them. Consistent with working memory declines that typically accompany advancing age, older adults have been shown to be particularly influenced by the order of response alternatives. That is, they have a bias toward selecting the last response alternative, probably because they have difficulty maintaining the others in a sufficiently activated state in working memory. For example, when asked "Should divorce in this country be easier to obtain, stay as it is now, or be more difficult to obtain?" older adults were much more influenced by the order of the alternatives than were the younger adults. Indeed, they were more likely to respond "be more difficult to obtain" when it is the last alternative than when it was in the middle position.[4] Interestingly, this pattern was virtually eliminated when the question and response alternatives were presented visually, because under this condition there was a good deal of environmental support for maintaining the different alternatives in memory.

Use Notes to Compensate for Declining Capacity

One simple way to counteract the effects of aging on working memory capacity is to use notes. Jotting down notes gives you the environmental support necessary to keep the relevant components of a problem activated. For example, if you are weighing the costs and benefits of moving or changing jobs, it would be helpful to actually write these down. In this way, notes can help you make more reasoned decisions and judgments.

Focus on the Most Relevant Information

In situations where it isn't possible to take notes, older adults can use an alternative strategy to minimize the adverse consequences of their reduced working memory resources. For instance, in one experiment participants were asked to develop the most efficient route around town for visiting stores and offices during the hours they were open. This experiment compared younger adults, who have fairly high levels of working memory resources, with older adults, who tend to have lower levels of these resources. Somewhat surprisingly, although the participants were not allowed to jot down notes, the older adults were able to plan as effectively as the younger subjects.[5]

How did these older adults achieve such high levels of performance? They restricted their information-gathering to the physical layout of the town and the hours of operation of those stores directly related to the required errands. In contrast, younger adults were much less judicious in the information they focused on and retained. That is, the older adults didn't saturate their working memories with irrelevant information. Instead, they focused their limited working memory resources on the most relevant information. Thus, as we age, we can compensate for limits in working memory resources by using our experiences to select only the most relevant information for consideration.

Working Memory and the Susceptibility to Distractions

Another factor that may compromise working memory resources even further is the human susceptibility to distraction. Thus, as Figure 4.1 shows, assuming equal levels of working memory resources, those who are more easily distracted have fewer functional resources available for pursuing their cognitive goals. If, for example, you are in an auditorium listening to a speaker, your comprehension and retention of the speech will be much better if you devote all your working memory resources to the speaker. But if you are distracted by the noises around you, your plans for the weekend, an upsetting conversation you recently had with someone, or your thoughts about how to renovate the kitchen, your working memory capacity will be reduced. You will have fewer resources left over to process the speech. Thus, if your goal is good comprehension and memory, you should try to devote 100 percent of your working memory resources to the task at hand. In fact, from this perspective, one of the nicest things that someone can say to someone else is, "You have one hundred percent of my working memory resources."

Aging Increases Sensitivity to Distraction

So, what happens to our sensitivity to distractions as we get older? As described in Chapter 2, one prominent theory of aging is that our ability to keep irrelevant thoughts out of working memory diminishes as we get older. According to Hasher and Zacks, during normal cognition we employ an inhibitory mechanism that functions to suppress or dampen off-task information; that is, information that is irrelevant to our cognitive goals. Consider again listening to a speech in an auditorium. Presumably, your major goal is to follow the speech

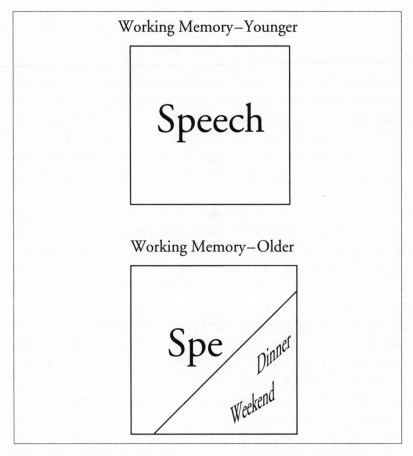

Figure 4.1 How problems in inhibition can affect one's functional working memory capacity.

and understand it. However, there are all kinds of distractions that can potentially interfere with your full attention or full processing of the lecture. Thus, it is quite adaptive to have a properly functioning inhibitory mechanism that inhibits thoughts that are irrelevant to the task at hand. A second major function of the inhibitory mechanism is to clear working memory of no longer useful or relevant information. This function is also quite important because if you can't remove something from working memory that is no longer relevant or is only marginally relevant, this will interfere with full processing of the speech.[6]

In summary, the current thinking is that two of the important functions of this inhibitory mechanism are to prevent irrelevant information from entering working memory and to delete no longer or marginally relevant information from working memory. Further, an impressive body of scientific evidence supports the idea that aging disrupts the efficient functioning of the inhibitory mechanism such that older adults are less able to keep off-task thoughts out of working memory.[7]

Consider, for example, an experiment by Connelly, Hasher, and Zacks in which they asked younger and older people to read texts that were either entirely relevant (control texts) or contained irrelevant distraction.[8] The task in this experiment was to read the passage aloud, and participants also knew that they would be tested for their comprehension of the passage. When receiving passages containing distracting information, they were further told to read only the text in italics and to ignore distracting material, which appeared in nonitalic font. Sample passages from this experiment are presented in Demonstration 4.2—before going further, try to read them in order to gauge your own performance. Although all participants were slower in reading the text containing distraction as compared to the control passage, older participants in particular were slower to read the passage containing italic text. These results are consistent with the idea that older adults have difficulty mentally suppressing irrelevant information.

A recent study by May also supports the view that aging disrupts the effective inhibition of irrelevant information. She presented participants with a modified version of the Remote Associates Test. As Figure 4.2 shows, in this task people were presented with sets of three words and for each set were asked to come up with one word related to all three words. This type of problem tends to be difficult because the three words are not obviously related to one another. In order to discover the relationship among the words, one needs to explore the less common interpretations of each of the words (hence the name Remote Associates Test). The interesting aspect of May's research is

Demonstration 4.2 An actual passage from the Connelly, Hasher, and Zacks study

1. Time yourself as you read this passage.

Control Passage

The car ride was getting bumpy now that George had left the main road to use the dirt road. He was out of school, not having to study during the summer break. He was glad to get out of the stuffy offices of the archaeology department and get out into. . . .

2. Now, time yourself as you read the passage below. Read only the italicized words and try to ignore the others.

Passage with Distraction

The car ride river *was getting bumpy* jeep *now that* religious *George had* religious *left the main* digging tools *road to use the* religious *dirt road. He* digging tools river *was out of* jeep *school, not having* digging tools *to study* digging tools river *during the summer* jeep religious *break. He was* jeep river *glad to* digging tools *get out of* jeep *the stuffy* religious *offices* river *of* religious *the archaeolgy* religious *department* river jeep *and get out into.* . . .

3. If you are like most people, you found the irrelevant words in the second passage distracting. These tend to slow down reading and reduce comprehension

Source: S. L. Connelly, L. Hasher, and R. T. Zacks, "Aging and Reading: The Impact of Distraction," *Psychology and Aging* 6 (1991): 533–541.

Normal Version of the Remote Associates Test
The task is to find the concept that relates all three cue words. As you can see, this is a difficult task because the unifying concept is only remotely related to each of the cue words.

Cue words	Solution
ship, outer, crawl	space

Misleading Distraction
As you can see, the distractor items in parentheses bias the dominant interpretation of each of the cue words. Thus, to the extent that you cannot ignore the distraction, it will be more difficult to discover the solution.

Cue words	Solution
ship (ocean), outer (inner), crawl (floor)	space

Leading Distraction
In this case, the distractors encourage the relevant interpretaion of each word for solving the problem. Thus, problems in ignoring the distraction in this condition should improve performance.

Cue words	Solution
ship (rocket), outer (atmosphere), crawl (attic)	space

Figure 4.2 Materials from the Remote Associates Test.

that she varied whether the words appeared with distraction and the kind of distraction that was present. Thus, on some trials participants received only the cue words (the typical form of the Remote Associates Test). On the irrelevant distraction trials, the distractors reinforced the primary interpretation of each word, which would likely interfere with solving the problem. On other trials, participants received relevant distraction or distraction that biased the interpretation of the cue words in the direction of a meaning that encouraged a solution to the problem. On these trials, processing of the distractor information was expected to facilitate discovery of the solution.[9]

Importantly, *all the participants were instructed to ignore the distracting words* that appeared within parentheses. Thus, to the extent that people were able to ignore the distraction, they should have been minimally affected by it. But, if they weren't able to suppress or inhibit the distraction, they should have been either helped or harmed by the distractor items. The results were entirely in line with Hasher and Zacks's theory that aging disrupts inhibitory processes. Specifically, relative to the control condition, younger adults were minimally affected by the relevant and irrelevant distractors. By contrast, older adults were more affected by the distractor items such that they showed substantial decrements in performance with the irrelevant distractors and marked improvements in performance with the relevant distractors. These results provide further evidence for the existence of age-related deficits and a diminishing ability to inhibit or suppress irrelevant information.

Reduce Distraction and Increase Working Memory Capacity

Given that irrelevant and distracting information can take up valuable working memory resources, what can you do to minimize these influences? First, you can eliminate distractions.

- Turn off the television or radio in the background.
- Go somewhere where you can do your work in a quiet place.
- Take care of annoying concerns before you take on a challenging task. If there is something you are dying to tell a friend or if the height of your lawn is really bothering you, it is probably wise to take care of these matters first; otherwise, they are likely to intrude on your thoughts and occupy your valuable working memory resources.

In summary, try to minimize the presence of both external and internal (mental) distractions.

Second, research has shown that closing your eyes can help you disengage from distraction in your visual environment. Some studies have found that people who close their eyes either during learning or while trying to remember information improved their performance by as much as 33 percent over groups in which people had their eyes open while looking at distracting information. Thus, closing your eyes may be a relatively simple way of preserving working memory resources for cognitively demanding tasks such as encoding and retrieving.[10]

Third, effortful actions tend to recruit mental resources and thus reduce the amount available for thinking and learning. Thus, your memory of a conversation is likely to be poorer when riding a stationary bike or lifting heavy packages. This may be obvious, but research has also shown that even walking can interfere with learning. Walking is something that for most of us is relatively automatic, which means that we have learned it so well that it can be done with minimal working memory resources. Walking can become effortful, however, such as when you are walking in a very crowded area where you have to watch your step or if you may have a physical ailment that makes walking difficult. Under these conditions, walking can demand working memory resources and interfere with the effective processing of information.[11] To the extent that walking has become less automatic for you, you may no longer have sufficient working memory capacity to perform strenuous mental operations while walking. Under these conditions, it is worthwhile to delay important conversations until you are comfortably seated.

Circadian Rhythms and Sensitivity to Distraction

The word "circadian" comes from the Latin *circa,* meaning "around," and *dies* meaning "day," and refers to a rhythm that our bodies follow over twenty-four-hour intervals. These rhythms are fairly regular in each of us and they influence a number of physiological processes, including pulse rate, hormonal secretions, and body temperature. For example, human body temperatures tend to be lowest around 4 a.m. and reach a peak sometime in the late afternoon or early evening,

Demonstration 4.3

Fill out the Morningness-Eveningness questionnaire below. After you are done, use the information at the end of the questionnaire to determine whether you are a "morning" or "evening" type.

Morningness and Eveningness

Instructions:

1. Please read each question carefully before answering.
2. Answer *all* questions.
3. Answer questions in numerical order.
4. Each question should be answered independently of others. Do *not* go back and check your answers.
5. All questions have a selection of answers. For each question place a cross alongside *one* anwer only. Some questions have a scale instead of a selection of answers. Place a cross at the appropriate point along the scale.

1. Considering only your own "feeling best" rhythm, at what time would you get up if you were entirely free to plan your day?

   a.m. 5------6------7------8-------9------10------11------12

2. Considering only your own "feeling best" rhythm, at what time would you go to bed if you were entirely free to plan your evening?

   p.m. 8------9------10------11------12------1------2------3

3. If there is a specific time at which you have to get up in the morning, to what extent are you dependent on being awakened by an alarm clock?

   _____Not at all dependent
   _____Slightly dependent

(*continued*)

Demonstration 4.3 Continued

_____Fairly dependent
_____Very dependent

4. Assuming adequate environmental conditions, how easy do you find getting up in the morning?

_____Not at all easy
_____Not very easy
_____Fairly easy
_____Very easy

5. How alert do you feel during the first half hour after waking in the morning?

_____Not at all alert
_____Slightly alert
_____Fairly alert
_____Very alert

6. How is your appetite during the first half hour after waking in the morning?

_____Very poor
_____Fairly poor
_____Fairly good
_____Very good

7. During the first half hour after waking in the morning, how tired do you feel?

_____Very tired
_____Fairly tired
_____Fairly refreshed
_____Very refreshed

8. When you have no committments the next day, at what time do you go to bed compared to your usual bedtime?

_____Seldom or never late
_____Less than one hour later

_____One to two hours later
_____More than two hours later

9. You have decided to engage in some physical exercise. A
   friend suggests that you do this one hour twice a week, and
   the best time for him is between 7 and 8 a.m. Bearing in
   mind nothing else but your own "feeling best" rhythm, how
   do you think you would perform?

   _____Would be in good form
   _____Would be in reasonable form
   _____Would find it difficult
   _____Would find it very difficult

10. At what time in the evening do you feel tired and, as a re-
    sult, in need of sleep?

    p.m. 8------9------10------11------12------1------2------3

11. You wish to be at peak performance for a test that you
    know is going to be mentally exhausting and lasting for
    two hours. You are entirely free to plan your day. Consider-
    ing only your own "feeling best" rhythm, which *one* of the
    four testing times would you chose?

    _____8 to 10 a.m.
    _____11 a.m. to 1 p.m.
    _____3 to 5 p.m.
    _____7 to 9 p.m.

12. If you went to bed at 11 p.m., at what level of tiredness
    would you be?

    _____Not at all tired
    _____Slightly tired
    _____Fairly tired
    _____Very tired

13. For some reason you have gone to bed several hours later
    than usual, but there is no need to get up at any particular

(*continued*)

time the next morning. Which *one* of the following events are you most likely to experience?

_____Will wake up at usual time and will *not* fall asleep
_____Will wake up at usual time and will doze thereafter
_____Will wake up at usual time but will fall asleep again
_____Will *not* wake up until later than usual

14. One night you have to remain awake between 4 and 6 a.m. in order to carry out a night watch. You have no commitments the next day. Which *one* of the following alternatives suit you best?

_____Would *not* go to bed until after watch was over
_____Would take a nap before and sleep after
_____Would take a good sleep before and nap after
_____Would take *all* sleep before watch

15. You have to do two hours of hard physical work. You are entirely free to plan your day. Considering only your own "feeling best" rhythm, which *one* of the following times would you choose?

_____8 to 10 a.m.
_____11 a.m. to 1 p.m.
_____3 to 5 p.m.
_____7 to 9 p.m.

16. You have decided to engage in hard physical exercise. A friend suggests that you do this for one hour twice a week, and the best time for him is between 10 and 11 p.m. Bearing in mind nothing else but your own "feeling best" rhythm, how well do you think you would perform?

_____Would be in good form
_____Would be in reasonable form
_____Would find it difficult
_____Would find it very difficult

17. Suppose that you can choose your own work hours. Assume that you work a *five*-hour day (including breaks) and that your job is interesting and pays by results. Which *five consecutive hours* would you select? (Circle them on the scale below)

12-1-2-3-4-5-6-7-8-9-10-11-12-1-2-3-4-5-6-7-8-9-10-11-12
midnight   noon   midnight

18. At what time of day do you think you reach your "feeling best" peak?

12-1-2-3-4-5-6-7-8-9-10-11-12-1-2-3-4-5-6-7-8-9-10-11-12
midnight   noon   midnight

19. One hears about "morning" and "evening" types of people. Which *one* of these types do you consider yourself to be?

_____ Definitely a "morning" type
_____ Rather more a "morning" than an "evening" type
_____ Rather more an "evening" than a "morning" type
_____ Definitely an "evening" type

Morningness and Eveningness Answer Key

1. 5—5 to 6:30 a.m.
    4—6:30 to 7:45 a.m.
    3—7:45 to 9:45 a.m
    2—9:45 to 11:00 a.m
    1—11:00 a.m. to 12:00 noon

2. 5—8 to 9 p.m.
    4—9 to 10:15 p.m.
    3—10:15 to 12:30 p.m.
    2—12:30 to 1:45 a.m.
    1—1:45 to 3 a.m.

3. 4—Not at all dependent

     3—Slightly dependent
     2—Fairly dependent
     1—Very dependent

4. 1—Not at all easy
    2—Slightly easy
    3—Fairly easy
    4—Very easy

5. 1—Not at all alert
    2—Slightly alert
    3—Fairly alert
    4—Very alert

(*continued*)

Demonstration 4.3 Continued

6. 1—Very poor
    2—Fairly poor
    3—Fairly good
    4—Very good

7. 1—Very tired
    2—Fairly tired
    3—Fairly refreshed
    4—Very refreshed

8. 4—Seldom or never late
    3—Less than one hour later
    2—One to two hours later
    1—More than two hours later

9. 4—Would be in good form
    3—Would be in reasonable form
    2—Would find it difficult
    1—Would find it very difficult

10. 5—8 to 9 p.m.
    4—9 to 10:15 p.m.
    3—10:15 to 12:45 p.m.
    2—12:45 to 2 a.m.
    1—2 to 3 a.m.

11. 6—8–10 a.m.
    4—11 a.m.–1 p.m.
    2—3–5 p.m.
    0—7–9 p.m.

12. 0—Not at all tired
    2—Slightly tired
    4—Fairly tired

6—Very tired

13. 4—Will wake up at usual time and will *not* fall asleep
    3—Will wake up at usual time and will doze thereafter
    2—Will wake up at usual time but will fall asleep again
    1—Will *not* wake up until later than usual

14. 1—Would *not* go to bed until watch was over
    2—Would take a nap before and sleep after
    3—Would take a good sleep before and nap after
    4—Would take *all* sleep before watch

15. 4—8 to 10 a.m.
    3—11 a.m. to 1 p.m.
    2—3 to 5 p.m.
    1—7 to 9 p.m.

16. 1—Would be in good form
    2—Would be in reasonable form
    3—Would find it difficult
    4—Would find it very difficult

17. 1—12 midnight to 4 a.m.
    5—4 to 8 a.m.
    4—8 to 10 a.m.

3—10 a.m. to 5 p.m.
2—5 to 10 p.m.
1—10 p.m. to 12 midnight

2—Rather more an
"evening" than a
"morning" type
0—Definitely an
"evening" type

18. 1—12 midnight to 4 a.m.
5—4 to 8 a.m.
4—8 to 10 a.m.
3—10 a.m. to 5 p.m.
2—5 to 10 p.m.
1—10 p.m. to 12 midnight

19. 6—Definitely a "morn-
ing" type
4—Rather more a "morn-
ing" than an "evening"
type

Morningness-Eveningness Type Scores	
Definitely evening	16–30
Moderately evening	31–41
Neutral	42–58
Moderately morning	59–69
Definitely morning	70–86

although this varies from individual to individual. There is good evidence that our cognitive processes also have peaks and declines such that we have an optimal time of day for performing certain cognitive operations. This is consistent with our intuitions, as most of us feel that we are more capable of getting our work done at a particular time of day.

The standard for measuring one's optimal time of day is Horne and Ostberg's Morningness-Eveningness questionnaire.[12] This is a nineteen-item paper-and-pencil questionnaire that is quite reliable, and the scores from this questionnaire correlate with physiological measures of arousal. Morning types generally wake up about two hours earlier than evening types and they go to bed earlier as well. Also, upon rising in the morning, the body temperature of morning types rises more rapidly such that body temperature peaks are significantly earlier in the day for morning types. Demonstration 4.3 shows this questionnaire, as well as the method of scoring. So, take a break from reading at this point and figure out your optimal time of day.

An interesting question is whether one's optimal time of day changes as a function of age. The answer to this is a definitive yes. Data collected from 1,264 younger adults and 430 older adults indicate that 73 percent of older adults (ages 60 to 75) fall into the "moderately morning" or "definitely morning" category. This contrasts with 5 percent of college students (ages 18 to 23) who fall into these categories. Whereas most college students fall in the "neutral" category, 38 percent show tendencies of being evening people, while only 2 percent of older adults do. In fact, it is probably fair to say that many older adults burn the "midnight" oil at 9 p.m.! Many college students, by contrast, claim that they wish they could stretch the scales so that they could list 1 or 2 or 3 in the afternoon as their preferred time for rising and 5 or 6 a.m. as their preferred time for going to bed! It is interesting to note that this pattern of change in optimal time of day across the life span has been found in many other cultures (including England, Italy, Japan, and Spain) besides our own.[13]

Be in Synchrony with Your Optimal Time of Day for Better
Learning and Memory

An interesting question is whether your optimal time of day actually influences your ability to learn and retain information. The answer to this question also seems to be yes, as shown by May, Hasher, and Stoltzfus.[14] As the top section of Table 4.1 shows, they tested younger evening types and older morning types either in the morning (8 or 9 a.m.) or in the late afternoon/early evening (4 or 5 p.m.). Thus, they tested both younger and older adults either at their optimal time or their nonoptimal time. As indicated in the figure, when a younger evening-type person was tested in the evening, that person was "in synchrony" with his or her optimal time. When an older morning-type person was tested in the morning, that person was "in synchrony" with his or her optimal time. In this experiment, participants were presented with ten short stories to read and later were given a recognition test that involved determining whether particular sentences had appeared in the short stories. This was a fairly difficult task because the false sentences were ones that did not appear in the stories

Table 4.1 Memory of sentences from stories as a function of performing at optimal and nonoptimal times of day

Design of their experiment

| | Time of testing | |
	Morning (8 or 9 a.m.)	Evening (4 or 5 p.m.)
Young (evening types)		In synchrony
Old (morning types)	In synchrony	

Results of their experiment: corrected recognition

| | Time of testing | |
	Morning (8 or 9 a.m.)	Evening (4 or 5 p.m.)
Young (evening types)	46.2	65.0
Old (morning types)	47.2	30.4

Source: Design and results of experiment by May, Hasher, and Stoltzfus (1993).

but could have plausibly been there. The bottom section of the table lists the recognition results for the various conditions. The important point to realize is that time of day had large effects on learning and re-membering in this task. The younger evening types performed signif-icantly better in the evening than they did in the morning. Con-versely, the older morning types performed significantly better in the morning than they did in the evening. These results strongly suggest that it is important to be in synchrony with your optimal time of day when performing complex cognitive tasks.

Time of Day, Sensitivity to Distraction, and Inhibition

Thus far, the research indicates that being in synchrony with one's optimal time has significant benefits for learning and memory. An important question is whether we are better at *all* tasks at our optimal time of day. Research results suggest that being in synchrony with our optimal time of day affects our inhibitory processes and thus primarily benefits performance on tasks that require good inhibition (i.e., ridding working memory of distracting information). By contrast, performance on tasks that are well-learned, very familiar, and often practiced shows few benefits of performing them at our optimal time of day.

A variety of data reinforce this interpretation. For example, in the Remote Associates study in which participants were presented with three cue words (examples were shown in Figure 4.2) and asked to find the word they were all related to, older adults were much more susceptible to distraction. While that is in fact the case, both younger and older adults were more affected by the distracting words (in both positive and negative ways depending on the condition) at their nonoptimal time of day. Thus, regardless of age, people had more difficulty ignoring the cue words at their nonpreferred time.[15]

Interestingly, one's optimal time of day doesn't seem to affect access to well-learned and highly familiar material. Thus, performance isn't affected by time of day when measuring the speed with which you can name colors, your ability to define vocabulary words, and the speed with which you can make category judgments (e.g., deciding that a chair is an article of furniture). It seems that it is complex tasks requiring complete and sustained attention (and thus the ability to inhibit distractions) that benefit most from being performed at their optimal time. Consider, for example, the task shown in Demonstration 4.4. In the top panel, the task is simply to name the color of the blocks as quickly as possible. See how many of these you can name in thirty seconds. Now try the bottom task, which is to name the color of the ink (and to ignore the word) as quickly as possible. Again, see how many of these you can do in thirty seconds. The second task is more complex and requires that you constantly keep in mind that you are naming the *color* of the words and that you inhibit your tendency

Red	Blue	Green	**Red**	Blue	**Red**	**Green**	**Green**	Blue	Blue
Red	Blue	**Green**	Blue	Red	Green	**Red**	Blue	**Green**	**Red**
Red	Green	Blue	Red	**Green**	Blue	Blue	**Green**	Red	**Green**
Green	Red	Blue	**Green**	Blue	Red	**Red**	Blue	Green	**Red**
Red	**Green**	Blue	Green	**Red**	Blue	**Green**	**Red**	Blue	Green
Blue	**Green**	Blue	**Red**	Blue	**Green**	Red	Green	Blue	**Green**

to automatically read the words. As you might expect from the theme of this chapter, performing at your optimal time of day doesn't affect performance on the first task, but it does affect performance on the second task.[16]

Similarly, consider the task in Demonstration 4.5. The top task simply requires you to connect the circles following the numbers in order. The requirement in the bottom task is to connect the circles but to alternate between numbers and letters. Thus, the sequence of connection should go from 1 to A, to 2 to B, to 3 to C, and so on. Again, the bottom task is more complex and requires that one inhibits the number 2 after thinking of 1 and connects it with the letter A. Consistent with the overall pattern of results presented thus far, performing at your optimal time of day has little or no effect on performing the top task but significantly affects performance on the task in the bottom panel.[17]

Drinking a Cup of Caffeinated Coffee at Your Nonoptimal Time

There are a lot of reasons for not drinking coffee (e.g., possible negative health effects, caffeine may interfere with your sleep), but if these do not worry you, you should consider drinking coffee to improve your memory performance at your nonoptimal time of day. In one study, Ryan, Hatfield, and Hofstetter tested the memory of coffee-drinking older people (over 65 years old) who were morning types. Their memory was tested in the morning (8 a.m.) and in the late afternoon (4 p.m.). What was new about their research is that they varied whether people drank a twelve-ounce cup of decaffeinated or caffeinated coffee thirty minutes prior to testing. The researchers measured memory of a list of words about twenty minutes after they had last recalled the list. After drinking decaffeinated coffee, the typical time-of-day effect was found; that is, the morning-type older participants remembered more in the morning than in the afternoon. After drinking caffeinated coffee, however, the memory of the participants improved in the afternoon but not in the morning. Thus, drinking a cup of coffee at their nonoptimal time produced memory performance that was equivalent to memory performance at

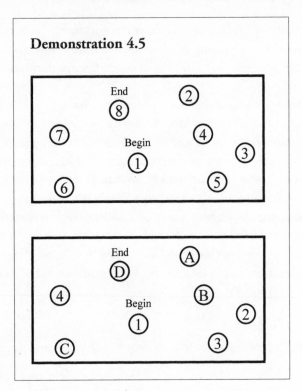

Demonstration 4.5

their optimal time. One interpretation of these results is that morning types typically feel sluggish in the afternoon, and ingesting a stimulant like coffee improves memory by increasing one's general level of arousal.[18]

It should be emphasized that the participants in this study were people who drank coffee on a daily basis. The authors caution us that non–coffee drinkers may experience distracting side effects of caffeine consumption (e.g., anxiety) which may actually show negative effects of drinking a cup of coffee.

Summary and Implications

The emerging picture is that older adults are generally more susceptible to distraction and that all people are more affected by distraction at their nonpreferred time of day. This picture has many practical implications:

1. *Consider your optimal time of day when planning your daily activities.*

   Complex cognitive tasks, ones that benefit from the ability to inhibit distraction and focus attention, should be performed at your optimal time, whereas simpler tasks that involve access to well-learned, familiar, or well-practiced information will not suffer from being performed at your nonoptimal time. For example, if your peak time of day is in the morning, you should try to schedule complex tasks such as serious reading, important conversations, and writing for the morning hours. By contrast, you can schedule, without cost, relatively simple tasks such as social conversations, ironing, and weeding the garden for your nonoptimal time of day.

2. *If you are a coffee drinker and need to perform a complex cognitive task at your nonoptimal time of day, consider drinking a cup of coffee.*

3. *Eliminate distractions from your physical environment.*

   Try to work in quiet rooms that are free of distractions like the television or radio. Also, if you are trying to learn something or retrieve a memory in a setting with lots of visual distraction, you will be more successful if you close your eyes or look away at something that is not distracting.

4. *Try to clear your thoughts of personal concerns.*

   Otherwise, these thoughts can take up some of your working memory resources. Similarly, if some actions—like walking or standing—are effortful for you, make sure that you are comfortable as you engage in tasks that are mentally difficult.

5. *Use notes in situations where it is difficult to keep all your ideas in mind.*

   If it is important to make several points in a conversation, write them down so that you are sure to cover all of them. Or, when working with complex problems, make notes and that will help you keep the relevant dimensions in mind. Some older adults believe that using notes is a sign of weakness. They see it as a crutch that undermines the exercising of the brain. This is not the case. In fact, notes provide wonderful external support and help you overcome the limits of your working memory capacity and keep more relevant thoughts activated.

CHAPTER FIVE

Most Memories Are There

THE TRICK IS FINDING THEM

At your fiftieth high school reunion, you have trouble recalling the names of some of your former classmates. For fun, the organizing committee has gathered the high school yearbook photographs from your graduating class and a list of names. You and your classmates are challenged to match the names with the photographs. Much to your surprise you find that you are able to nearly perfectly match the names with the faces.

This vignette, based on an actual study, illustrates that in many instances information we cannot remember is still in long-term memory.[1] The difficulty is getting the information out of long-term memory, a process psychologists term "retrieval." Today, psychologists believe that a good deal of our forgetting is the result of retrieval failure. To convince yourself of this, try Demonstration 5.1.

As described in Chapter 2, aging disrupts the ability to retrieve information from long-term memory.[2] Although retrieval failures are often frustrating, it should be comforting to know that it is normal to experience difficulty in calling up information not recently or fre-

Demonstration 5.1

Get a sheet of paper and a pencil. Read aloud each word in the list and after you say the word, write down a word that relates to or is associated with the word you read. Do *not* write down the word you read. Spend about 5 seconds on each word. Once you have written down a response word, say the next word. Once you have completed the list, take several minutes to relax.

Speech	Clove
Brush	Robber
Cheek	Mast
Fence	Fiddle
Honey	Chapel
Flame	Sonnet
Sheep	Witch
Flour	Roach
Knife	Brake
Copper	Twig
Glove	Grin
Monk	Drill
Daisy	Moan
Miner	Claw
Cart	Singer

On a new sheet of paper, try to recall as many of the words from the list above as you can. Do not look at your other sheet of paper while trying to recall.

Once you have recalled as many words as you can, take out your response sheet. Using these responses, again try to recall the words on the list.

You should find that you can recall much more of the list with your own sheet of responses than without it. This shows that most of the words you studied were stored in long-term memory. The forgetting that you experienced when trying to recall the words the first time was a retrieval problem. Getting the words out of long-term memory was greatly facilitated when you had retrieval cues to help.

quently used. It seems that our memory system is designed to reduce the accessibility of memories that are no longer current or relevant. In this way, memory serves us more efficiently as our environment and our circumstances change. For instance, if you move to a new city (or a new part of the city), your new telephone number becomes more important than your old telephone number, and you adapt by retrieving your new number instead of your old one. Your memory helps you adapt by making your old number less accessible so that the new one can be more easily retrieved.

But this adaptive design feature of memory comes at a cost. Things that you haven't thought about for a while become less accessible. Names, titles of movies, places visited—any pieces of information you haven't had to retrieve for some time—typically become more difficult to recall. This is not necessarily a sign that your memory is failing—on the contrary, it is just a normal consequence of the way memory works. The good news is that memory is designed to quickly "reset." An item not retrieved for a long while can again become easily retrieved with just one exposure to that item.[3] That one exposure essentially signals that the information is again currently important, and our memory responds by increasing the accessibility of the information.

The implications for getting the most out of your memory are straightforward. If you anticipate that you will need to recall some information you haven't used in a while, then try to bring that information to mind before you are put on the spot. For instance, if you are going to a party where you expect to meet acquaintances you haven't seen for some time, think about their names, and perhaps the names of their family members, before you get to the party. Of course, a key question here is how to retrieve that "forgotten" name, movie title, or vacation hotel in the first place. The rest of this chapter focuses on this critical question.

Cues Facilitate Retrieval and Reduce Age Differences

For all of us, especially as we age, excellent memory performance is possible when retrieval is facilitated. This fact has been dramatically demonstrated by a study conducted in Sweden similar to that shown in Demonstration 5.1.[4] Participants were presented with a list of 600 words to study, with just 20 seconds to study each word. During that 20 seconds they had to write down three words describing the word being studied. It took over 3 hours for people to go through the set of 600 words. Afterward, the participants were asked to recall the entire list of words. To help recall, they were given the descriptive words they had written down.

After spending half a day looking at 600 unrelated words, how many do you think you could remember? Maybe 100 if you were having a very good day? With the help of the descriptive words, people were able to correctly recall, on average, 543 words! The person with the worst performance recalled 523 words. You might be wondering whether the descriptive words given to aid recall simply allowed people to guess the studied words without having to actually remember the words. This possibility was addressed by giving people who had not seen the word list the descriptive words used by the participants in the experiment; they were able to guess an average of 104 words. Thus, only a small portion (less than 20 percent) of the 500-plus words that participants were correct on could have been guesses. The rest were remembered.

In this study, retrieval of the 600 words was facilitated by allowing the participants to use *retrieval cues*—the descriptive terms written down while studying the list. When we take photographs or keep a written log of our vacations, we are creating retrieval cues to help us remember those experiences. Looking at the photographs or reading our log even years later helps us remember details of experiences that we stored in memory but cannot recover without those retrieval cues. When friends recount events at a party that occurred several years ago, they are providing us with cues that help us remember a celebration we had forgotten. Retrieval cues are essential for recovering memories.

With increasing age, retrieval cues are especially important for memory. It has been shown that when these cues are present, memory levels in older adults are nearly as high as or even equivalent to those in younger adults.[5] The results shown in Figure 2.5 demonstrate this clearly. When individuals were told to recall an entire list of items presented earlier, with no retrieval cues provided, substantial age differences were seen. By contrast, when participants were given good retrieval cues (as in recognition tests when participants are re-presented with the original items), the memory improvement for the older adults was especially remarkable.

There are two lessons here. First, good retrieval cues are extremely effective in producing great memory. Second, with good retrieval cues, the negative impact of age on memory can be minimized. What is a good retrieval cue? Research has provided an answer.

Effective Retrieval Cues Are Those That Were Present During the Original Experience

Among the best retrieval cues are those that remind you of what you were thinking about during learning. Imagine, for example that you were trying to learn the word "cat" in an experiment, and that when you encountered the word, you thought of the "catlike" moves of Michael Jordan. If this were the case, then "Michael Jordan" would be a good cue for retrieving the word "cat," whereas something that is highly associated but not thought of during learning (e.g., "dog") would not be a good cue. To experience this phenomenon, try Demonstration 5.2. The memory power of cues that reestablish your original thinking as opposed to cues that are highly associated but do not reestablish your original thinking has been shown repeatedly in scientific studies.[6] The lesson here is that cues that remind you of what you were thinking about during learning are very effective.

The following cues will stimulate retrieval of forgotten information:

- Returning to the physical environment in which the forgotten information originated can provide excellent retrieval cues. For example, have you ever walked into the kitchen and forgotten your reason for going in there? You are likely to recover your memory by walking back to where you were before you walked into the kitchen. Visiting an old neighborhood can

Demonstration 5.2

Read each pair of words in the list below and try to remember the capitalized words. Pay attention to the cues paired with each capitalized word, as they might help you remember the word during a memory test.

ground	COLD
head	LIGHT
bath	NEED
cheese	GREEN
stomach	LARGE
sun	DAY
pretty	BLUE
cave	WET
whistle	BALL
noise	WIND
glue	CHAIR
command	MAN

Cover up the capitalized words. Looking at the cues, try to recall the words. Now that you've had some practice, try it agin with the longer list below.

fruit	FLOWER
home	SWEET
grasp	BABY
butter	SMOOTH
drink	SMOKE
beat	PAIN
cloth	SHEEP
swift	GO
lady	QUEEN
blade	CUT
plant	BUG

wish	WASH
hope	HIGH
stem	SHORT
whiskey	WATER
moth	FOOD
cabbage	ROUND
glass	HARD
country	OPEN
tool	HAND
memory	SLOW
covering	COAT
barn	DIRTY
spider	BIRD

Below, the cues words are listed in a different order. Use them to try to recall the capitalized words you just studied, then write them on your sheet of paper.

wish
whiskey
lady
tool
hope
drink
glass
fruit
barn
blade
cloth
butter

Do not score your recall just yet. Below is another list of cue words, each cue related to one of the capitalized words in the list you just studied. Using these cues, try to recall as many more capitalized words as you can. Turn your recall sheet over

or get a fresh sheet of paper to write down the words as you recall them.

stop
insect
closed
eagle
long
bitter
cat
fast
square
lining
infant
ache

Now go back to the study list and count how many words you
recalled with each set of cues. What you should find is that you
recalled more with the first set of cues than with the second set
of cues, even though the second set of cues is more strongly associated with the capitalized words.

produce a flood of memories for forgotten events. In writing
her autobiography, Doris Kearns Goodwin used this technique to retrieve memories of her girlhood in Baltimore.

■ If you can't place yourself in the actual physical environment,
then creating a visual image of that environment can be just as
effective a retrieval cue.[7] For instance, if you can't remember
where you put your wallet, you might prod your memory by
imagining each physical location you were in during the day
and your activities at each place.

■ Re-create the sensory backdrop that was present when the information was stored. It has been shown, for example, that

playing the same songs or providing the same smells that were present when something occurred will increase our ability to retrieve the memory of that event. Again, in the absence of the actual song or odor, imagining it can be helpful.[8]

■ Get in the mood you were in during the storage of information. Mood cues seem to be most effective for retrieving information that is congruent with the mood. So, it is easier to retrieve pleasant memories when you are in a happy mood, whereas unpleasant memories seem to be most often retrieved when your mood is more gloomy.[9]

■ Repeat the kinds of thoughts you had when you were storing the information to give yourself retrieval cues. Many times this involves re-creating the mindset you had at the time. For instance, if you are trying to remember the contents of a book on Geronimo in a conversation with a friend, you can try to duplicate the frame of mind you were in when you read the book. You might have had an interest in the history of the Southwest. Or you might have had an interest in the treatment of Indians by the white settlers. Or you might have had an interest in the Hispanic influence on the Indians. By re-creating your frame of reference, you will generate the kinds of thoughts that were present at the time of reading. These will serve as good retrieval cues.

The More Specific the Cue, the Better

Cues that are highly precise and specific are more effective in retrieving information than are cues that are more general. In one study, college students and older adults were presented a set of sentences describing a particular man doing something (e.g., a hungry man, a brave man, a fat man, and so on). Later, the participants were given either general or specific cues for retrieving the adjective that was paired with each particular man (Figure 5.1). Not only were the specific cues more helpful than the general cues in retrieving the adjectives, but the specific cues eliminated the age differences in memory. In contrast, with the general cues, the older adults consistently re-

Participants: College-age students and older adults (mean age = 70)

Phase 1: Read sentences in which a particular person was doing something—e.g., The grimacing man held the cheese while the mousetrap sprang on his finger.

Phase 2: Memory test for the adjective describing the person. The test provided subjects with either a general or specific cue.

General cue: The _____ man held the cheese.

Specific cue: The _____ man held the cheese while the mousetrap sprang on his finger.

Results: The specific cue increased recall and eliminated age differences.

Figure 5.1 Specific retrieval cues are better than general cues. *Source:* K. E. Cherry, D. C. Park, D. A. Frieska, and R. L. Rowley, "The Effect of Verbal Elaborations on Memory in Younger and Older Adults," *Memory & Cognition* 21 (1993): 725–738.

membered fewer than half the adjectives that the younger adults remembered.[10]

To provide yourself with specific and precise cues you can:

■ Take notes and use them to retrieve needed details. For instance, when conversing with your doctor, jot down notes to use later as retrieval cues for remembering critical details. The more precise the notes, the better.
■ Take pictures or videos. As you age, these records can provide specific cues to help you retrieve and enjoy cherished times with family and friends, vacations, and so on. In fact, some

suggest that reviewing videos is an effective way for people with Alzheimer's disease to remember family members and shared events.

A Procedure to Maximize Retrieval

By itself, each retrieval cue described above may not provide a large boost in information retrieval. But when used together as an integrated technique, these cues can provide significant gains in remembering. A team of psychologists has developed such an integrated system to help victims and witnesses of crimes retrieve information about the event. Research has found that people who use this system can retrieve about 45 percent more information than those who don't use it. This research also showed that the system stimulates more memory retrieval than does hypnosis. Older adults who were instructed to use this system recalled significantly more of a story read three weeks earlier than did older adults who did not use this system.[11]

To use this system, try to activate the cues just discussed, simultaneously. Specifically, think back to:

1. The physical environment at the time of the event.
2. Your "internal state," which includes feelings, sensations, and moods present at the time of the event. Your internal state also can include your physical status at the time (had a cold).
3. Particular *thoughts* you might have had at the time.

Second, when you have activated these cues, focus your concentration on memory retrieval. Do not allow disturbances or interruptions to break your concentration. Be prepared to expend mental effort.

Third, continue to try to retrieve the memory, even if you are unsuccessful at first. Research shows that the more times you attempt to retrieve a memory, the more you will remember.[12]

Fourth, use partial information to help cue a specific memory.

For instance, if you can't remember a name, try to think about the length of the name, the number of syllables, the starting sound of the name, or the ethnicity of the name.

Use this system to help you maximize remembering.

Summary

The key lessons from this chapter are:

1. *Much forgetting is due to problems with retrieving information stored in long-term memory.*
2. *Retrieval cues can help us to access forgotten information.*
3. *As we age, retrieval becomes more difficult.* Therefore, the necessity for retrieval cues in maintaining good memory becomes ever more important as we age.
4. *Good retrieval cues are those that (a) help reestablish the context and the mindset you were in during learning and (b) are highly precise and specific*
5. *If retrieval is at first unsuccessful, keep trying.*

CHAPTER SIX

How to Learn and Remember Complex Material

ARTICLES, LECTURES, AND TEXTBOOKS

One of my students came to me in great distress. He had done poorly on a recent examination and could not figure out why. He had studied many hours for the examination, more hours than his friends. He had read the required chapters several times and gone over his class notes innumerable times. Yet he was disappointed with his grade and what he was able to remember.

The implicit belief that this student held was that the more one repeats information, the better that information will be remembered. This student is in good company. Many adults hold this belief, including professionals such as physicians. Even authors of books that provide advice on improving memory promote this belief. Yet, while this seems intuitively to be the case, experiments that have directly tested this theory clearly indicate that continuous rote rehearsal is *not* a very effective way to remember and learn new information.[1]

Using good strategies during learning is the key to good memory.

This is true for people of all ages. One study showed that college professors over 65 who were allowed to read an article outside their particular field of study only once could recall as much of the article as younger adults (including young college professors).[2] These older professors had not developed a better memory in general. They performed more poorly than the younger adults on material for which they had not developed effective strategies, such as remembering a list of names or faces. The older professors had developed powerful strategies for remembering technical material. Their secret is that they use a collection of techniques often referred to as "elaborative rehearsal." Elaborative rehearsal involves enriching and embellishing the material. This includes associating the material to related information, thinking about how the content relates to your existing knowledge, and forming images of the content. This chapter describes the techniques of elaborative rehearsal. With practice, you will be able to use these techniques to improve your own memory ability. If you make them your preferred thinking activity over rote rehearsal, you will be a more successful learner.

Essential to the application of elaborative rehearsal for older adults is that they may need more time to elaborate.[3] So, take more time if you need to, but be sure that you use that time for elaborative rehearsal and not rote rehearsal.

If you are dissatisfied with your memory, chances are that you are often reading quickly and listening without elaboration. For better memory, change this minimal processing approach. As we present the following elaboration strategies, think about how you would apply them in your daily life to improve your memory. For example, you could use them to remember information from a training manual, a seminar on financial planning, or a book.

The *Must:* Comprehension

A straightforward key to memory is comprehending what you are trying to learn. Students sometimes read assignments with an understanding of the words and the sentences but with little understanding of the overall message or of what the passage is about. When this occurs, memory will be poor and fragmentary. To give yourself a first-hand experience of how memory relies on comprehension, try Demonstration 6.1.[4]

The lesson here is clear and striking! The most basic ingredient for improving memory for articles, lectures, instructions, educational programs, and so on is to make sure that you understand the material. Here are things you can do to help improve your comprehension of the material you want to remember.

Tools to Increase Comprehension
Ask Questions

When somebody is presenting information, ask questions when you cannot understand the material. Don't be shy about asking questions. Remember that there are no stupid questions. When attending a talk, you might fail to ask questions because you fall into the trap of writing down words from the talk without understanding the information. Be sure that you understand what you are writing down. If you don't have time to write down all the important information, it might be better to listen for understanding, ask questions, and tape-record the lecture so that the details are available for later use.

Answer Practice Questions

Some training manuals and instructional guides may include practice questions or exercises. We suggest that you do these exercises. In general, test your comprehension of the material you want to remember. Often, you can't know what it is that you don't understand until you fail to produce a correct response. In the absence of practice questions, try to summarize sections after reading them.

Tell Somebody Else about the Material

After reading an informative article, a training manual, or an instruction booklet, recount the information to somebody else. In order to

Demonstration 6.1

Read the following passage.

If the balloons popped the sound wouldn't be able to carry since everything would be too far away from the correct floor. A closed window would also prevent the sound from carrying, since most buildings tend to be well insulated. Since the whole operation depends on the steady flow of electricity, a break in the middle of the wire would also cause problems. Of course, the fellow could shout, but the human voice is not loud enough to carry that far. An additional problem is that the string could break on the instrument. Then there would be no accompaniment to the message. It is clear that the best situation would involve less distance. Then there would be fewer potential problems. With face to face contact, the least number of things could go wrong.

Now turn away from the page and try to recall the ideas in this passage—try to say it aloud to yourself.

If you were unable to remember more than several of the ideas from this passage, you are not alone. Most people—both young and older adults—find it very difficult to remember any of the ideas from this passage. Notice that although the passage contains sentences that are individually easy to understand, the sentences do not relate to form a coherent message. Thus, it is nearly impossible to comprehend what the passage means. Next, experience what happens when you are provided with a context that allows full comprehension of the passage. Look at the picture on the next page, and then reread the passage.

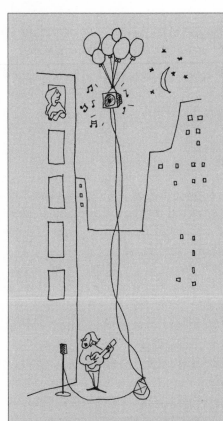

Try to recall the passage again.

You no doubt noticed that once you were able to fully comprehend the passage, your memory for the ideas in the passage improved significantly. In fact, experiments have shown that memory for passages like this one nearly doubles once the passages are presented in a context that allows full comprehension.

teach something, you really have to understand it. If you cannot explain the material to somebody else, then you haven't understood it. This technique will also help identify the gaps in your understanding. Additionally, telling somebody about the material forces you to retrieve the information from memory. As discussed later, retrieval itself is a potent memory technique.

Relate the Material to Your Knowledge

As Demonstration 6.1 illustrates, you understand better when you connect new information with material that you already know. You would fail to understand the demonstration passage if you had no knowledge of balloons, microphones, and so on.

Sometimes what you already know can serve as an analogy to understanding new information. Indeed, many scientific discoveries have been stimulated by analogy. In 1596, Johannes Kepler was trying to understand why the outermost planets move more slowly around the sun than do the innermost planets. The prevailing view was that spirits caused the planets' motion. Kepler suggested that maybe there is one spirit radiating from the sun that gets weaker as the distance from the sun became greater. But how could there be such a power that could not be seen yet exert an effect at a considerable distance? Kepler developed his understanding of this new concept by relating it to light. Light from a lamp shines less brightly on objects that are farther away than on objects that are nearer. Kepler used this known property of light to refine and support his understanding of the new information about planetary motion. Of course, Kepler's understanding was the precursor of the present-day concept of gravity.

More generally, research has clearly shown that new information related to what we already know is remembered much better than is new information not related to prior knowledge. As already mentioned in Chapter 2, older adults generally have more knowledge (semantic memory) than do younger adults. By relating your storehouse of knowledge to the material you are trying to learn, you will be able to exploit one benefit of age.

Ask *Why?*

An effective procedure for relating new material to existing knowledge is to pose the question "Why?" In a series of experiments conducted by one of the authors, students from Canada were given a set of Canadian social studies facts to learn, such as: "There are more unions in British Colombia than in any other province." Students who constructed reasons for why the fact might be true remembered almost twice as many facts as students who were told to simply study the facts for a later test. The "Why?" students did not even have to succeed at constructing a reason—just thinking about possible reasons produced better memory for the facts.[5] Attempting to relate new information to existing knowledge will improve your memory for that information.

The *Techniques:* Elaborative Rehearsal Tools
Organize Information

By organize, we mean relate the information together and establish groups of related information. For example, to help the students in my memory course remember the research findings about memory, I advise them to group the experiments in terms of what kind of memory store the experiment is about: sensory memory, short-term memory, long-term memory. Further, I tell them that rather than view each new fact as a separate piece of information, they should relate it to the theories that they are learning about the different memory stores.

Organization is perhaps one of the strongest techniques for supporting memory over long-term time spans. The authors' research has directly compared organization strategies against other elaboration techniques. The interesting finding is that when testing is immediate, organizing a list of words or trying to better organize the information presented in a prose passage does not necessarily produce better recall of the material than do other elaboration techniques. Yet when testing is delayed for a day or more after study, organization produces the best recall of the material. Organizational strategies help older as well as younger adults improve their memory for studied information.[6]

Sometimes you have to work a little bit to find some dimension on which to-be-remembered information shares some similarities. For an example of this and of how powerful organization is, try Demonstration 6.2.[7]

Create an Organizational Theme

If the information you're trying to learn has no apparent organizational scheme, you might make up a sentence or story about the information. To this day, the only way I can remember the order of the planets around the sun is to recite the sentence I used in elementary school: "My Very Enthusiastic Monkey Jumped Straight Up Near Pluto" (Mercury, Venus, Earth, Mars, Jupiter, Saturn, Uranus, Neptune, and, of course, Pluto).

Use Visual Imaging

Generating visual images of the material is a time-honored strategy for improving memory. Over 2,000 years ago, Aristotle advocated this technique. In the early 1900s a Russian who gained some notoriety for his phenomenal memory feats relied on visual imagery for storing information in long-term memory. It seems that this individual was able to easily, almost involuntarily, generate vivid visual images. Even if you don't have exceptional imagery ability, the act of trying to create a visual image of the information you want to remember will improve your memory. Forming a visual image forces you to make the information more specific or more particular, making the meaning of the information more precise and less arbitrary.

As a concrete example of how you might use imagery for learning new information, consider the two kinds of photoreceptors on the retina of the eye: rods and cones. The rods are specialized for vision under conditions of low illumination but are not sensitive to color. The cones are the receptors that are used to perceive color. To remember this information you could form a visual image of a black and white photograph of someone fishing in the evening with a fishing rod.

Demonstration 6.2

Study each of the words in the list for about 5 seconds. Then on a piece of paper try to recall as many of the words as you can.

Pea	Grasshopper	Lawn	Dollar
Parsley	Clover	Tea	Lake
Gasoline	Wine	Ketchup	Syrup
Horn	Train	Drum	Thunder
Rattle	Siren	Canoe	Oak
Blocks	Bookcase	Table	House
Pilot	Kite	Bee	Time
Robin	Flag		

Most of us would find recalling this word list difficult. In the authors' experiments, younger adults rarely recall more than half of the words, and their recall is usually worse than 50 percent.

Now study the words again (again, give yourself 5 seconds per word), but do so by trying to relate groups of words together according to some dimension on which they share a similarity. To give you some help, you might think about the dimensions of "things that are green," "liquids," "things that make noise," "things made of wood," and "things that fly." Then try to recall the word list.

We expect that you found it easier to remember the words after you imposed some organizational structure on the list. Try doing the same thing for new information you want to remember. You will find welcome improvements in your memory.

Then form another image of someone eating a colorful, many-flavored ice cream cone. These images combine the names with the functions of the two kinds of photoreceptors, thereby making this information easier to remember.

Forming visual images not only improves memory but also enhances understanding. Used in this way imagery can simulate the ideas you're trying to understand and learn. For example, to increase his insight and understanding of relativity and the consequences of traveling at the speed of light, Albert Einstein used visual imagery. To approximate the actual experience, Einstein imagined himself riding a lightning bolt or falling in an elevator at very fast speeds.

With some tweaking, the visual imagery technique can become an even more powerful aid for remembering. One study had students view images in which to-be-remembered words were interacting or presented separately. For instance, one group might be shown a picture of a CART carrying LETTERS that had STAMPS affixed. The other group might see a picture of a CART, LETTERS, and STAMPS positioned separately side by side. The interactive-imagery group remembered substantially more of the target words than did the individual-imagery group. Further, memory benefits are observed regardless of whether the interactive images are bizarre or common.[8]

Employ the "Why?" Technique

As mentioned, asking yourself "why?" questions is helpful in comprehending material. The authors' research has revealed that asking "why?" is also an extremely effective technique for elaborating information so that it is better remembered.[9] The advantage of the "why?" technique is that it is easily applied to a wide range of material that you need to remember. For instance, in learning about the cardiovascular system, one fundamental fact you might want to remember is that arteries are thick and elastic and that veins are thin. This fact is more easily remembered if you attempt to answer "why?" One answer is that arteries carry blood away from the heart and thus are subjected to spurts of blood produced by the heart's pumping motion. To work well, muscular, elastic walls are needed. Muscular walls can withstand the pressure created by spurts of blood pumped by the heart, and elasticity can produce the action of a one-way valve thereby preventing blood from flowing back toward the heart. Veins, in contrast, return blood to the heart. Located farther away from the heart's contractions, they are not as directly influenced by the heart's pumping motion. Blood flows more evenly, so the walls need not be elastic or thick. With this understanding, information is more likely to become knowledge-based rather than memorized, and thus is more likely to be retained in semantic memory. As we know, semantic memory functions well even as we age.

To illustrate the range of the "why?" technique, consider a set of facts as in the Bill of Rights. One amendment many people don't remember is the Third Amendment, which prohibits quartering of soldiers without due compensation. This amendment is probably difficult to remember because it is unrelated to our daily lives. Asking "why?" guides elaboration of this amendment so that it directly relates to our existing knowledge. "Why is quartering of soldiers without due compensation part of a Bill of Rights?" A plausible answer is that under the governments of the 1700s, martial rule commonly posed great financial hardship for some individuals who were forced to house and feed soldiers. This Third Amendment guarantees that such burdens will not be required of individuals living in the United States. Generating answers to "why?" questions will not only help you remember the information, but also may well stimulate additional interest in the material you are studying. As you might expect, research suggests that material that is more interesting is better remembered than is information that is considered boring.[10]

All the above techniques will help you remember information, but sometimes you may need additional help, especially if part of the requirement is to remember their order. To memorize things that are difficult to relate to prior knowledge or must be remembered in order, use the Method of Loci.

Try the Method of Loci

When my sister Marisa was faced with having to learn the Bill of Rights for an exam, she complained that, unlike me, she "had a life." She did not want to waste her valuable time trying to memorize the constitutional amendments by repeating them over and over as her classmates were repetitively doing.

I told her that she could learn the material by using a powerful memory technique developed by the ancient Greeks known as the Method of Loci. Because materials for writing were expensive, the Greeks memorized their public lectures and speeches. Good oratory was highly prized, so the Greeks were committed to developing effective memorization techniques. One of the benefits of being alive today is that the Method of Loci is perfectly legal. In ancient Greece it was against the law for political candidates to hire a memory coach (who would teach the Method of Loci) to help the candidates memorize their political speeches. At that time it was believed that a memory coach conferred an unfair advantage to the candidate over his opponents. With this method, each successive main idea is related in turn to a familiar landmark (a locus) among a familiar route. Practitioners typically construct an interactive image that relates an idea to the landmark.

Having decided to follow my advice and use this method, my sister used different parts of our house as the loci, and imaged an activity that incorporated each one of the first ten Amendments with a particular part of the house. First she imagined a member of a religious organization at the doorstep wanting to discuss his religion with her. This represented the First Amendment: The right to free speech and choice of religion. Having tired of the conversation, Marisa imagined reaching into the front hall closet to grab a rifle to encourage the visitor to leave. This represented the right to bear arms, the Second Amendment. Next, the kitchen: Marisa imagined it overrun by a troop of soldiers demanding to be fed. This violates the Third Amendment: no quartering of soldiers against one's will. The soldiers raided the cupboard and did not pay for the food. This violates the Fourth Amendment: no unreasonable search and seizure. And so it went.

Each successive part of the house was related to another amendment. At the time of the test, Marisa mentally "walked" through the house and recovered the image she had associated with that part of the house. This not only prompted memory of each amendment but also preserved the order of the amendments, which was a requirement for the exam.

No matter what your age, you can effectively use the Method of Loci. This was proven when a group of German researchers taught the Method of Loci to older adults ranging in age from 65 to 83, instructing them to use the method in studying a list of forty words. In order to have enough loci to connect to each word, the adults used landmarks around the city of Berlin. The improvement in memory was fantastic. Before learning the Method of Loci, these same adults recalled on average no more than about three of forty words in a list (but note that this is not much worse than younger adults' recall, which was about five of forty words). After practicing the Method of Loci, the participants were then challenged with remembering a new list of words and preserving the order in which the words were originally presented. Participants were given only ten seconds to study each word. Even under these demanding study conditions, older adults averaged twenty-three words recalled. After learning how to use the Method of Loci on word lists, the participants then demonstrated that they could use the method to remember lists of historical events and their dates.[11]

Now, try Demonstration 6.3 to convince yourself that this is an extremely powerful memory technique. Having learned about the Method of Loci, you can use it to remember information that is not easily structured or for which correct ordering is important.

- Material for a course
- Important chronology, such as a family tree
- The key points of a speech you are giving
- The order of procedures for new policies at work or for operating a new piece of equipment
- A grocery list, when pencil and paper are not handy

Demonstration 6.3

Use the Method of Loci to study the following grocery list. Use interactive imagery. Making the images bizarre can be helpful as well.

hot dogs,   cat food,   tomatoes,   bananas,   chicken, juice,   broccoli,   lunch meat,   pasta,   bread,   cherries

Hint: Try using successive parts of your house as the loci, such as

1. Driveway	5. Living room	9. Den
2. Garage	6. Bathroom	10. Bedroom
3. Front door	7. Dining room	11. Study
4. Hall closet	8. Kitchen	

On a sheet of paper try to write down the grocery list.
You should find that you can recall most or all of the items.
If you are still having trouble with the method, here are some images you might form to link each grocery item to a locus.

First, imagine your driveway with a big *hot dog* across it
Then an image of a *cat* eating her *food* in your garage
Your front door with *tomatoes* smashed against it
The front hall closet with a bunch of *bananas* hanging on the coat rack
A *chicken* sitting on your living room couch, reading
Juice coming out of the faucet in the bathroom sink
Broccoli hanging from the dining room ceiling
Lunch meat wrapped around your kitchen refrigerator
Pasta insulating the walls of your den
Loaf of bread sleeping in your bedroom
Three slot-machine *cherries* on your computer screen in your study

Recalling these grocery items is now a simple matter of taking a mental walk around your house and trying to re-create the images you initially formed.

Allocate Your Time

Once you've settled on the elaboration techniques that appeal to you, you can take several more steps to improve their effectiveness.

First, for remembering large amounts of information, such as the contents of a training manual or a textbook chapter, try to divide your study time into several sessions or days instead of using all your time in one block. Massing study time is not as effective as using the same amount of time in several, shorter sessions. The idea here is exactly the same as learning a skill like playing tennis or learning to play a musical instrument. One long practice session once a week is not as effective as many shorter sessions spread out over the week.

Second, focus your study time on the material you're having trouble remembering. You do not need to devote time to information you've already learned. This recommendation seems obvious, so why mention it? Well, research has been done on how participants studied a list of items so that they would improve their performance on a memory test for that list. Remarkably, many people tended to spend more time studying items they had gotten correct on previous tests than on items they had not previously memorized. In some ways this finding makes sense, because by studying items you've successfully remembered, you are rewarded by easily recalling them on a memory test. Clearly, however, this strategy doesn't help you improve your performance. The better strategy is to identify information that is difficult to remember and then spend your study time on those difficult items.

Finally, try to study during a time of day when you feel the most alert—what researchers term your optimal time of day. Especially for adults over the ages of 60, thinking and remembering decline at nonoptimal times of day. Most older adults report preferences for morning over evening times. Exciting new research indicates that when older adults are given memory tasks at the optimal times (i.e., morning), their performance declines little or not at all relative to younger adults. Chapter 4 provides more details on this new insight into the cognitive abilities of older adults.

The Rest of the Battle

Getting information *into* memory is only half the battle. Getting information *out* is the other half. Evidence suggests that much of the information we store in long-term memory lasts a lifetime. Many of us have had the experience of feeling that we know the material we are trying to remember, and might even remember where in the book that material appeared or in what lecture the material was presented. Still, we are not able to bring to mind the desired information.

As described in Chapter 5, the challenge of retrieval becomes more pressing as we age. Aging tends to diminish the ability of the individual to retrieve information from long-term memory. It's likely that the memory changes you notice as you age have to do with increased difficulty in bringing to mind (retrieving) information stored in memory.[12] Retrieval might be said to be the weak link in memory. The good news is that techniques exist that can facilitate retrieval and that are extremely effective even for older individuals with declining memory capabilities.

Practice Retrieving the Target Information

One powerful technique is to practice retrieving the information you want to remember. If you can anticipate what that will be, then try bringing that information to mind without your notes or the original reference in front of you. That is, practice what you will be required to do later during a speech, at work, or on a test: retrieve information from memory. I once gave a talk in which I had selected a particular word to use at a critical juncture in the talk. The word kept escaping me, so I periodically retrieved it. When giving the talk, at the critical juncture the word came to mind immediately. Our research has shown that the act of retrieving information is one of the best ways to ensure that information will be remembered.[13] It "greases the gears," so to speak.

The retrieval practice technique is so powerful that it has been successfully used in exciting research that has improved Alzheimer's patients' memory for necessary information (see Chapter 13 for more extensive discussion of this technique). In the technique used with Alzheimer's patients, the patient is prompted to remember the target information twenty seconds after hearing it. If that retrieval is successful, then the next prompt occurs forty seconds later and so on until the interval has reached five minutes or so. Individuals who are able to retrieve the target information after a five-minute interval are also likely to remember the information a week later![14]

You could try adopting a similar technique for retrieval practice, but of course use longer time intervals. Try to retrieve the information you want to remember at a short interval after study, perhaps after fifteen minutes. If successful, then try increasingly longer intervals until you can easily retrieve the material after several days' delay from last exposure.

Generate Retrieval Cues at Test

It is well established that retrieval is greatly improved when cues are provided. To convince yourself of this, try Demonstration 5.1 (in Chapter 5). As noted in that chapter, commonsense retrieval cues can include written notes or photographs. But in many settings, it is difficult to provide yourself with retrieval cues. For example, you may find yourself in the enormous parking lot of the mall, without a pad and pencil to mark down the spot where you've parked. When you return to the parking lot after a long day of shopping, how will you remember where you left your car? In cases like these, you can exploit particular cues to help stimulate your memory.

Use What You Already Know

Your knowledge base can be a good source of retrieval cues, especially if during study you have hooked or linked the material being tested to your previous knowledge. Previous knowledge is more easily retrieved than is newly learned material. That easily retrieved information can act as a cue to stimulate further retrieval about the topic, and you may be able to access the required information. It is also important that you don't just keep thinking about the identical information on the topic, but that you try to keep retrieving different facts. Memory theorists believe that retrieval of the wanted information can become blocked if you concentrate on the same piece of information. For instance, the other evening I was trying to recall the name of a representative for a retirement fund. The name "Jim" kept coming to mind. As I tried to retrieve other names, I kept coming back to "Jim." I realized that "Jim" was not correct and was blocking access to the right name. I went to bed, forgot about "Jim," and the next morning as I thought about the person, his name came to mind: "John."

Use Physical or Environmental Cues

You probably know from your own experience that the physical environment can stimulate retrieval of information from memory. Perhaps you returned to childhood surroundings, such as the house you grew up in or your high school, and found that many memories came to mind. Indeed, it may have surprised you how many things you remembered that you thought had been completely forgotten. It's a safe bet that most of those memories had to do with people and humorous or poignant events associated with those locations.

The important question for present purposes, however, is whether environmental cues are effective in stimulating retrieval of technical information, such as facts required on an exam. The answer is yes, they seem to be. Some research has compared the scores of students who took an essay test (which requires recall) in the same classroom where they heard the lecture material against the scores of students who took the test in a different classroom.[15] Students who took the test in the same classroom as the lectures scored somewhat higher than did students who took the test in a different classroom. Students typically take tests in the classrooms where their lectures are held. So, if you find that you cannot retrieve some needed information, you might try looking around the room and envisioning the feel of the classroom, the students you were sitting with, and other features present during the lecture that contained the information being tested.

By the same token, you may be required to remember material in a different physical environment from the one where you first encountered it. You can provide yourself with environmental cues by envisioning the physical environment in which you heard the information. Research shows that cues derived from visualizing a study environment can be as effective as the physical presence of those cues.[16]

Get in the Mood

Your internal state during studying can actually serve as a retrieval cue in a test situation, provided you can recapture that state at the time of the test. One aspect of your internal state is your mood. Some studies have reported that a particular mood present during encoding (e.g., happiness, sadness) can facilitate retrieval if the mood is recaptured during retrieval, whereas other studies have not found that mood can serve as a retrieval cue for technical information. Most studies agree, however, on the fact that when mood is induced through music, it can indeed act as an effective retrieval cue. For example, if the mood inspired by background music during studying is stimulated during an exam, then consistent improvement in performance has been reported. So, if all else fails during that important test, you might want to try re-creating the mood you were in when you studied the information you are having trouble retrieving.[17]

Returning to the Classroom: The SQ3R Method

For many reasons, middle-aged and older adults are returning to the classroom. Some are doing so in conjunction with retraining at their current place of employment, some are entering a new career, and some are simply interested in learning for the sake of learning. All the techniques presented in this chapter can be used to better remember and master school-related material or new business-related material.

You may find, however, that returning to the classroom presents especially difficult memory demands. Many older students returning to school, as well as younger students just entering college, mention as one of their most daunting tasks the memorization of large quantities of textbook material. This is not surprising, because very little in our day-to-day routine prepares us for reading, digesting, and remembering large amounts of information from books.

To meet this challenge, you can use the SQ3R method. SQ3R, which stands for "survey, question, read, recite, and review," is an easily implemented, systematic, and effective way to guide your learning from textbooks or any other written material. It integrates in step-by-step fashion the techniques you have already learned about in this chapter.

Survey

When starting your reading assignment, the first step is to skim or survey the material in order to get a broad overview of the content. Often, you can read the subheadings provided in a chapter to get an idea of what the main topics are. Sometimes reading the first sentence of each paragraph in a section can give you a good sense of the general points addressed in the chapter. Regardless of the particular strategies you use to skim a chapter, your objective is to map out the territory covered in the book. As a concrete example, consider surveying a chapter on intelligence in a developmental psychology text. By looking at only the first two levels of subheadings and reading some initial paragraph sentences, you can see that the chapter will cover the definition of intelligence, changes that come with age, how to measure intelligence, factors that influence measurement of intelligence, importance of intelligence, and information processing.

Notice that in "surveying" the chapter, you have created a structure or framework to contain the detailed material you are about to read. Indeed, the purpose of surveying is to help you organize the material. As you know, organization is one of the key steps in producing good memory.

Question

Next ask yourself questions about the material you have surveyed. It is important that you ask the kinds of questions that will further stimulate your own interest in the material. When you become interested in an assignment, the material is easier to absorb. Many people report that they feel more "in flow," happier, and more like themselves when they are absorbed in a productive task.[18] Further, good questions will stimulate elaboration and use of the "why?" technique. Consider again that chapter on intelligence. Clearly, it would not be a good idea to ask yourself, "I wonder how many pages I have until the end of the chapter?" This type of question is bound to throw water on any embers of interest you might have about the material. Better questions about a chapter on intelligence might be: "What determines intelligence—nature or nurture?"; "I wonder if there's something I can do to increase my kids' intelligence?"; "Will my intelligence increase as I age?"

Read

After asking questions, carefully read the chapter. Just read. Do not take notes or underline. The objective here is to understand the material. Underlining or taking notes can interrupt your attempt to create a cohesive understanding of the chapter.

Recite

Next, you should test your knowledge at the end of a section or chapter. Tell yourself, a friend, or your mate about what you've read. Instead, or in addition, answer any study questions that are included at the end of the chapters or sections of your book. Reciting serves two major goals. First, it provides retrieval practice, a tried-and-true memory improvement technique. Second, it helps you identify what you did not understand or what you are not able to remember. This allows you to more effectively focus on the next step.

Review

Review the material, especially the material you did not understand or remember well. Approximately 50 percent of your review can be conducted with the book closed. After doing so, you might find that using the book to take notes or underline is effective in helping you learn and remember the specific information you found difficult on initial review. The SQ3R recommendation is that underlining and taking notes be left for the review period. This recommendation fits in with the research findings indicating that students sometimes study inefficiently because they spend time on material they can already remember. By postponing the time-consuming note-taking or underlining process until review, you can reserve that last step to focus on information you have *not* already learned from surveying and reading.

Should the SQ3R process be conducted on whole chapters or section by section? There's no scientific evidence to support one approach over the other, but studying a chapter section by section seems to be the more effective method.

A Final Word

A piece of advice for those of you who are going back to school or taking classes that require remembering lectures and texts: all the techniques discussed in this chapter are effective only to the degree that you devote your attention to implementing them. During your study periods you need to avoid distractions that compete for your attention. Turn off background noise like the television, radio, or clanking washing machine. Try to find quiet, uninterrupted periods of time when you can fully concentrate on the material. Many experiments have demonstrated that divided attention during study substantially reduces memory. This is true even when participants are instructed to use elaborative rehearsal techniques during periods of distraction. The same advice holds for remembering lecture material. While listening, don't let your mind wander to worries, social engagements, anticipated vacations, or that book that you just read about improving your memory.

CHAPTER SEVEN

Remembering Tough Things

A few years ago, the authors were filmed for an educational video series designed for introductory psychology students. The topic was memory, and as part of the video, several older adults were assembled to chat about their memory problems. One gentleman noted that a memory failure that he was unhappy about was forgetting where he set down his keys. His wife retorted, "But, Honey, in all of the years that I've known you, you've always forgotten where you put your keys."

Some things are tough to remember for all of us, no matter what our age. Where we put our keys, the name of a person to whom we've been introduced, a new vocabulary word we want to remember, the title of a book someone has recommended to us, or a short list of items to buy at the store—these details are perhaps not crucial, but forgetting them can cause inconvenience and create frustration. This chapter presents the memory strategies you need to substantially improve your memory for things that are tough to remember.

First, it's important to identify the fundamental characteristic that makes things tough to remember. Things that have a high degree of "arbitrariness" are hard to remember. Some people set their keys

Demonstration 7.1

Have somebody read you the list of words, or try reading them yourself, spending one or two seconds per word. Then attempt to recall the words in any order.

DRUM, CURTAIN, BELL, COFFEE, PENCIL, PARENT, MOON, GARDEN, HUT, FARMER, NOSE, BUZZARD, COLOR, HOUSE, RIVER

To get a sense for how your memory compares to that of the general population, count how many words you correctly recalled. When a list like this is read to adults at the rate of one word per second, recall averages about seven words. Adults 70 years of age and older recall an average of about four words.

Source: Adapted from the Rey Auditory-Verbal Learning Test.

down anywhere in the house or office. For these people, there is no rhyme or reason for where keys can be placed—it's arbitrary. Similarly, a person's name is arbitrary. With the exception of some nicknames, there is usually no inherent association between a name and a person's appearance. A standard memory assessment is to give people a list of fifteen unrelated words at a fairly rapid pace (one word per second), after which recall is attempted. Remembering all the words is not easy because they have no obvious meaningful relationships. Stop now and try this yourself with Demonstration 7.1.[1]

To remember tough things, one general strategy is to try to take the "arbitrary" out of the information you need to remember. If you made an attempt to create meaningful associations for the words in the demonstration, you were making the items less arbitrary. You could do this by thinking of how each word relates to things that are personally relevant. For "drum" you might think of your nephew who

Demonstration 7.2

Read the list of words or have somebody read you the list. While reading or listening to the list, try to form associations with the words. As suggested in the text below, you could tie the words together in a story. Or think about a personal experience that involves that word.

DESK, RANGER, BIRD, SHOE, MOUNTAIN, GLASSES, TOWEL, CLOUD, BOAT, LAMB, GUN, SCHOOL, CHURCH, FISH

You should find that your recall has improved relative to your performance on the first list in Demonstration 7.1.

Source: Adapted from the Rey Auditory-Verbal Learning Test.

is a whiz at playing the drums, for "curtain" you might remember operating the curtain at the school play, for "bell" you might remember your mother ringing the bell for dinner, and so on. Or you could build meaning into the list by constructing a scene or story that incorporates the words in the list. You might imagine a "farmer's house" on the "pencil"-thin "river" with the "moon's nose" just going down over the "curtain" of the "garden" and the "coffee" smells waking you with the "bell." By linking up the words in a meaningful way, the words become less arbitrary, and recall for the list improves considerably. I used this story strategy and was able to recall thirteen of the fifteen words. On a similar list, without using the strategy I recalled fewer than five words. If you didn't create associations the first time, try doing so with the new list in Demonstration 7.2. You should experience a dramatic improvement in your ability to recall the words.

A second general strategy for remembering tough things is to periodically practice retrieving that information (pulling it out of long-term memory; see Chapter 5). Every so often during the day or the week, retrieve the name of a new friend or client you want to remember. For that important point you want to make at a meeting, every so often rehearse your presentation of it. For that joke you want to remember at the next party, practice retrieving it occasionally. A common belief is that we need to study a lot in order to cement arbitrary information into long-term memory. Research has shown, however, that periodic retrieval of newly encountered information can be just as effective, and often is more effective, for creating abiding, accessible long-term memories (see Chapter 6 for more on this point).[2]

Remembering Names

"It's one of the most uncomfortable social situations we face, and it happens over and over again: We see someone we've met once or twice but can't recall the person's name."[3] This is one writer's lament, shared by many. In fact, for people whose business depends on networking, forgetting peoples' names can add economic loss to embarrassment. Aside from being arbitrary, names are challenging because of the social context in which we meet new people. Social introductions are often accompanied by distraction. For example, we may be preoccupied by anxiety about how we are presenting ourselves and about what we are going to say. We may be attending to the person's appearance as well. Thus, when we hear a person's name we may be paying attention to everything but that. The upshot is that the person's name is not stored in memory and we have forgotten it within seconds of hearing it. Using the terms introduced in the overview of memory presented in Chapter 2, you might say that with all these distractions the person's name resides in our auditory sensory memory for several seconds and never receives the attention and working memory "resources" necessary for more permanent memory storage.

The first and most obvious step, then, in remembering names is to pay attention to the name. A simple technique is to immediately say the person's name in your response to being introduced: "Bob. How do you do, Bob?" Saying the person's name requires you to concentrate on it, thereby increasing the likelihood you will store the name in long-term memory. This may be difficult to do at first, but keep working on it. Eventually it will become habit.

Step two is to reinforce the name in long-term memory. You can do this by periodically using the person's name during the course of your conversation. This requires that you retrieve the name from memory occasionally, and such retrieval practice is a powerful way to help remember the name (see Chapter 6 for more on retrieval practice).

Probably the most effective way to store a name in long-term memory is to reduce the arbitrary nature of the name. Pick out a trait or physical feature of the person that would make the name fit (or a similar-sounding word fit). When meeting "Ward," for example, you might notice a wart on his hand and then make the association between "Ward" and "wart." When meeting "Gil" you might concentrate on the creases or wrinkles on the side of his neck, which remind you of gills. Maybe "Steve" has big forearms, like those of a stevedore. "Angela" could be so named because she has the appearance of a sweet, innocent angel. "Debbie" might dress like a debutante.

This technique works because it provides a familiar relation for the name, making it less random, and also because it uses people's physical characteristics, which are effective retrieval cues (see Chapter 5 for more on retrieval). Some years ago, I was interviewed on a local television show to discuss memory. Not wanting to forget the name of our host, Mary, I noticed that she had very close-cropped hair and related that to her name. "Not hairy" became a cue for remembering Mary. Under the glare and stress of the television cameras, I could simply look at Mary's hair and have her name immediately come to mind. It has been years since the taping of the show, and the only thing I remember is Mary's name.

Often individuals do not have these distinguishing features, however. The solution is to use visual imagery to add those features or to accentuate existing features.[4] For instance, you can form a mental image of gills on the person named Gil. This is a good approach to remembering the name of somebody you've not met in person. For example, my friend had to remember the name of a business colleague he had not yet met named "Lockheart." One way to make this name more meaningful or logical, and hence more memorable, would be to envision a man clutching his chest as if his "heart" had "locked."

You can reduce the arbitrary nature of a name by adding personal relevance to it, just as you might have done for Demonstrations 7.1 and 7.2. Clearly, you can relate a new person's name to that of a family member; for example, "Richard" is the name of my uncle. You can also relate a new name to a movie, television, or book character whom you really like (or dislike).

In summary, to remember names you need to:

- Pay attention to the name when introduced.
- Practice retrieving the name by using it after being introduced.
- Make the name less arbitrary by associating it with a physical or personality trait.

Last Resorts

If you haven't used these techniques when being introduced to a new acquaintance, don't give up on being able to recall his or her name. The trick here is not to think harder (which usually doesn't work) but instead to generate possible retrieval cues. One choice is to use the letters of the alphabet as a prod, considering names that start with "A" and moving on until your memory is jogged. A friend of mine was telling me about the younger brother of bluegrass musician Bill Monroe, whose name he couldn't remember. He tried the alphabet strategy, and upon reaching "C" he remembered the man's name: Charlie Monroe.

Sometimes you'll have a vague feeling that a name (or any word you're trying to retrieve) did start with a particular letter. This impression can be a good cue, and you can focus on generating names starting with that letter. Even if you don't get the name, the words you generate can themselves become a thread that leads you to the name you're trying to remember. For instance, an older friend of mine was trying to recall a name. He had the feeling that the name started with "k" and started to think of names. He came up with "King," knew that wasn't correct, and then used "King" to think of "Queen." "Queen" wasn't correct, but "Queen" (perhaps in combination with "King") cued "Royal." "Royal" was the name my friend was trying to remember.

Other times trying to think of facts that are related to a person (or any name you're trying to remember) can help trigger your memory for the name. For example, you might think about when you last saw the person, what he or she looks like, where you met them, who their friends are, what activities they like, and so on. A woman who successfully used this technique relates: "My daughter lives in a new subdivision in town that has a special name, which I have trouble remembering. I wanted to tell my neighbor. I thought, 'Maybe if I think of some related information, it will help.' I thought about the entry sign to the subdivision that has a cannon on it. 'It must have something to do with the Civil War.' It came to me—Gettysburg!"[5]

One more suggestion is to write down the names of people you see infrequently but want to remember. So, after meeting a new couple at a party, jot down their names and information about them in a journal that you keep of your friends. The next time you anticipate seeing them, you can refresh your memory for their names and prior conversations with a quick glance in your journal.

Remembering Where You Put Things

Word has it that the average person spends a total of about five days of the year looking for his or her keys. We do not know if this figure is accurate, but it underscores how easily we can forget where we left a needed object like keys, glasses, or a wallet, or even where we parked the car. The best remedy is to establish a single location where you consistently put your keys, glasses, or other easily misplaced objects when you are finished with them. In my house we have a small key holder attached to the kitchen wall where I routinely hang my keys after getting home. If I neglect to do so and see the keys lying around later, I put them on the holder immediately. This small organizational step can save you hours of frustration.

Sometimes it isn't convenient to put your glasses in the same spot or to find the same parking space. Usually we "forget" where we put these things because we are preoccupied with other thoughts when we deposit these objects. So, this information never reaches our long-term memory in the first place. Like remembering names, the solution is to stop for a moment and pay attention to your surroundings when you place something somewhere. To make yourself pay attention, say aloud the place where you put your object. As you set your keys down in the living room, say aloud to yourself, "I am now putting my keys on the coffee table in the living room." One older gentleman told us proudly that he now never forgets where he has parked his car. As soon as he gets out of his car, he routinely pauses and pays attention to the landmarks on each side of his car.

Putting objects down in your house can create a more challenging memory problem because the landmarks are so familiar that they lose their effectiveness as cues. In this context, you may need to create a more elaborate association between the object and its location. For instance, if you put your keys by the computer, pause immediately and create a story. "I was excited to check my e-mail so I went straight to the computer and threw my keys down." Again, it helps to say the story aloud. Or you can imagine the computer taking your keys from you as you sit down. These elaborations help memory in two ways. They force you to attend to where you have placed the object, and they create a rich set of cues, any of which can provide a link to your memory.

Finally, if you are like the man described at the beginning of this chapter who had a long history of forgetting where he had left his keys, you might try adding perceptual markers to the objects. You could tie a flag to the antenna on your car to allow easy visual location. For smaller objects, products are available that provide perceptual cues as to the whereabouts of the lost object. One such product is a key chain that beeps when you clap your hands. This solution can have its own drawbacks, however. The key chain can beep when other random sounds are made (a television), and then you have to fetch the key chain in order to turn off the beeper. Indeed, this defect can be so annoying that people stop using the beeping key chain, in which case the memory techniques listed above may be preferred.[6]

In summary, to remember where you put things:

- Find a location where you can consistently place the object.
- If this is not possible, pay attention when you deposit the object by saying it aloud.
- Associate the location with the object by creating a meaningful story or a visual image.

Learning New Vocabulary

There are times when you want to learn the meanings of new vocabulary words. For example, you may want to learn some basic vocabulary to facilitate traveling in a foreign country, you might be taking a foreign language course, or you might simply be trying to build new vocabulary in your native language. Remembering the meaning of new words can be difficult because the relation between the vocabulary word and its meaning is often arbitrary. Memory for vocabulary meanings can be enhanced by using a simple memory strategy known as the key-word technique.

The key-word technique involves two steps. First, identify a familiar word that is embedded in the new word or sounds like the new word (or part of the new word). For example, in the word "penurious" you can find several familiar sound-alike words—"pen," "penny," "furious." These familiar words are your key words. Second, form a visual image of the meaning of the familiar key word interacting with the meaning of the new vocabulary word. Continuing the example, select "penny" as your key word. The new word "penurious" means "stingy," so you would form an image of a stingy man interacting with a penny. One image might be a man who is clutching a penny. Our research has shown that a bizarre image can often be more memorable, in which case you could form an image of a man with his arms wrapped around a giant penny. If forming visual images is difficult for you, a verbal description of the scenario will serve the same purpose.[7]

Now you have a strong memory record of the meaning of the new word, as well as an easily available cue to that memory record. The next time you see or hear the new word, identify your key word and use it to think of your image, which will contain the meaning of the new word. The key word serves as a strong cue to your image (or scenario), provided that your image contains the two meanings interacting together or related in some logical way. That is, the key word is not as effective if you envision the meaning of the key word next to that of the new word (e.g., a penny next to a man).[8] Also, sometimes you will need to play with the sounds in the new word in order to find a key word. For instance, the Spanish word *perro* has no clear English word embedded in it. But "per" sounds like "pear," so it could be the key word that is used to form an interactive image with the meaning of *perro* (dog). So, for example, you could imagine a dog eating a pear or a dog who has pear-shaped ears. Later, when you see *perro,* the sound "per" should cue the image of the dog.

You may have encountered books and tapes that use the key-word method to help people successfully learn foreign vocabulary (e.g., the "Linkword Language System"). Many scientific studies have consistently confirmed the power of the key-word technique for learning foreign vocabulary and learning new vocabulary words in one's native language. In one typical study, college students were able to remember the meanings of 80 percent of sixty-one previously unknown English words after spending only fifteen seconds applying the key-word method to each word. To get a sense of how easy and effective this technique is, try it now on the list of English vocabulary words shown in Demonstration 7.3. Use this technique to your advantage anytime you are trying to remember new vocabulary meanings.[9]

In summary, the key-word technique works as follows:

- Find a known word—the key word—that is embedded in the new word or is similar to the new word.
- Form an interactive image of the meaning of the known key word and the meaning of the new word.
- Later, use the key word to remember the image that contains the new word's meaning.

Demonstration 7.3

Spend about 10 seconds applying the key-word method to each of the words (skip the ones you already know). If you need help with selecting key words, we have provided possible key words in parentheses by the vocabulary word. Otherwise, try finding your own key words. Then cover up the key words and the meanings with a sheet of paper, and try to recall the meaning of each vocabulary word as you read it. You may be surprised at how much you remember with the key-word technique.

Vocabulary Word	Definition	Key word
CLAYMORE	sword	(CLAY)
LOGGIA	balcony	(LOG)
INUNDATION	flood	(NUN)
SUNDER	split	(SUN)
PENURY	extreme poverty	(PEN)
SURREPTITIOUS	secret	(SYRUP)
PERNICIOUS	causing harm	(PERM)
HABILIMENTS	attire	(BILL)
POLYGLOT	speaker of several languages	(POLLY) (the parrot)
VERDANT	green	(ANT)
DESCRIED	discerned	(CRIED)
DISSEMBLE	disguise	(CYMBAL)
SOPORIFIC	sleepy	(SOAP)
DROMEDARY	one-humped camel	(DAIRY)
DUCTILE	easily bent	(DUCK)
DULCET	soothing	(DOLL)
EBULLIENT	high-spirited	(BULL)
STENTORIAN	extremely loud	(TENT)
DIAPHANOUS	transparent	(FAN)
TRENCHANT	cutting	(TRENCH)
FULSOME	offensive	(FOOL)
CONFLAGARATION	a burning	(FLAG)

Remembering Numbers

Telephone numbers, license plate numbers, identification numbers, street numbers, ZIP codes, bank codes, social security numbers—our society finds many uses for numbers. Because numbers are difficult to remember, we normally write them down for later use. Sometimes, however, it is inconvenient or impossible to write down a needed number, and sometimes we tire of continuously having to find that slip of paper in our purses, pockets, or drawers. So, at least occasionally, we do need to rely on our memory to retain a number. This section presents some methods to help you remember numbers well.

First, it is important for you to know that the memory technique people adopt as children and continue to rely on throughout their adult years is not very effective. Most people attempt to remember numbers by repeating them over and over. Although this so-called rote rehearsal technique (see Chapter 6) does keep the number active in short-term memory, it does little to support recall of the number from long-term memory.[10] Short-term memory fades within a couple of seconds. This means that if you can't continuously rehearse the number, it will be lost from your memory almost immediately. The other problem is that short-term memory holds a limited amount of information (about seven numbers). So, although you might be able to retain a seven-digit telephone number in short-term memory with rehearsal, it is unlikely that you could accurately retain a new telephone number with its area code, which involves ten digits, in short-term memory. Most of you will have already discovered this lesson: rote rehearsal is a poor method for committing numbers to memory.

The general principle for remembering numbers reflects the theme of this chapter: reduce the arbitrary nature of the number. Following are some ways to make a number less arbitrary.

Find logical patterns in the number—describe the number to yourself as a pattern. Two real-world examples illustrate how effective this method can be. One of my relatives has the following telephone number: 335-3978. I noticed that both groupings of numbers begin with a number in the 30s. The first grouping is easy because 3s are repeated (33); then all I have to remember is 5. The second grouping includes another number in the 30s that, when doubled (39 + 39), equals the final two numbers. I don't dial this number often, but last summer I needed it as I put my children on the plane to visit this relative. Not having the number with me, I had to recall it from memory. Remembering was easy because I had once taken the time to describe the number as part of a logical pattern. The second example involves my friend's telephone number at work: 864-2173. This number simply starts at the highest even digit and follows with each even digit in turn. Then the number begins going up by odds, but with 7 in the middle.

Find groupings (chunks) of numbers that overlap with number strings you already know. My home telephone number begins with 254-. Having learned that number, I use the first chunk of my home number to help remember the number of the telephone in my office (277-2547). I rarely need to dial my own work number, so I don't use it much. Even after more than eight years, I still remember it by relying on the knowledge of my home phone number. My helpful description is: "Starts with 7s, home number, ends with 7."

More generally, you can add meaning to numbers by associating them with your knowledge base. If you are a runner, you could relate digits to running times. The number 3492 could be thought of as a near world-record time of 3 minutes and 49.2 seconds for running the mile. For those of use who are not runners, we might associate a to-be-learned number with driving times for certain distances, the ages of several friends, or notable dates in our personal or national histories. After much practice with this technique, you could even use it to become a memory performer. With 250 hours of practice perfecting this technique, one individual was able to remember strings of over 80 digits that were presented at a rate of one per second. For the much shorter strings of digits we commonly need to remember, the technique is applied with little practice. All you need is a ready knowledge base to associate with numbers.[11]

In summary, to remember a string of numbers:

- Do something to make the numbers less arbitrary.
- Periodically practice retrieving the numbers from long-term memory. Periodic retrieval practice helps strengthen numbers

in memory, making them easier to access from memory. It also helps you easily generate the specific retrieval cues attached to the number (e.g., "world-record running time," "decreasing sequence of evens followed by odds").

Remembering Steps for Operating Electronic and Computer Devices

"I recently purchased a new VCR, read the instructions, and tediously followed them to record my favorite TV show. The next time I tried to record a show, I couldn't remember what to do and had to reread the instruction manual."[12] Most of us have experienced similar frustrating episodes of forgetting how to operate an electronic or computer device. This problem is compounded when we additionally cannot remember where we placed the instruction manual! Incidentally, you can remedy this latter problem by putting all instructional documents for appliances and electronic equipment in one location (e.g., a folder in a particular drawer).

You can implement two basic techniques to better remember the steps to operate your new electronic gadget. The first technique is to make yourself do more than just read and follow the instructions when you first use the device. To remember what to do, take time to elaborate the instructions and to make them less arbitrary. Various ways to do this include:

- Translate the directions into your own words. Say the translated directions aloud or explain them to somebody else. You can also translate the directions onto a sheet of paper, which can serve as a quick reference to refresh your memory for later uses.
- You might be able to make the control dials and buttons more meaningful by attaching small labels that identify the purpose of each one in words you understand.
- Comment on the steps. To finalize a recording time in my VCR, I have to proceed through two steps that to me seem unnecessary and redundant. I remember these steps by saying

to myself, "OK, now I'm finished, except that I still have the two unnecessary steps to do."

■ To make the directions less arbitrary, figure out the importance of each step. That is, produce elaborations that establish cause and effect relations between the step and what the device is doing (see Chapter 6 for more on elaboration).

■ Try to organize the steps themselves. Elaborate so that the order of the steps has some logic to it.

Usually, we forget how to operate a gadget because we don't use it on a regular basis. Thus, the second technique for remembering is to practice using the gadget periodically. Some concrete guidelines for practice are the following:

■ Try to space your practice sessions, especially for devices that have a number of different functions that all have somewhat different steps. I recently got a hand-held computer device for scheduling appointments, keeping telephone numbers and addresses, and jotting down notes. There were a lot of different steps to remember. Instead of practicing all of the steps at once, I practiced a few every day.

■ Limit practice sessions to about thirty minutes, especially if you are an older adult.[13]

■ Some researchers suggest practicing the device (or for whatever it is you're trying to learn the steps) once a week to maintain the steps in long-term memory. To help you stay with it, you can enter a time on your weekly calendar for practicing.[14]

■ It may be that you want to get "up-to-speed" on the device rather quickly. In this case, for the first several weeks, you can practice operating the device every other day. Afterwards, if you don't use the device often, then a booster practice session every several months will be needed.

The key point here is that you should do anything you can to make the information you want to remember less arbitrary. By using the techniques described in this chapter, you will improve your ability to remember tough things in all kinds of situations.

CHAPTER EIGHT

Remembering to Remember

MEDICATIONS, APPOINTMENTS,
THINGS TO PACK . . .

I was on a trip to give a research talk at another university. The morning after I arrived, I was selecting the sports coat, slacks, and tie that I would wear to meet the students and faculty. As I rummaged through my suitcase to find my dress shoes, I was feeling confident and excited about my talk later in the day. At first I was perplexed when I couldn't find them. Then to my horror I realized I had forgotten to pack them. Later that day, there I was at my talk trying to remain calm while dressed in tennis shoes. The ultimate irony and embarrassment was that I was giving a scholarly talk on remembering to remember!

How are we to understand this kind of memory failure? In this case, I had not forgotten that I needed dress shoes. While deciding what I needed to bring the day before, I had several times thought about these shoes. My lapse was that I failed to remember the shoes at the appropriate time during packing. Many of our daily memory tasks are of this type. We have to remember to pick up bread on the way home, to take our medication at the appropriate time, to show up for appointments, and to give our spouse or housemate a telephone message. Whenever we forget in these situations, it is rarely because we have forgotten that we need bread, that we have to take medication, or that we need to relay a simple telephone message. We have not forgotten the critical information. We have forgotten to call up the critical information at the appropriate moment. This type of memory is known as "prospective memory."

Surveys we have conducted with groups of younger and older adults show that on a day-to-day basis, most people are more prone to prospective memory failures than to any other types of memory failure.[1] This trend does not diminish with age. In some cases, such as forgetting to buy bread on the way home, prospective memory forgetting produces only minor irritation. But this kind of forgetting can have serious consequences as well. With age come more health-related problems that often require remembering to take medication—a prospective memory task. Remembering to turn off the stove when food is done or locking doors before departing for vacation are also prospective memory tasks that, if forgotten, can spell disaster.

Although prospective remembering is intertwined in our daily lives and poses increasing challenges as we age, memory experts and books on memory rarely address this aspect of memory. The authors of this book, however, have been conducting research on prospective memory for over a decade. This emerging research will help you understand what you can do to prevent prospective memory failures. Contrary to popular belief, not all prospective memory diminishes with age. Aging seems to exacerbate the difficulty of performing only certain types of prospective memory. This chapter alerts you to several important kinds of prospective memory tasks that are especially challenging for older adults, and it describes simple techniques to meet these challenges.[2]

Where's the Cue?

Previous chapters in this book have emphasized that memory involves retrieving the desired information from a long-term memory store. They have also emphasized that retrieval is facilitated by cues. A simple rule of thumb is that the more cues you have, the better your memory will be—and this is especially true for older adults. For example, your friend asks you if you remember a character from a particular movie you viewed a long time ago. Upon this direct "request to remember," you may find yourself stuck for the answer. But if your friend then provides you with helpful details about the character's appearance, role, and actions, you can use these as cues to help you remember the character.

When a task requires you to draw on your prospective memory, however, there is no request to remember—no friend to ask you to retrieve information or to supply you with cues. This leaves you with the most difficult of all memory tasks—having to retrieve information in a virtual vacuum. For instance, if you have to remember to give your friend a phone message, there is no cue telling you that you should retrieve something from memory. That is, nobody asks you to remember, so you don't have the advantage of being in a "memory mode" (where you can try to generate cues to prompt retrieval if necessary, as described in Chapter 5).

Once you understand this basic problem, it is easy to see that developing successful prospective memory involves taking extra steps to make sure that you provide yourself with appropriate cues. Before learning these steps, be alert to a second major difficulty with prospective memory. People sometimes resist taking the necessary extra steps not because they're being irresponsible but because tasks involving prospective memory (such as remembering to relay a simple phone message) seem so easy. When the authors have asked adults in their experiments if they try to do anything extra to remember a prospective memory task, they often indicate that there is no need to. Most people believe that they will not forget an action they intend to perform sometime later. The authors' research shows, however, that no matter how vivid a thought seems to be at the moment, it can be forgotten within a few seconds. The lesson here is: do not be seduced by the apparent simplicity of prospective memory tasks. These tasks, by their nature, strip away the cues we ordinarily rely on to prompt successful retrieval. It is very important that you build useful cues into prospective memory tasks.[3]

Provide Your Own Cues

To remember to do things that require prospective memory, add external cues to the environment to serve as reminders. Some commonly used external cues are making entries on calendars or writing a note to oneself. These cues are certainly helpful and work for many people. However, they are not fail-safe methods, as I learned the hard way. My daughter asked me to bring home a blank computer disk from the office. Being a memory expert, I knew that this was a prospective memory task and therefore would be difficult to remember. Accordingly, I wrote myself a note as a reminder and placed it in my briefcase, which I always carry to work. But I still forgot to bring the computer disk home . . . because I forgot to check my note. The danger here is that after writing a note or making an entry on the calendar, we may figure that the task is as good as completed and don't bother checking notes or calendars.

The best prospective memory cues are physical cues that serve as alerts. Some examples are:

- Tape your reminder note over the opening of your briefcase.
- Set a timer as a reminder to check the oven, pick up your child from practice, or leave for an appointment.
- Put a shoe (or other object) by the door as a reminder to take the trash out or to put your check in the mailbox before leaving the house for the day.
- Tie a red piece of yarn on the cabinet as a reminder to grab your lunch from the refrigerator on the way out.

To maximize the "attention-grabbing" potential of your cues, use unusual cues or display cues in an unusual manner. For instance, if you ordinarily leave your shoes by the door, then placing a shoe at the door as a reminder is not likely to attract your attention. Make the cue something out of the ordinary. For instance:

- Instead of placing a shoe at the door, hang your shoes on the doorknob or place a clock turned upside down at the door as a reminder to do something before leaving the house.

■ Put a pan upside down in the middle of the kitchen floor as a reminder to check the oven.

It also stands to reason that the cue should be placed in a prominent location. It does little good to turn a clock in your den upside down if you rarely go into the den. Likewise, a note to yourself that is buried in a clutter of materials on the counter is not likely to be noticed. The cue must be placed in a position so that you will encounter it and pay attention to it in the course of your daily activities.

Finally, the cue will be most effective if it relates meaningfully to the prospective memory task. That is, the cue should be *informative in terms of suggesting the action you are trying to remember.*[4] For example, every two weeks I must remember to put the empty water container on the porch so that the water company will give me a full container. The day of the week on which the delivery is made is not consistent, so the task is not routinely tied to a particular day. To remember the task, I put the empty water container by the door the night before. Other concrete examples are:

■ Place the check you want to mail by the door (instead of a shoe).
■ To remember to get your lunch from the refrigerator, tie a piece of red yarn to the refrigerator door (instead of a cabinet).
■ To remember to take out the garbage, put a piece of crumpled scrap paper by the front door.

Summary

To remember a prospective memory task, take these steps:

■ Use an external cue.
■ Position the cue in a prominent position so that it alerts you.
■ Try to use an informative cue that relates directly to the prospective memory task.

Create Imaginary Cues

For some tasks requiring prospective memory, you may have difficulty adding external cues. At a restaurant with no cloakroom, for example, you may slip your hat, scarf, or other item under the table while you eat and have to remember to pick up your belongings after eating. All of us have walked out of a restaurant without remembering to gather some item, and perhaps even lost something of value. Notice that this situation is a perfect recipe for forgetting. Your hat or scarf is out of sight so there is no external cue to remind you to grab your belonging. Also, in this situation you are unlikely to be able to use unusual external cues. Even if you could, you might not feel comfortable putting a bizarre object on the table at a restaurant. In situations like this where external cues are sparse, use an imagery strategy to create cues. Immediately after depositing your belongings, find a landmark that will be prominent as you leave (the door works well). Then imagine these items in some bizarre interaction with the landmark. Here are several examples to get you started:

- To remember your umbrella, imagine the exit door blocked by a giant umbrella.
- To remember your hat, imagine the door as a big tunnel in the shape of a hat that you have to slide through.
- To remember to stop at the store to buy bread on the way home, imagine the intersection where you have to turn blocked by a huge loaf of bread.

Several features of this imagery strategy help you to remember. First, of course, a neutral object (e.g., the door) has now been embellished so that it will grab your attention and thus serve as a reminder cue. Second, the extra attention required to think of and form the image keeps the thing you want to remember more "alive" in memory so that it more easily comes to mind later. Research shows that the imagery strategy can indeed be quite effective in helping us remember to remember. The authors have found that participants who were instructed to use imagery strategies remembered significantly more than participants who were not told about the imagery strategy. Indeed, this strategy can be as effective for prospective remembering as can adding external cues.[5]

Form Implementation Intentions

Consistent with this advice that establishing good cues is important is compelling research by Gollwitzer and his colleagues showing that it is critical to go beyond forming general intentions—specifically, it is important to also think of where and when you will perform the intended actions. Gollwitzer makes the point that when we set goals, we often do not accomplish them, not because we don't want to succeed but rather because we simply do not think of our intended goals and actions at the appropriate times. In one study, for example, one group of women was taught about the importance of breast self-examinations and strongly encouraged to perform them. Another group was also encouraged to perform the examinations but this group was additionally asked to form what Gollwitzer calls an implementation intention. Rather than simply thinking about the general intention of performing self-examinations, these women were encouraged to imagine exactly *where* and *when* they would perform the examinations—for example, while taking a shower in the morning. Although both groups of women were highly motivated to perform the examinations, the results indicated that the women who formed the implementation intention were much more likely to remember to perform the task over the next month.[6]

Implementation intentions have been shown to be effective in a variety of situations including helping people remember to eat healthful foods, engage in exercise, and stop smoking. Moreover, implementation intentions have been shown to be effective with older as well as younger people and even to be helpful with people who have certain types of memory problems.

Research demonstrating the effectiveness of implementation intentions is so impressive that it caused me to be a little overbearing (I believe my wife called it obnoxious) this past New Year's Eve. When discussing New Year's resolutions with my friends, in the spirit of helping them succeed I tried to get them to form implementation intentions. For example, after one of my friends told me that his New Year's resolution was to exercise more often, I told him about the research on implementation intentions and told him that he should take his resolution a step further and specifically think about the exact conditions under which he would perform the desired behaviors. Implementation intentions take the form of imagining, "When situation X arises, I will perform action Y." I told him that he needed to convert his general intention, "I want to exercise more often," into an implementation intention, "Every day after my eleven o'clock class, I will go the gym and run for twenty-five minutes on the treadmill." In addition, I asked him to mentally imagine himself doing that. Memory is very associative, and by thinking in advance of the specific situation in which you are to perform an intended action, the thought to perform the action will automatically come to mind when you are in that situation.

For practice, before you move on to the next section, take the time to form an implementation intention for a behavior you want to remember to perform. You might want to remember to do something later on today or you might want to change a routine behavior in some way such as increasing the amount of exercise you get by using the stairs rather than taking the elevator. Again, the key is to imagine yourself performing the behavior in that particular situation.

Do It When You Think It

Be aware of another potential pitfall in remembering to perform tasks that draw on prospective memory. Thus far, this chapter has provided you with strategies to bring to mind at the appropriate time the prospective memory task. Having successfully accomplished this memory feat, you may feel that you are home free. Not necessarily! This e-mail circulating among older adults humorously illustrates the problem:

> This is how it goes: I decide to wash the car; I start toward the garage and notice the mail on the table. OK, I'm going to wash the car. But first, I'm going to go through the mail. I lay

the keys down on the desk, discard the junk mail and I notice
the trashcan is full. OK, I'll just put the bills on the desk and
take the trashcan out, but since I'm going to be near the mailbox anyway, I'll pay the bills first. Now, where is my checkbook? Oops, there's only one check left. My extra checks are
in my desk. Oh, there's the Coke I was drinking. I'm going to
look for those checks. But first I need to put my Coke farther
away from the computer. Oh, maybe I'll pop it into the
fridge to keep it cold for a while. I head toward the kitchen
and my flowers catch my eye—they need some water. I set
the coke on the counter and uh-oh! There are my glasses. I
was looking for them all morning! I'd better put them away
first. End of Day: The car isn't washed, the bills are unpaid,
the Coke is sitting on the kitchen counter, the flowers are half
watered, and the checkbook still has only one check in it.

For many of us, this amusing caricature is painfully accurate. The authors' research confirms that keeping intended actions in mind in the
midst of distraction becomes increasingly difficult with age.[7]

In technical terms, once the prospective memory task has been
retrieved from long-term memory, it must be maintained in working
memory until the task has been executed. The natural limitations of
working memory, however, introduce a new set of challenges. Because working memory can maintain information only for several
seconds (unless the information is rehearsed), once retrieved, the intended action will stay in mind only briefly before it leaves our awareness (see Chapters 2 and 4).

The rub here is that once the intended action leaves awareness
you are faced with the difficult task of remembering to remember the
intended action again. This may now be doubly difficult because the
external cues you relied on initially are sometimes no longer present.
For instance, you turn off your oven buzzer that signals the food is
done, then someone calls you to another room before you can take
the food out of the oven. This brief distraction can be enough to cause
you to forget that the food is still cooking. Despite implementing a
good strategy, you've ended up with burned food. Another common

experience is to think about taking your morning medication (or vitamins) while in the kitchen, but on your way to the bathroom to get the medication you get distracted by some clutter in the living room. If you do eventually get to the bathroom, you now are no longer thinking about the medication and instead you brush your teeth out of habit.

The authors' research confirms that intended actions are difficult to maintain in awareness (i.e., working memory) for even brief time periods. In several studies, participants were provided with external cues that were so attention-grabbing that they rarely forgot to perform the prospective memory task. In some conditions, after seeing this effective external cue, participants were prevented from executing the prospective memory task immediately. Instead, these participants were distracted and had to delay execution of the prospective memory task by five to thirty seconds, during which time the cue was removed. These short delays caused a significant number of participants to fail to execute the prospective memory task.[8]

For older adults, having to briefly delay execution of an intended task was disastrous. When the older participants (those over 60 years of age) were allowed to perform the prospective memory task at the time the effective external cue was present, they forgot little or anything. But when execution was delayed by as little as five seconds after the cue was removed, they forgot to perform the task about half the time.[9] This degree of forgetfulness is dramatic considering that in some cases no distractions were presented after the five-second delay. How can we understand this? As mentioned in Chapter 4, working memory declines significantly with age. Perhaps it is these type of memory failures that give rise to the common observation that we get "absentminded" as we age.

The key lesson here is to recognize that our memory is not good at handling scenarios in which a retrieved intention must be held briefly before being executed. This is especially true when the brief delay is full of distraction, when the delay is associated with removal of the external cues we ourselves have provided as reminders, and as we age. Here are some straightforward ways to succeed under any of these conditions:

- Whenever possible, as soon as you retrieve the intention, *perform the task.*
- If you get interrupted before you are able to follow through on your intention, then create an external cue: you can set or reset a timer, quickly jot a note, or place some nearby object in an uncommon position.
- If you cannot create an external cue, then take a moment to imagine a mental cue. For instance, if a ringing telephone interrupts you, quickly imagine setting the handset on your hand with enough pressure to cause some discomfort. Hanging up the telephone should then cue the image and thereby remind you that something was unfinished when you started the conversation. Alternatively, you might try crossing your legs or your fingers as a cue.

Habitual Prospective Memory Tasks: When Practice Does Not Make Perfect

Prospective memory tasks that are performed repeatedly become habitual and therefore may not be expected to pose memory problems. Remembering to take a medication that is prescribed for a period of time is a common and important example of a habitual prospective memory task. At first you may forget to take the medication, in which case you can use one of the memory strategies already described. After awhile, however, taking the medication becomes part of the daily routine and is not likely to be forgotten. So, where's the memory problem here?

After days of repeatedly taking the medication, you do it without even thinking about it. Then one day, as evening approaches you cannot remember whether you have taken your medication earlier in the day. This memory failure presents a serious quandary. If you took the medication and then take another dose for safe measure because you cannot remember, you might be in danger of overmedicating. If you didn't take the dose but memories of taking the medication from previous days convince you that you really did take the dose that day, then you will forgo that day's medication.

Research conducted in the authors' laboratories has shown that both these types of memory errors can occur when the prospective memory task becomes habitual. These findings are reinforced by studies that suggest that adherence to a medication regime can be hindered by such memory problems. The authors' research has found that people, and especially older adults, are particularly susceptible to forgetting that they have performed the habitual prospective memory task when they are engaged in distracting activity at the time they perform the task. In other words, under conditions in which they are very busy, older adults are very likely to repeat an action (the equivalent of repeating a medication).[10]

A very effective measure to address this specific memory problem is to put your medication in a pillbox that has separate compartments for the different medications you take throughout the day or for each day of the week. These pillboxes are inexpensive and widely available. The presence or absence of the medication in that day's compartment tells you directly whether you have taken the pill or not. If your pillbox is not transparent, consider the following story. A friend of the authors' has an 80-year-old mother who eats dinner out frequently, and when she does, she places her pillbox upside down in front of her dinner plate to remind herself that she hasn't yet taken her pill with her meal. She turns it right-side up after she swallows her pill.

- You can also use a tear-off calendar with daily pages. When you take the medication, tear out that day's page.
- You can make a chart and mark checks when you take your medication.

If you do not want to fool with pillboxes or other external aids, then there are several steps you can take

- Keep your focus on the task (taking the medication). Do not allow distracting thoughts or conversations to intrude as you perform the task. The more attention focused on the task, the better you will remember having performed it.
- Try to perform the task in some unusual or different way each

Table 8.1 Summary of How Age Affects Prospective Memory and How to Improve It

Prospect Memory Task Characteristic	Age Effects	Solution
Good environmental cue: Take book back to library—library book placed by the door	Minimal	Not needed
Poor environmental cue: Pick up a friend or relative at a certain time, or take food out of oven after a certain amount of time, no set alarm	Substantial	Create environmental cue: —Associate with a daily event (after lunch) —Set timer alarm
Maintaining intention over brief delays Remembering to take your medication as you are about to take out the garbage	Very substantial	Do it when you think of it: —Take the medication before taking out the garbage
Habitual: Daily medication taking	Moderate to substantial confusion over whether action performed	Use external records: —Pillbox —Daily calendar or check sheet

day. For instance, one day you might cross your arms as you place the pill in your mouth. The next day you might place one hand on your head as you place the pill in your mouth with your other hand or you might swirl the juice around in your mouth to make the event more distinctive and memorable. These extra and atypical movements will help elaborate the event, and thus make it memorable.[11]

Summary

Table 8.1 summarizes different prospective memory situations, how they are affected by age, and how to improve prospective memory in those situations. In general, you should follow the simple steps below for successful prospective remembering.

- Create an "attention-grabbing" external or internal (imagery) cue.
- Do *not* delay performing the intended action once it has been brought to mind (e.g., by a cue).
- If interrupted after the intention comes to mind, try to "reset" your cue or quickly create a new cue.
- For a prospective memory task that is habitual (like taking medication), to remember that you actually executed the action use external records or distinct movements in executing the action.

CHAPTER NINE

Mental Exercise and Memory

USE IT OR LOSE IT

I have an aunt who is well into her 80s. I see her only occasionally, but when I do I am always impressed by how alert and vital she is. She is an animated conversationalist. She can talk about a wide variety of topics, and she remembers information well. The last time I saw her at a family wedding, I asked her what her secret is. She informed me that she tries to stay mentally active. I wondered what she meant by that, and she said she has a group of friends that gets together during the week to play games like bridge. She studies the Scrabble™ dictionary to memorize uncommon words and brings out the game when company calls. She's unbeatable. In fact, sometimes they make up new rules to add some variety to their games.

My aunt of course is not an isolated example. The *New York Times* recently described a 102-year-old man whose life is anything but dull.[1] He works at the Institute for Clinical Science at Pennsylvania Hospital, edits a medical journal, keeps two secretaries busy, and plays a 1694 Stradivarius violin. Another 102-year-old works at a zipper factory in Los Angeles making sales calls and grappling with the challenges of cheap imports. A 92-year-old man works forty hours a

144

week as an efficiency expert at a plant making strings for banjos and guitars. One idea about why these people have maintained their cognitive abilities is that they continue to challenge and use those abilities. This reflects the increasingly popular notion that memory ability follows the "use it or lose it" principle. The scientific evidence provides guidelines for the kinds of activities that are most likely to keep your memory abilities intact.

A central theme of this book is that memory is not a unified "thing." Rather, there are distinct kinds of memory. This property of memory suggests that there are two possible interpretations of the use-it-or-lose it principle. The "specialist" interpretation holds that although using or practicing a particular kind of memory will in fact keep that memory ability from degrading, it will not do much to maintain other memory abilities. An analogy is that training for tennis certainly helps maintain specific tennis skills but does little to increase swimming speed. Similarly, spending more days swimming may make you a stronger swimmer but it probably wouldn't do much to help your tennis skills.

In contrast, according to the "generalist" interpretation, doing intellectual or memory tasks that are challenging provides a generally positive effect on all memory abilities. The generalist position is illustrated by people who do the daily crossword puzzle in the belief that it will help them learn and remember information in general. Is there any truth to either interpretation of the use-it-or-lose-it belief?

Maintaining Specific Memory Abilities Across the Life Span

The evidence supports the idea that continued use of particular types of memory skills will keep those skills functioning well into old age. Research presented at a conference several years ago examined the memories of both active and recently retired older architects. Architects routinely are engaged in looking at and remembering floor plans. In this study, both active and just-retired architects were given a complex and novel floor plan to study and later to recall. Recall accuracy for the spatial layout of the plan was as good for the older architects as for the younger ones. But when older architects who had been retired for several months were given the same recall task, performance was not nearly as high as for the older employed architects.

This finding suggests two key points. First, the ability to remember spatial information can remain high into old age as long as the person keeps using that kind of memory. Second, when that kind of memory is no longer practiced, it is quickly lost. This certainly supports the use-it-or-lose-it principle. This early research leaves one important question unanswered: Were the good memory abilities displayed by older and unretired architects limited to spatial memory (the "specialist" view) or could it have been the case that many types of memory were still intact in the older and unretired architects (the "generalist" view)?

An observation from an Alzheimer's patient is consistent with the specialist view.[2] As expected, this patient performed poorly on a variety of memory tasks, "flunking" most of them. The surprising finding was that this patient performed perfectly on a task in which he had to put together shapes to form various target patterns presented by the neurologist. This task likely involves visual working memory skills in holding the target patterns in mind while working with the shapes. Why wasn't this memory skill devastated by the Alzheimer's disease as were the other memory tasks? As it happens, this patient had been an artist. The implication is that because he had used his visual/spatial skills extensively, he did not easily lose these skills, even with the devastation of Alzheimer's.

An experimental finding with older and actively working college professors also supports the view that the particular kind of memory ability being used is the kind of memory that will stay intact as we age (this is the specialist view). One daily activity of college professors is to read articles or listen to talks that contain new information and to try to integrate this new information with their existing knowledge. Other chapters in this book have mentioned that trying to relate new facts to existing knowledge produces good memory for new information. Following that reasoning, it could be assumed that college professors are practiced at reading technical articles and books in such a way that they can remember the information from those sources. Sure enough, researchers have found that older college professors from 60 to 71 years of age could recall scientific passages about the earth's atmosphere and about the anthropology of tribal cultures as well as younger professors. These older professors could also recall a fictional prose passage as well as the younger professors. This study also compared the memory for these kinds of materials among younger and older people who were not professors. In this case, the older people showed worse recall for the passages than did the younger people.[3]

The bottom line is that older adults who stayed active at reading and remembering new information (college professors) did not show any decline in the ability to gather and remember information presented in articles. Older adults who were not as actively involved in this kind of memory task showed definite declines in memory. The lesson here is that practicing and using a specific kind of memory does help maintain that particular memory ability at high levels.

Here are some everyday examples of this memory-specific use-it-or-lose-it effect. One older retired woman recently took up bridge again after years of not playing. She found that she was not as able as she had been to remember the bidding and play of particular cards, and this was frustrating to her. This can be a lot of information to remember, and the memory task is more difficult because the bids and the cards can fly by pretty quickly (for those who don't know bridge, once a "trick" of cards has been played they are turned over so that the players cannot see which cards have been played). After playing regularly for several months, the woman was quite pleased that she was able to do well at remembering the bidding and the cards that had been played throughout the hand. By practicing weekly during her bridge session, she was able to regain her ability to remember and use necessary information to play a good game of bridge.

A retired professor who was still coming into campus several days a week found that he was starting to forget where he had parked his car in the campus parking lot. Incidentally this kind of memory problem is not uncommon as we age. This professor realized that his memory no longer quickly and automatically recorded the landmarks that signaled where his car was parked. To address this problem, he made himself pause after getting out of his car. He then forced himself to pay attention to what was in front of his car, behind his car, and beside his car (but not the other cars—they might move). He was trying to store in memory the landmarks of where his car was in the parking lot. At first he found it hard trying to commit to memory the landmarks of the parking lot. But just like the bridge player, after repeatedly practicing remembering this information he found that he was easily able to remember where his car was parked. In fact, in telling this story, the man smiled and remarked that now he doesn't even have to think about remembering where his car is parked. Noticing and remembering the parking lot landmarks feels like an easily performed habit. Again, practice at remembering this kind of information not only improved memory but also made the process less effortful for this older adult.

With these examples in mind, identify the particular situations where you would like to improve your memory. Once you identify the situation, think about activities or tasks that would force you to use that kind of memory. Then make sure that you regularly practice or schedule those activities. If you follow this plan, you should experience memory improvement. Remember that at first it may take a lot of effort, but if you stick with it you are likely to find that the amount of effort lessens as your memory skills begin to return.

Evaluating the Generalist Position
Evidence from Career Activities

Let's return to the issue of whether staying intellectually active provides protection for all memory abilities. One research strategy for testing this issue has been to examine the general memory abilities of older college professors, who, by virtue of the nature of their job, remain intellectually engaged while they are still working. According to the generalist position, older college professors should score highly on all tests of memory ability. Two studies showed that older professors did *not* perform as well as younger professors on a variety of memory tests. So, this research suggests that staying intellectually active does not help prevent loss of a wide range of memory abilities. Phrased in terms of an everyday example, the results suggest that daily practice at crossword puzzles may not prevent loss of memory in general. In fact, one study directly found that the amount of time older adults spent solving crossword puzzles was not associated with the preservation of their intellectual functioning.[4]

Another set of studies suggests a different conclusion. Researchers at the National Institutes of Mental Health conducted a remarkable study in which adults' thinking and memory abilities were followed for thirty years. The study focused on the complexity of people's work and its influence on thinking and memory. Complex work is work that is intellectually challenging, requires making decisions, and demands some self-direction. For example, work that primarily involves following instructions, performing routine activities, or handling a tool on an assembly line would not be complex work. Work that includes problem solving about dealing with people and other unpredictable things, having to come up with original ideas, or setting up new machines and equipment is complex. The results were telling. Complex work was related to higher thinking and memory scores on standard tests. These tests were not directly linked to particular work activities. That is, we see "general" increases in intellectual functioning and memory when people's daily job activities demand thinking. Even more encouraging is that older workers well along in their careers showed significantly more memory benefits of complex work on memory and thinking than did younger workers. Similar findings have now been reported in Japan, Poland, and Ukraine. The lesson from these studies is clear. Using your brain daily in complex activities is important—especially so as you age—for keeping your memory and thinking skills sharp.[5]

In sum, in studies that have focused on the effect of mental engagement from a job or career on memory, the results are mixed. Further, a majority of older adults do not work for pay.[6] Thus, before drawing any conclusions, we need to review additional research.

Research on Everyday Activities

Recent scientific research has given us a better idea of everyday activities that could possibly serve as "aerobic mental exercise." In one study, researchers collected information over a six-year period about how often older adults engaged in a variety of everyday activities.[7] These included physical activities (e.g., jogging and walking), social activities, hobbies, home-maintenance activities, and challenging or novel cognitive activities (learning a language or playing bridge). All these adults were also periodically tested to evaluate memory functioning throughout this time period. The memory tests measured recall of facts (semantic memory), recall of words, recall of stories, and working memory.

The findings showed that activity levels did tend to change over the six years. Importantly, not all activities helped buffer these older adults from declining memory. Social activity and typical hobby activities had very little association with how well the older adults maintained memory functioning. The activities that were significantly associated with good memory functioning were those that required intellectual engagement. Adults who participated in demanding intellectual activities were more likely to maintain their memory abilities than did those adults who did not participate in such endeavors. The results also showed that it is important to keep challenging oneself intellectually. Those older adults who continued to engage in intellectual activities over the six-year period were less likely to show the decline in memory ability that was evident in adults who did not do so.

Similar results were found in studies that examined adults ranging in age from 41 to 88 years after time spans of twenty to thirty years. One long-term study followed Canadian war veterans. Memory and cognitive measures were taken at the time of entry into the army and compared with similar measures some thirty years later. Those men who were more involved in intellectually challenging activities showed less decline in memory and cognitive functioning than did men who were less challenged. Importantly, research has also found that frequent participation in cognitively stimulating activities is related to reduced incidence of Alzheimer's disease. One study involving older Catholic clergy found that those engaged in frequent stimulating cognitive activity were half as likely to develop Alzheimer's (in a five-year follow-up) as those who infrequently engaged in these activities.[8]

Summary

Two important lessons are to be gained from the scientific research:

- It appears that keeping active can be important in maintaining memory functioning. "Use it or lose it" seems to be a valid principle, in both a general and a specific sense. There is some promising support for the generalist idea that challenging your mind with a variety of intellectual activities will help keep your memory decline at a minimum. The evidence more strongly suggests that memory benefits from "specializing" in intellectual activities that specifically challenge your memory. Borrowing an analogy from sports, running will help you keep generally fit, which may keep your swimming abilities from declining. My swimming coach used this reasoning when the pool at school was being repaired. He made the team participate in cross-country runs. But once the pool at school was fixed, our workouts consisted only of swimming. Specializing in swimming improves swimming more so than running improves swimming. The larger lesson here is to stay especially active in the mental activities you care most about maintaining.
- Current evidence strongly suggests that your mind needs to be challenged with "demanding" intellectual activity to keep your memory functioning well. Learning a new language or playing games that demand thinking (like bridge or chess) may help keep general memory abilities sharp, whereas passively watching television will not. The most critical point is that it is not what you do, but the degree to which you mentally challenge yourself in that activity. For instance, consider again watching television. This might well provide intellectual

engagement if you are analyzing the styles of the actors, figuring out the motivations of the characters, anticipating what comes next, and searching for a deeper meaning to the story.[9]

To help you include more brain-building activities in your life, Figure 9.1 provides a list of common activities that require high levels of intellectual engagement.[10] For comparison, Figure 9.2 lists common activities ranked not very highly in terms of intellectual engagement.

The scientific evidence discussed here encourages mental activity as a way to help maintain memory ability as we grow older. There are, however, important qualifications to this evidence. Scientists have not been able to conduct the experiment that would prove (or disprove) that increased mental activity has a causal effect on protecting against age-related memory decline. In such an experiment, individuals that have approximately equal memory scores would be required to engage in different levels of mental activity for an extended period of time and afterward would be tested on a range of memory tests. Instead, scientists have shown that individuals who engage in more mental activity tend to have better memory. This result could mean that better memory ability makes a person more eager to engage in mental activity—not that mental activity produces better memory. Further, some reports have failed to find a positive relation between mental activity and memory performance in adult humans.[11] Nevertheless, it seems that the news at this stage is positive. Maintaining an active and mentally engaged life as we age is possible, and people who do so seem to better maintain their memory function.

Yet, some claims you may hear speculate well beyond this scientific evidence. For instance, in one popular book on brain fitness, the authors suggest that doing routine activities in new ways will help build "mental muscle," presumably for improving memory and cognitive functioning.[12] Two examples are brushing your teeth with your nonpreferred hand or wearing your watch upside down and on the other wrist. Also proposed are exploring books on tape if you normally read, or getting news on-line if you normally watch your news on television. In the authors' opinion, such advice is overly simplistic.

Playing cards
Playing chess
Doing jigsaw puzzles
Playing knowledge games
Playing word games
Reading newspapers and books and thinking meaningfully about
    them
Career reading
Using the library
Watching educational TV
Letter writing
Creative writing
Programming software
Using software or a calculator
Balancing your checkbook
Preparing your taxes
Doing math
Attending a lecture
Giving a talk
Doing business activities
Job training
Taking a course
Learning a language
Debating an issue on the meaning of a movie with someone
Relating what you have learned to someone

Figure 9.1 Common activities requiring a high level of intellectual engagement.

It is quite unlikely that brushing your teeth with your nonpreferred hand, wearing your wristwatch upside down on the other wrist, and trying something different for breakfast will provide intellectual challenge.

Variety Is the Spice of Memory

The final ingredient in the recipe for better memory through mental exercise is to build a routine that includes a mix of activities that challenge your intellect. Focusing on just one activity does not seem to give the degree of mental exercise needed to keep the brain fit. For instance, simply increasing your hours per week doing crossword puzzles is not associated with improved cognitive performance.[13] Variety is key. Those who engage often in a variety of the activities such as the ones listed in Figure 9.1 are more likely to slow or even arrest their age-related memory losses. The list in Figure 9.1 should not be viewed as a strict guideline. The central guideline is to create and find activities that are intellectually demanding. The goal is to try to integrate into your life activities that demand problem solving, thinking, and remembering. To get you started, here are some examples of how you might increase the intellectual challenges of activities you are already doing.

- Social activities per se are not necessarily intellectually demanding (see Figure 9.2). To help memory, inject an intellectual activity into social get-togethers. For instance, some groups regularly discuss an assigned novel. Others may discuss a movie. Older adults participating in these book (or movie) discussions well into their 80s and 90s tend to be mentally alert and energetic.
- There is evidence that not just any reading provides the kind of demanding intellectual activity that will help slow memory loss with age. Reading tabloids, celebrity, or movie magazines does not require the kind of deep, evaluative thinking that helps keep your mind and memory working well. One 75-year-old head of a company, for example, reads Shakespeare to

Physical: gardening, jogging, sailing, playing tennis

Self-maintenance: preparing a standard meal, doing housework, shopping, caregiving, owning pets

Hobbies: maintaining your car, repairing your house, assembling an item, woodworking, photography, sewing, singing

Social activities: eating out, going to a party, visiting relatives

Entertainment: watching game shows, comedies, soap operas on TV, listening to the radio, watching a sporting event, watching a movie, going to a concert

Figure 9.2 Common activities that do not require a high level of intellectual engagement.

keep his mind challenged. Preparing outlines of what you've read can also stimulate your mind and slow memory loss. Of course, if you are among the many who don't want to write an outline of what you're reading, then get in the habit of summarizing what you've learned to your friends and relatives. Or write your summaries, thoughts, and critiques of what you've read during the day in a journal.[14]

■ Increase the level of intellectual engagement your hobbies presently require (see the list in Figure 9.2). For instance, to increase the mental exercise of playing a musical instrument, work on memorizing a favorite piece. Try to learn a new style of playing, like improvisation. Learn the music theory that underlies the music you enjoy playing.

■ Inject more intellectual challenge in your self-maintenance activities (Figure 9.2). Try experimenting with new meals and dishes. Think about how changing ingredients would change the taste or consistency, then put your hypotheses to the test.

CHAPTER TEN

Physical Exercise and Memory

NOT EXERCISING IS RISKY BEHAVIOR

My research on this chapter quickly convinced me of the multiple benefits of exercise at any age, so much so that I became an impassioned crusader for the value of exercise in older adulthood. During my early research, I discovered that this thinking is counterintuitive for people who grew up in another era. For example, one woman told me that her father, who had been an avid athlete, quit playing tennis when he turned 50. His thinking and the advice given at the time were that demanding athletic activities were too vigorous and that older adults should not push their cardiovascular systems. After hearing several stories like this, I realized that the traditional view of aging was that older adults should conserve energy and avoid any activities that could possibly do harm. This mode of thinking about aging has a long history. Sir Francis Bacon, a philosopher and scientist who lived in the 1500s and 1600s, believed that human longevity is determined by how quickly we use up our vital spirits. According to this view, a long and healthy life results from inactivity and conserving one's resources.

I used to think this way too. My view was shaped by events like the one that happened to my favorite teacher while I was an undergraduate. He died from a heart attack while shoveling snow from his driveway, and I later learned that this is the leading cause of death from snowstorms. Incidents like this led me to believe that activity is unhealthy for older adults. While it is true that strenuous exercise is dangerous for older people who have been leading sedentary lives, it is also true that developing a regular exercise regimen in older adulthood is one of the most important things you can do for your physical and mental health.

In recent years, there has been a reversal of thinking about the value of exercise in older adulthood. We are at a point today where prestigious organizations like the National Institute on Aging, the International Longevity Center, the Centers for Disease Control and Prevention, and the American College of Sports Medicine are strongly touting the virtues of exercise for high-quality functioning in later life. It is obviously unwise to lead a sedentary life and then suddenly engage in strenuous physical activities such as snow shoveling. But there is complete agreement today that when training is built up gradually and done properly, it is dangerous *not* to exercise. Despite these urgent calls and the emergence of convincing evidence of the benefits of exercise for both physical and mental health, however, it is estimated that less than 10 percent of older adults engage in exercise that is sufficient to maintain and enhance endurance and muscular strength.[1]

This chapter describes some of the physical declines that occur with age, along with the powerful benefits of exercise on physical health for people of all ages. It then explores research testing whether exercise facilitates mental functioning. To foreshadow, there is strong recent evidence that exercise improves some cognitive functions. The end of this chapter presents strategies for beginning and sustaining a balanced exercise program.

Physical Changes with Age: The Bad News
Cardiovascular and Respiratory Systems

All of us who are over 40 know that aging profoundly affects our bodies. Major changes occur in our cardiovascular and lung capacity. The cardiovascular system, consisting of the heart and blood vessels, transports substances (oxygen from the lungs, nutrients from the digestive system, hormones from the glands, antibodies from the immune system) to the cells in our bodies and carries waste products to the kidneys and lungs. This nourishment of the body's cells is accomplished when the heart pumps oxygen-rich blood through the arteries and into the capillaries of the body's organs. The capillaries have highly permeable walls that allow the transfer of oxygen and nutrients from the blood to the organs.

Advancing age produces some declines in cardiovascular efficiency. Normal aging tends to have small effects on the functioning of the heart at rest, but it does reduce the maximum efficiency of the cardiovascular system (that is, its top efficiency while exercising). Starting in middle adulthood, the walls of the coronary arteries tend to narrow, and they become less flexible and more rigid. With both age and negative lifestyle-dietary choices, the level of cholesterol in the blood tends to increase. These factors lead to progressive blockage of the arteries, making it more difficult for the blood to pass through the system. These conditions force the heart to work harder, raise blood pressure, and increase the probability of a heart attack and stroke. A heart attack occurs when the coronary arteries (vessels that supply the heart with oxygen and nutrients) are prevented in some way from supplying the heart with blood (e.g., because of clogging). A stroke (the equivalent of a brain attack) occurs when brain cells don't receive their normal blood supply (e.g., because of clogging of arteries that supply blood to the brain).

Aging also affects the respiratory system. It reduces the amount of oxygen that is taken up by the blood in the lungs. Also, older individuals cannot breathe in and exhale as much air. The consequence is decreased "maximal oxygen consumption," which represents the body's maximum capacity to transfer oxygen throughout the body and to use it during exercise. To measure maximal oxygen consumption, people are asked to exercise on a machine (such as a stationary bike) and are asked to breathe through a large tube placed in the mouth. This allows measurement of the body's consumption of oxygen. As you continue to exercise at increasing workloads, the rate of oxygen uptake keeps increasing but eventually reaches a plateau, and this represents your maximum ability to take in oxygen and transport it throughout your body. Maximal oxygen consumption is thought to be the best estimate of cardiovascular fitness, and it decreases from 5 to 15 percent in each decade of life after the age of 25.[2]

Muscular and Skeletal Systems

In addition to developing wrinkles as we age, we lose bone calcium. As our bones become more brittle, we are at greater risk for breaking bones from falling. As a result of bone loss and spine compression, we lose a bit of height between the ages of 30 and 70 (men lose about one and a quarter inches, whereas women lose up to two inches).[3] The loss of bone mass is more pronounced in women after menopause, and this puts them at greater risk for osteoporosis (a severe loss of bone minerals and increased bone brittleness).

Also well documented is the loss of muscle mass (this loss is called sarcopenia), which causes a loss of muscle strength as we age. We lose about 30 percent of our muscle strength between the ages of 30 and 70, and the rate of loss is thought to be even more precipitous after 70. These losses often have severe consequences, ranging from interfering with our ability to perform routine chores around the house to threatening our ability to walk or rise from a chair independently.

We also have reduced muscular and joint flexibility, which means that our range of motion becomes more limited as we get older. There are corresponding declines in our postural stability, which means that we are at greater risk for losing our balance while standing and for falling while walking. This is a serious problem for older adults, as falling is the number one cause of accidental injury in people 65 and older. And, given the increased brittleness of bones, falls often have much more severe consequences (e.g., bones break more easily) in older adults.[4]

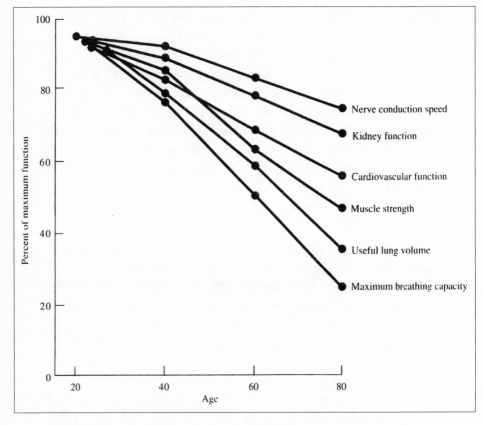

Figure 10.1 Age-related declines in the major biological systems.

Summary

Thus far this section has presented a rather depressing list of physical declines that accompany typical aging. As can be seen in Figure 10.1, the declines are quite general in the sense that they affect all our biological systems.[5] This news is not good. When left to its own, the body experiences a gradual decline in lung capacity, oxygen consumption and transportation, bone density and muscle mass, and flexibility. These declines along with some aches and pains often lead older people to restrict their activity even further, which in turn leads to increased losses in strength, bone mass, flexibility, and endurance. These conditions lead to a vicious cycle that has the effect of severely limiting one's activities and quality of life.

What are we to make of this? Should we lie back and wait for the inevitable to occur? Absolutely not! Although history has been marked by those looking for miracle antidotes to aging (such as Ponce de Leon, who searched in vain for the Fountain of Youth), today it is becoming increasingly clear that there are no miracle potions to redress the effects of age. The strong consensus today is that your health in your older years is determined to a substantial degree by how you lived your life in your younger years. This is a somewhat cruel circumstance, because nearly all of us feel healthy in our youth and often do not realize the strong need to control our diet and engage in exercise. With the benefit of today's research, however, we now know that—other things, such as genetics, being equal—those who lead a life free of alcohol abuse and smoking, maintain a balanced diet that is low in fat, and exercise regularly are not only likely to live longer but also much more likely to maintain their strength, endurance, and flexibility into their older years.[6]

The data are crystal clear in showing that people of any age (even those over 90) can benefit from exercise. As noted above, the younger you are when you begin to exercise, the better. But it appears that exercise at any age produces improvements in health and functioning.

Effects of Physical Exercise on the Body

As Table 10.1 shows, balanced exercise programs can significantly slow down nearly all the age-related physical declines described in the previous sections. Some believe that most of the physical declines we see with advancing age are actually due to our increasing inactivity as we get older and not to steady and irreversible physical deterioration. These people point to data like those in Figure 10.2 showing that exercising older adults have relatively "young" physical systems. It should be heartening to realize that the cardiovascular capacity of 75-

Table 10.1 Effects of Age and Exercise on Various Bodily Conditions and Characteristics

	Effects of Age	Effects of Exercise
Cardiovascular system		
Cardiovascular disease	Increases	Decreases
Stroke	Increases	Decreases
Blood pressure	Increases	Decreases
Cholesterol	Increases	Decreases
Body fat	Increases	Decreases
Aerobic capacity	Decreases	Increases
Muscular and skeletal systems		
Muscle strength	Decreases	Increases
Muscle endurance	Decreases	Increases
Muscle mass	Decreases	Increases
Flexibility	Decreases	Increases
Bond density	Decreases	Increases
Base rate of metabolism	Decreases	Increases
Depression	Increases	Decreases

Source: Adapted from R. Dustman, R. Emmerson, and D. Shearer, "Physical Activity, Age, and Cognitive-Neuropsychological Function," *Journal of Aging and Physical Activity* 2 (1994): 143–181.

year-old athletes is similar to that of slim but sedentary 25-year-olds. Indeed, the benefits are so pronounced that master athletes in their 50s and 60s today actually perform at levels comparable to those of the gold medal winners in the 1896 Olympics. As shown in Table 10.2, the 1979 champion in the 65- to 69-year-old age category would have won the 1896 Olympic marathon by nearly six minutes![7]

It is important to realize that it is not only master athletes who can maintain their function. *Exercise is beneficial at all ages, even light and moderate forms of exercise.* So even if you are out of shape and in your 80s, exercise may prevent or delay cardiovascular disease or osteoporosis. It may also help you recover the ability to get up by your-

Table 10.2 Running Times of Older Athletes in 1979 in Comparison to Those of Olympic Champions in 1896

Event (measurement units)	Best time in Olympic games of 1896[a]	Unofficial world record in 1896[b]	Age category (years) for master athletes in 1979[c]				
			50–54	55–59	60–64	65–69
100 m (s)	12.0	10.8	11.4	11.6	12.0	13.2
200 m (s)	22.2	21.8	23.6	23.6	24.9	27.9
400 m (s)	54.2	48.2	52.9	54.6	59.1	65.1
800 m (min/s)	2:11.0	1:53.4	2:01.1	2:11.4	2:19.9	2:27.2
1,500 m (min/s)	4:33.2	4:10.4	4:14	4:20.4	4:53.2	4:59.2
Marathon (hr/min/s)	2:58.50	—	2:25.17	2:26.35	2:47.46	2:53.03

[a]Data from "Olympic games" (1985).

[b]Data from zur Megede (1987).

[c]Data from Stones and Kozma (1981).

Source: Adapted from K. A. Ericsson, "Peak Performance and Age: An Examination of Peak Performance in Sports," in *Successful Aging: Perspectives from the Behavioral Sciences,* ed. P. Baltes and M. Baltes.

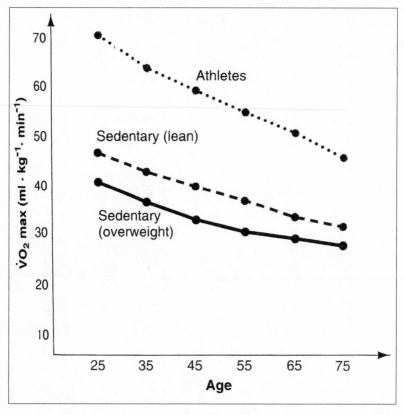

Figure 10.2 Maximal oxygen consumption over the life span for sedentary and athletic older adults.

self, climb a set of stairs, and twist the cap off a jar. If you are still capable of performing these tasks, exercise will help you maintain that ability for as long as possible. Beyond avoiding the negatives, exercise can improve your level of activity, relieve depression, and in general enhance the quality of your life.

Endurance or Aerobic Exercise

Aerobic exercises are the ones that elevate your breathing and heart rate (and metabolic rate), creating major health benefits when they are done for extended periods of time. Examples include jogging, brisk walking, and swimming, as well as activities related to your lifestyle like raking leaves, vacuuming the house, and dancing. All these activities, when done at sufficient pace and when maintained over time, improve the functioning of your heart, circulatory system, and lungs.

As indicated earlier, the best measure of cardiovascular performance is thought to be maximal oxygen consumption during strenuous exercise. Research shows that older adults, just like younger ones, demonstrate the same significant benefits in maximal oxygen consumption with prolonged endurance training. And, as Figure 10.2 shows, athletes maintain their maximum oxygen consumption across the life span. Endurance exercise training has also been shown to lower blood pressure in older adults with hypertension, to the same degree as in younger adults. Interestingly, light to moderate training is often just as effective as vigorous training. Exercise training of this sort also improves the composition of the body. Studies show a 1 to 4 percent decrease in the percentage of body fat, a variable associated with other risk factors for cardiovascular disease.[8]

A 1996 study conducted at the National Institute on Aging illustrates the importance of exercise for cardiovascular functioning.[9] This study compared two groups of men—people in both groups were healthy and free of heart disease—between the ages of 58 and 62. One group consisted of sedentary men who committed to an exercise regimen for twenty-four to thirty-two weeks. The other group consisted of athletes, who stopped exercising for twelve weeks. Initially maximal oxygen consumption was 55 percent higher in the trained than in the sedentary group. After exercising, maximal oxygen consumption of the sedentary group increased significantly whereas maximal oxygen consumption of the athletes dropped significantly. The result was that by the end of the regimen, the new maximal oxygen consumption was only 16 percent higher in the athletic group. This one study shows both effects of endurance exercise training—that exercise increases cardiovascular health, and the lack of exercise reduces it. So, the benefits of exercising are great, and you need to stick with it to maintain those benefits.

Strength or Resistance Training

While many people are aware of the value of aerobic conditioning, fewer appreciate the many benefits of strength conditioning. Weight training was once practiced by only a few muscular individuals. Now, there is growing recognition that this type of training is vital for maintaining and enhancing good health. When you visit a gym these days, you see people of all ages and all shapes working out with weights and weight machines. As you would expect, strength training enhances the strength of the muscles.

Studies have shown that older adults can increase their strength by two- or threefold in a three- to four-month training period. Indeed, older adults tend to show as much gain in strength, if not more, relative to younger people. Studies have also shown that this kind of conditioning improves balance. As mentioned earlier, strength training can mean the difference between walking independently and using a cane and the difference between doing your own chores and relying on others. Better yet, the increased strength and balance will minimize the probability of falling and injury.[10]

A second important benefit of strength training is that it increases bone density. In fact, studies have shown that resistance training in addition to taking calcium supplements is very effective at increasing bone density in older adults.[11]

A third benefit of weight or resistance training is that it increases one's resting metabolic rate. Thus, in addition to reducing body fat and building muscle mass, the increased metabolic rate can help you maintain or lose weight.[12]

Benefits of Exercise on Emotional Health

Depression becomes more prevalent as we age. About 15 percent of older adults report depressive symptoms, and the suicide rate is relatively high among depressed older adults. A good deal of literature shows that those who exercise tend to be less depressed than those who do not. One study that assessed people's lifestyles and measured their depression over a two-decade period found that inactivity is associated with depression. Interestingly, increases in cardiovascular exercise were associated with decreased depression, whereas decreases in physical activity over a twenty-year period were correlated with an increased probability of depression. Similar findings were reported in another study that examined men and women over 65 years of age.[13]

One factor that contributes to depression is a sense that we have lost control over our lives. As we lose abilities and simply cannot perform the tasks we once could, we become more dependent on others. To the extent that exercise enables you to maintain your physical capabilities, this should positively affect your sense of personal control and thus your emotional outlook on life—with the result that depression may be reduced or avoided altogether. It is not surprising then that exercise is frequently prescribed by physicians for their patients suffering from mild depression.[14]

Effects of Endurance or Aerobic Exercise on Cognition

You might be wondering how exercise can possibly improve cognitive processes. The general theoretical idea is that increased oxygen to the brain results in improved cognitive functioning. Cardiovascular exercise has been shown to increase the stroke volume of the heart and oxygen transportation to the brain. Moreover, some provocative research involving younger and older rats shows that exercise stimulates the growth of new capillary networks in the brain, thereby allowing greater oxygen delivery to the cells of the brain. In one study, for example, Greenough and his colleagues raised younger and older rats in an environment that encouraged exercise but not intellectual stimulation. Relative to a control group in which rats were exposed to a rich variety of stimuli but had no opportunities to exercise, the group that exercised showed more capillary development and the group that had the intellectual stimulation showed greater neuronal development (more synaptic connections, receptor sites on the dendrites, and so on). Capillaries are tiny, thin-walled, permeable vessels through which oxygen and nutrients from the blood reach the tissues of the body. Increased capillary development, therefore, allows more oxygen to flow

to the brain. These data strongly suggest that exercise imparts important biological advantages to the brains of both younger and older animals.[15]

Indirect Evidence for an Exercise-Memory Link

Whereas the research shows that cardiovascular exercise significantly
improves oxygen flow to the brain, an important additional issue is
whether this translates into measurable benefits in cognitive functioning. Researchers have tackled this question from several perspectives. One approach (correlational) has been to compare the cognitive
abilities of people who engage in cardiovascular types of exercise (e.g.,
brisk walking, water aerobics, jogging) on a regular basis with those
who are the same age but do not exercise. Although it should be noted
that a few studies have shown no relation between exercising in older
adulthood and measures of cognitive performance, the majority of
studies show that exercisers perform better on cognitive tasks than do
nonexercisers. For example, studies have shown that exercisers perform at a higher level than sedentary folks on a variety of tasks including those that measure reaction time, the ability to learn and
recall a list of unrelated words, reasoning, the ability to hold information in memory while distracted over brief periods of time (see the
working memory task in Demonstration 4.1), and the ability to inhibit distractions or strong responses (see Demonstrations 4.4 and
4.5 for tasks that measure abilities related to inhibiting distraction).[16]

A closer look at a study by Hill, Wahlin, Winblad, and Backman
reported in 1995 captures the nature of the findings in this area.[17]
These scientists studied 253 adults who were 75 years of age and older
and who showed no signs of dementia. They collected a lot of information from the participants including their age, their education,
and the amount of exercise they engaged in on a weekly basis. Then,
they had the participants learn and recall several lists of words. After
statistically controlling for differences in age and education, they
found that exercise was associated with higher performance in learning and recalling the list of unrelated words without using cues of any
kind. When the participants received categorized lists (e.g., three an-

imals, three musical instruments, three articles of clothing, and so on) and when they were given cues at recall (e.g., the category names), there were no differences in performance between those who did and did not exercise. These results are fairly typical in that older adults who exercise tended to do better on some cognitive tasks but not on all tasks. In this study, exercising had benefits primarily on the more difficult memory task in which participants were not given any cues to guide their retrieval. As mentioned in Chapters 2 and 5, aging tends to reduce the ability to retrieve information from memory on one's own, and exercise may protect against this reduction.

In general, then, in comparing older adults who exercise with those who don't, the exercisers appear to benefit from exercise on a wide variety of tasks. Most exciting, the pattern of results suggests that exercise may confer the most benefits on the kinds of mental tasks that are most affected by aging.

Direct Evidence for Cognitive Benefits of Exercise

One problem in interpreting the results from these kinds of studies is that older adults who exercise may differ from nonexercising older adults on important dimensions that may themselves be the cause of the difference in cognitive performance. For example, perhaps exercisers generally take better care of themselves or perhaps their biological systems are simply genetically less affected by the aging process. And, it may be these factors and not exercise per se that cause the difference on tests of cognitive ability. This criticism highlights the limitation of the correlational approach to studying the effects of exercise on the mental faculties of older adults.

Another method for studying the link between exercise and levels of cognitive functioning is the experimental approach. The key differences between these methods is presented in Table 10.3. With the experimental method, you take groups of nonexercising older individuals and put some of them on an exercise program for several months (typically two to six months) and then compare the groups on various cognitive tests. The control group in this type of research is usually given some kind of exercise (e.g., stretching, muscle toning)

Table 10.3 Approaches to Studying Whether and How Exercise Affects Memory and Cognition

Correlational	Experimental
Select people who are already exercising and compare them with those who are not.	Select people who are not exercising and randomly assign some to an exercise group and the others to a control group.
Give them a battery of memory tests. When comparing the groups, try to statistically control for other possible differences that exist between the groups (such as education level and health).	Give them a battery of memory tests (pretest) and after a period of exercise give them the battery of tests again (posttest). Because of random assignment, assume that the groups are equal on the memory tasks at the beginning of the experiment. This can be verified by examining performance on the pretest.
The possibility always exists that variables other than exercise differ between groups and contribute to differences in performance.	With this method, you can assume that the differences that emerge between the groups after the exercise program were caused by exercise.

that does not have cardiovascular benefits but does require the same number of sessions with the experimenter. Thus, the control group gets as much attention and interaction with the experimenter as the group receiving cardiovascular exercise. Also, participants are randomly assigned to exercise and control conditions (random assignment is the technique scientists use to equate groups approximately). Thus, the groups should be equal at the start of the experiment in their cognitive abilities, and this is typically verified with pretests. If the exercise group shows a greater improvement (or less of a decrement) on the cognitive tests after the conditioning program than the control group, we can infer that the difference was due to cardiovascular exercise. Experiments of this sort have shown that exercise can produce substantial benefits on some tasks but not on others.[18]

The general conclusion from examining these studies is that the positive effects of exercise on cognitive performance are selective. A very well done study conducted by Kramer and his colleagues reveals an interesting pattern that helps us understand which cognitive tasks are most positively affected by exercise. In examining prior studies, these researchers noticed that exercise mainly helped individuals perform tasks that believed to be subserved by the frontal lobes of the brain. This is interesting because there is strong evidence today that our frontal lobes show the earliest and greatest amount of age-associated losses. This evidence comes from a variety of sources but includes studies showing that the frontal areas of the brain lose the most volume with age. Consistent with this, tasks that draw on cognitive processes performed by the frontal lobes are especially affected by aging.[19]

What are the cognitive processes controlled by the frontal lobes? Among other functions, the frontal lobes are thought to be responsible for working memory and executive control processes. Working memory is the system that performs the very important function of maintaining information in memory in the midst of distraction (Chapters 2 and 4 cover this in some detail and indicate how it is measured; see Demonstration 4.1). Our executive control processes are involved in selecting tasks to be performed and coordinating their performance. The frontal lobes are also thought to control inhibitory processes or the ability to suppress task-irrelevant information. As described in Chapter 4, inhibitory processes are important to cognition in that they serve to limit the entrance of irrelevant information into the working memory (see Demonstrations 4.4 and 4.5 for tasks that are sensitive to inhibitory ability). Taken together, these frontal lobe processes and functions are critical in order for us to function effectively. Figure 10.3 lists some real-world capabilities that are to a large extent controlled by the frontal lobes.

To test their hypothesis, Kramer and his colleagues gave partici-

• Effective conversation because this requires that you keep your current concerns and ideas sufficiently activated while you are listening to the conversation. If you can keep your ideas sufficiently well in mind, you will be able to express them when there is a pause in the conversation.

• Mentally performing math problems where you have to hold products in mind while performing other arithmetic operations.

• Reading because comprehension of a sentence often requires that we relate the current phrase to previous phrases.

• Cooking a meal that involves planning and coordinating several recipes for different food items so that nothing is forgotten and that all of the foods are ready at the same time.

• Switching back and forth between tasks such as might be demanded in a busy office.

• Listening to a talk because inhibitory processes help you ignore distractions and focus on the speaker.

Figure 10.3 Examples of real-world tasks that are thought to be at least partially controlled by the frontal lobes.

pants a battery of tests that did and did not involve the frontal lobes. Approximately half the 124 participants, who ranged in age from 60 to 75, were randomly assigned to a walking group (for this group, the object was to improve cardiovascular fitness). The others were assigned to a toning group (for this group, the object was to improve the fitness and flexibility of the muscles but not cardiovascular fitness). Both groups met with trained exercise leaders three days a week over a six-month period for forty to sixty minutes each session. The toning group mainly stretched all the large muscle groups in their lower and upper body. The walking group started off with short fif-teen-minute light-intensity walking workouts. The duration and in-tensity of the workouts were increased to the point that participants were walking forty minutes at a moderate pace by the end of the six months.

The experimenter tested the participants on three measures of cardiovascular fitness (including maximal oxygen consumption, de-scribed in the beginning of this chapter) at the beginning and the end of the six-month training period. On all three measures, the walking group showed greater improvements than the toning group. In fact, over the six-month period, for the maximal oxygen consumption measure the toning group showed a slight decrease in fitness, whereas the walking group showed an improvement. These results are consis-tent with the findings presented earlier in this chapter. Older adults experience a natural decline in cardiovascular health, but exercise slows and can even reverse this decline. Importantly and consistent with expectations, participants in the walking group demonstrated significant improvements in the tasks that are thought to involve frontal lobe processes but no improvement in others tasks (again, see Figure 10.3 for real-world tasks that are thought to involve the frontal lobes).

This paragraph presents a concrete example of one of the tasks used in this experiment. If you are not interested in following the de-tails of this research, you can skip this material. The frontal lobes are thought to play a significant role in controlling and coordinating the activities required to switch back and forth between different tasks. To examine this phenomenon, Kramer and his colleagues used a task-switching paradigm in their study. Specifically, participants were pre-sented with a two-by-two matrix in the center of a computer screen. On each trial, they received a letter and a number, which appeared in either the top or bottom half of the matrix. If the items appeared in the top half, the participant was to decide as quickly as possible if the number was odd or even. If the items appeared in the lower half, the participant was to decide as quickly as possible if the letter was a vowel or a consonant. The order of the tasks was such that partici-pants received two number judgments followed by two letter judg-

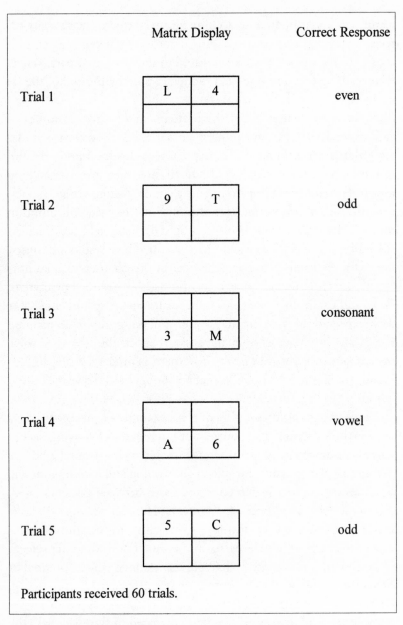

Figure 10.4 Sample trial sequence from the task-switching paradigm.

ments, a sequence that continued throughout the task. A sample sequence of five trials is shown in Figure 10.4. Participants received a good bit of practice making these number and letter judgments. Success was measured according to the average speed with which they made correct responses. The response time of the toning group actually slowed down from the pretest to the posttest (by 22 milliseconds—there are 1,000 milliseconds in a second), whereas the walking group lowered its average response time by 537 milliseconds (from 2,496 to 1,959 milliseconds).[20] These results are consistent with the theory that exercise helps on frontally mediated tasks.

It should be noted that improvements in cognitive functioning occurred among both the younger older adults and the more senior older adults. It's clear, then, that even relatively brief periods of exercise can significantly enhance abilities that are thought to be most negatively affected by the aging process. In fact, walking briskly for forty minutes just three days a week for a six-month period has been shown to improve mental functioning! Indeed, many of the studies that have shown the beneficial effects of exercise on memory used only two- and three-month training periods. This level of physical effort seems modest in light of the great cognitive rewards.

Research examining the effects of exercise on reducing and even reversing the effects of aging on mental functioning is increasing at a feverish pace. In the future, we should learn the answers to important questions such as: "What are the benefits of long-term and sustained cardiovascular exercise?" and "Do periods of inactivity lead to rapid reductions in mental processes?" Indeed, in 2001 Kramer reported that the benefits of exercise on memory are greater when people mix resistance training with cardiovascular training and with intense cardiovascular exercise relative to moderate exercise.[21] Further research is needed to confirm these possibilities. Although studies to date show that the improvements in cognitive functioning are somewhat selective, it may be that prolonged exercise (say, several years) might prove beneficial for an even wider variety of cognitive tasks.

Conclusions

The first half of this chapter documented the importance of exercise for physical conditioning. The latter half focused on the benefits of exercise on mental functioning. In the authors' opinion, when it comes to maximizing both your physical and mental functioning *it is downright risky behavior not to exercise*. The physical benefits are profound, and the psychological and cognitive benefits are very promising. Thus, it is important for older adults, especially, to commit to a well-rounded exercise program that includes a significant cardiovascular component. If you have access to the Internet, take a look at the Web site *www.NIHSeniorHealth.gov*. This site, which was developed by the National Institute on Aging, presents up-to-date and scientifically based information on a variety of topics that are of interest to older adults, one of which is exercise. It spells out the benefits of exercise and how to begin and maintain a successful exercise regimen. It is very well done, containing video demonstrations in addition to written descriptions. To get started, Figure 10.5 lists some tips and factors to keep in mind when you begin your program. Also from the National Institute on Aging is a guidelines Web site: *www.nia.nih.gov/ health/agepages/exercise.htm*. It is strongly recommended that you get your physician's approval if you are planning a vigorous exercise regimen, and that you begin slowly.

Exercise: Feeling Fit For Life

Adults young and old can help put an end to a major public health enemy: lack of physical activity. The crime: adding to disease and disability.

Here are some facts:

• Exercise can help older people feel better and enjoy life more, even those who think they're too old or too out of shape.

Figure 10.5 Advice about exercising from the National Institute on Aging.

- Most older adults don't get enough physical activity.
- Lack of physical activity and poor diet, taken together, are the second largest underlying causes of death in the United States. (Smoking is the #1 cause.)
- Regular exercise can improve some diseases and disabilities in older people who already have them. It can improve mood and relieve depression, too.
- Staying physically active on a regular, permanent basis can help prevent or delay certain diseases (like some types of cancer, heart disease, or diabetes) and disabilities as people grow older.

How You Can Help

Plan on making physical activity a part of your everyday life. Do things you enjoy. Go for brisk walks. Ride a bike. Dance. And don't stop doing physical tasks around the house and in the yard. Trim your hedges without a power tool. Climb stairs. Rake leaves.

The first step is to get at least 30 minutes of activity that makes you breathe harder, on most or all days of the week. That's called "endurance activity," because it builds your stamina. That way you can keep doing the things you need to do and the things you like to do. If you can't be active for 30 minutes all at once, get at least 10 minutes of endurance activity at a time. If you choose to do 10-minute sessions, make sure that they add up to a total of 30 minutes at the end of the day.

Even a moderate level of sustained activity helps. One doctor describes the right level of effort this way: If you can talk without any trouble at all, your activity is probably too easy. If you can't talk at all, it's too hard.

Studies show that endurance activities help prevent or delay many diseases that seem to come with age. In some cases, endurance activity can also improve chronic diseases or their symptoms.

Step two is to keep using your muscles. People lose 20 to 40 percent of their muscle—and, along with it, their strength—as they age. Scientists have found that a major reason people lose muscle is because they stop doing everyday activities that use muscle power, not just because they grow older. Lack of use lets muscles waste away.

When you have enough muscle, it can mean the difference between being able to get up from a chair by yourself and having to wait for someone to help you get up. That's true for younger adults as well as for people 90 and older. Very small changes in muscle size, changes that you can't even see, can make a big difference in your being able to live and do things on your own.

You can combine activites—for example, walking uphill and raking leaves both build endurance and some of your muscles at the same time. Or you can start an exercise program that makes sure you do the right types of activities. (One good reason to start an exercise program is that you will probably work muscles that you may have stopped using without even realizing it. Another is that exercise programs are likely to help you build up—not just maintain—your endurance and strength.)

Keeping your muscles in shape can help prevent another serious problem in older people: falls that cause broken hips or other disabilities. When the leg and hip muscles that support you are strong, you're less likely to fall. And using your muscles may make your bones stronger, too.

Step three is to do things to help your balance. For example, stand on one foot, then the other, without holding onto anything for support. Stand up from sitting in a chair without using your hands or arms. Every now and then, walk heel-to-toe (the toes of the foot in back should almost touch the heel of the foot in front when you walk this way.)

Step four is to stretch. Stretching won't build your endurance or muscles, but it may help keep you limber.

Who Should Exercise?

Just about anyone, at any age, can do some type of activity to improve his or her health. Even if you have chronic disease (cardiovascular disease or diabetes are just two examples) you can still exercise. In fact, physical activity may help your condition, but only if it's done during times when your condition is under control. During flare-ups, exercise could be harmful. You should talk to your doctor for guidance.

Check with your doctor first if you are a man over 40 or a woman over 50 and you plan to do vigorous activity (the kind that makes you breathe and sweat hard) instead of moderate activity. Your doctor might be able to give you a go-ahead over the phone, or he or she might ask you to come in for a visit.

If you have any of the following problems, it's important to check with your doctor before increasing your physical activity:

• a chronic disease, or a high risk of getting one—for example, if you smoke, if you are obese; or if you have a family history of a chronic disease
• any new, undiagnosed symptom
• chest pain
• shortness of breath
• the feeling that your heart is skipping, racing, or fluttering
• blood clots
• infections or fever
• undiagnosed weight loss
• foot or ankle sores that won't heal
• joint swelling
• pain or an irregular walking gait after you've fallen
• a bleeding or detached retina; eye surgery or laser treatment
• a hernia
• hip surgery

Saftey Tips

The following are some things you can do to make sure you are exercising safely:
• Start slowly. Build up your activities and your level of effort

gradually. Doing too much, too soon, can hurt you, especially if you have been inactive.

- Avoid holding your breath while straining—when using your muscles, for example. If you have high blood pressure, pay special attention to this tip. It may seem strange at first, but the rule is to exhale during muscle exertion; inhale during relaxation. For example, if you are lifting something breathe out on the lift; breathe in on the release.
- If you are on any medications or have any conditions that change your natural heart rate, don't use your pulse rate as a way of judging how hard you should exercise. "Beta blockers," a type of blood pressure drug, are an example of this kind of medicine.
- Use safety equipment, such as helmets, knee and elbow pads, and eye protection, to keep you from getting hurt.
- Unless your doctor has asked you to limit fluids, be sure to drink plenty when you are doing endurance activities that make you sweat. Many older people tend to be low on fluid much of the time, even when not exercising.
- When you bend forward, bend from the hips, not the waist. If you keep your back straight, you're probably bending correctly. If you let your back "hump" anyplace, you're probably bending from the waist, which is the wrong way.
- Make sure your muscles are warmed up before you stretch, or you could hurt them. For example, you can do a little easy biking, or walking and light arm pumping first.
- None of the exercises should hurt or make you feel really tired. You might feel some soreness, a little discomfort, or a bit weary, but you should not feel pain. . . . In fact, in many ways, physical activity and exercise will probably make you feel better.

How to Find Out More

Local gyms, universities, or hospitals can help you find a teacher or program that works for you. You can also check with local churches or synagogues, senior and civic centers, parks, recreation associations, YMCAs, YWCAs, or even local shopping malls for exercise, wellness, or walking programs.

There are many organizations that provide information for older people about physical activity and exercise. The following list will help you get started:

American College of Sports Medicine
P.O. Box 1440
Indianapolis, IN 46206
Internet: http://www.acsm.org

American Physical Therapy Association
111 North Fairfax Street
Alexandria, VA 22314-1488
Phone: 800-999-2782
Internet: http:www.apta.org

50-Plus Fitness Association
P.O. Box D
Stanford, CA 94309
Phone: 650-323-6160
Internet: http://www.50plus.org

The President's Council on Physical Fitness and Sports
DHHS/OS/OPHS
200 Independence Ave., SW
HHH Building
Washington, DC 20201
Phone: 202-690-9000
Internet: http://www.os.dhhs.gov

For more information about health and aging, contact:

American Geriatrics Society (AGS)

AGS is a nationwide, not-for-profit association dedicated to im-

proving the health, independence, and quality of life of all older people. AGS can send you a brochure, "What Is a Geriatrician?" as well as provide referrals to a geriatrician in your local area. Call 800-247-4779. Write: 770 Lexington Ave., Suite 300, NYC, NY 10021.
Visit the AGS Web site: http://www.americangeriatrics.org

National Institute on Aging (NIA)

NIA, part of the National Institute of Health, distributes Age Pages and other materials on a wide range of topics related to health and aging. For a list of free publications, call the NIA Information Center: 800-222-2225. Visit the NIA Web site: http://www.nih.gov/nia

Source: National Institute on Aging, US Department of Health and Human Services, Public Health Service, National Institutes of Health, 1998.

CHAPTER ELEVEN

Effects of Stress, Depression, Illness, and Medications on Memory

Several years ago, a student in one of my classes did poorly on her first exam. She was quite upset by her grade and came to see me to discuss strategies for improving it. She was eager to do better and agreed to meet with me several times a week to work on reviewing the material and improving her study techniques. She faithfully attended all the review sessions and seemed highly prepared each time, but she failed the second examination as well. I tried to reassure her that it sometimes takes a while for new and improved study techniques to yield benefits, and I encouraged her to keep working with me in an attempt to improve her grades in the course. She and I continued to review the materials over several sessions, and she seemed to really understand the material. I was quite surprised when she failed the third exam. Her poor grade caused her to question the value of our sessions, and she stopped coming to see me for review. To my astonishment, she made a B on the fourth exam and a B on the final exam. I had gotten to know her fairly well and was intrigued by her remarkable reversal of fortune in my class—especially because it seemed to coincide with reduced help from me. When I asked her how she had done so well on the last two exams, she revealed that she had been highly anxious about the tests and had simply taken the tranquilizer Valium before each of the last two examinations. Apparently, she had been using very effective memory strategies to learn the material, but her anxiety during the tests was interfering with her ability to remember the information required to solve the test problems. The lesson here is that emotional states can have powerful effects on memory.

It has been known for a long time that emotions can interfere with learning and memory. As reflected in the true story above, extreme levels of stress, arousal, and anxiety can be absolutely devastating to performance in general and memory in particular. This chapter focuses on the debilitating effects mainly of stress, but also of depression and illness, on memory. It also discusses strategies for overcoming their negative effects.

Our mental abilities are quite dependent on the state of our biological systems. At the end of this chapter are lists of common prescription medications that can influence memory. If you are currently taking one or more of these medications and if you believe that your memory is affected, you may want to talk to your physician about this possible connection and about other approaches to solving your medical problems.

Relationship Between Stress and Performance: The Yerkes-Dodson Law

A useful relationship to keep in mind when considering the effects of stress (which include anxiety and fear) is that proposed by Yerkes and Dodson in 1908.[1] As Figure 11.1 shows, the relationship between arousal and performance follows an inverted U-shaped function. What this means is that performance tends to be low with very low levels or very high levels of stress. Typically, the highest levels of performance occur with moderate levels of stress. A concrete example may help you understand this correlation. Imagine, for example, that I told my students that I was going to give them an exam and that I

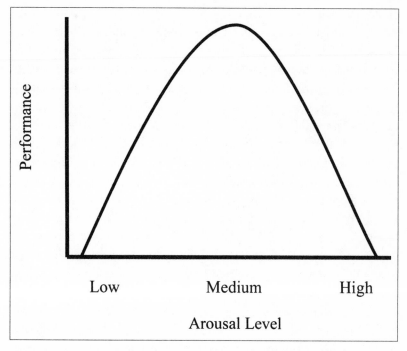

Figure 11.1 Yerkes and Dodson's inverted-U relation between arousal and performance.

was going to throw it away as soon as they finished taking it—without grading it! The prospects of taking this exam would induce very little stress, which would probably lead the students to read the questions quickly and not think about them very deeply. If, instead, I told the students that the results of this single exam would be used to determine their grade for the entire course, this might induce so much stress that it would interfere with performance on the test. According to the Yerkes-Dodson Law, the most effective level of arousal is a modest one in which the students know that the test is important so that they will be motivated to carefully read the questions, think deeply about the answers, reread their answers, and so on.

The debilitating effects of high levels of stress and/or anxiety on memory are fairly easy to document. In what would now be considered unethical research, Berkun conducted a study in 1964 in which he created high levels of anxiety in people before he had them recall.[2] Working with soldiers in the army, prior to the experiment he had them develop a list of personal belongings and taught them a series of procedures for what to do on a military aircraft in case of a crash landing. Sometime later, the soldiers were on a flight when the commander came out and told them that the plane was experiencing malfunctions and that a crash landing was almost a total certainty. In preparation for the crash landing and likely death, the commander asked the soldiers to make a list of their personal belongings and to list the steps in the ditching procedure. Of course, the plane did not crash, but it is likely that Berkun effectively manipulated the anxiety levels of these poor soldiers! Relative to a control group that experienced an uneventful flight, the soldiers who experienced high levels of anxiety had lower levels of recall both for their personal belongings and for their memory of the ditching procedure.

Although you are unlikely to experience levels of anxiety that are quite this extreme in the real world, we often do reach stress levels that interfere with recollection. For example, most of us have at one time or another had some anxiety or stress when interacting in a social situation. In such a situation, you may have had trouble remembering the name of someone you know well when you were about to introduce that person to someone else. The anxiety level rises even higher when the name doesn't come to us immediately, making it even more unlikely that the name will be retrieved. Another common experience that can produce debilitating levels of anxiety and poor memory is public speaking. Often, thoughts that seem to come to mind readily when we are relaxed are much more difficult to retrieve when we are in a public speaking situation. When I lecture on this topic in class, students often offer the example of trying to remember something for an exam with only a few minutes left. As they get more and more anxious with the realization that time is flying by, they have great difficulty retrieving the required information. Indeed, often the item does not come to mind before they have to turn the exam in. Immediately after giving the exam to their professors, however, their anxiety level decreases markedly and the sought-after memory suddenly comes to mind.

In addition to particular circumstances that can create stress, some people find themselves in an ongoing state of high anxiety. Highly anxious people tend to be consumed with worry or fear, a sense of imminent doom, panic attacks, restlessness, or irritability. These people are unable to maintain concentration or pay attention to the task at hand. Under these conditions, memory suffers, sometimes to the extent that daily functioning can be impaired. Guidelines for overcoming memory problems caused by anxiety and stress are presented later in this chapter.

How Do High Levels of Stress Affect Memory?

Eysenck and Calvo have proposed a theory that explains how anxiety affects cognitive processing in general and memory in particular. Although this theory was developed in a context of understanding the effects of anxiety, it could be used to explain the effects of other kinds of stress as well. Their basic idea is that increased levels of anxiety increase cognitive arousal or alertness, which can actually lead to improved performance on tasks that are fairly simple and not highly demanding. The other effect is that anxiety leads to thoughts of worry, which occupy a good portion of working memory capacity. The result is that less working memory capacity is left over for learning information or for retrieving it from memory. That is, fewer mental resources are available for thinking deeply about material and retrieving it. The concept of working memory is discussed in detail in Chapters 2 and 4, and it may be worthwhile to review this material at this point. In general, though, it is important to realize that the availability of working memory resources affects how well you can learn and how well you can remember, particularly with complex tasks. Further, it is thought that high levels of anxiety coupled with few available working memory resources result in a "narrowing" of attention such that you are able to focus only on the strongest or most salient aspects of a situation. The decreased working memory capacity that results from high stress or anxiety affects the range of cues available to you in solving a problem, interpreting a situation, and retrieving memories. This is likely to lead to decreased performance, especially in complex situations.[3]

A couple of examples should help you understand the effects of anxiety on performance. Imagine giving the problem below to groups of people who have either low, moderate, or high levels of stress.

Fill in the next number in the sequence: 64   16   48   12   36   9   ___

It is very likely that the group with a moderate level of stress will be able to solve the problem more quickly. Why might this be? It is likely that those with very low stress might put less effort and concentration into solving the problem and will not be very selective in the range of cues they consider in solving the problem. For example, they might see that the numbers 64 and 16 both contain the numeral 6 and try creative strategies that involve the numeral 6 in order to solve the problem. When very high levels of stress are present, very few working memory resources will be available for solving the problem (because the arousal or worry takes up a good deal of the resources), and this may lead to too much selectivity or focus in solving the problem. For example, when seeing that 64 is followed by 16, people in the high arousal condition may see that you can produce 16 by dividing 64 by 4. In this case, they get stuck because following this rule will not produce the next number in the sequence. The obstacle here is that these people have narrowed their focus too much. This problem is complex, requiring people to use two rules. Moderate levels of stress encourage the highest level of performance, stimulating participants to focus on the problem without restricting or narrowing the range of cues to solve the problem. Thus, moderately stressed people are more likely to realize that one solution to this problem requires that you divide the first number by 4, multiply the second number by 3, and repeat. Thus, the last number should be 27.

Another example may be helpful. In the early days of training people to skydive, students were taught how and when to pull the cord to release the primary parachute. They were also told that if for some reason the primary parachute did not open, they should pull the cord for the secondary parachute. Although many people did this, a number of accidents occurred in which people were found dead on the ground, clutching the cord to the primary parachute. Apparently, these folks had pulled on the cord for the primary parachute and when it failed to open, continued to tug frantically on the cord. It is as if they never thought to pull the cord controlling the secondary parachute. How can we explain this disastrous outcome? A good deal of anxiety is associated with skydiving (especially if you are a novice), and the stress level is likely to increase dramatically when a person discovers that her or his primary parachute will not open. Under conditions of extreme panic, very few working memory resources will be available, and the focus of attention narrows dramatically to the point that the only thing the person can think of is to pull on the main cord. As a result of incidents like these, it has become obvious that what we learn under low-stress conditions may not be remembered under high-stress conditions. Thus, among skydivers today the training is much more extensive, and people are overtrained to pull the secondary cord when the primary cord does not produce results. This overtraining ensures that the action of pulling the secondary cord is a strong response and will come to mind even under conditions of high stress and few available working memory resources.

Aging, Stress Hormones, and Arousal

Cortisol is a hormone that is released in the body when the mind senses stress, and this causes the arousal we feel. Unfortunately, aging lowers the levels of almost all the hormones in the body except for cortisol. Indeed, it has been shown that older adults often produce cortisol for more prolonged periods under stress than do younger people. The problem is that high levels of cortisol in the body interfere with learning and memory. Recent studies have shown people who were given cortisone tablets, which raise cortisol levels in the blood, had lower levels of recall than did those who were given placebo tablets. For example, de Quervan gave participants sixty nouns to learn for four seconds each and then gave them a recall test (recall all of the words that you can) followed by a recognition test (identify the words that were and were not presented). The results showed that taking cortisone tablets produced poorer memory than did taking a placebo. It is not only the ability to embed information in long-term memory that is affected by stress. As you might expect from this discussion thus far, studies have shown that other memory measures (e.g., working memory; see Chapters 2 and 4) are especially sensitive to elevated levels of cortisol.[4]

So, as we age, increased cortisol production makes us more vulnerable to stresses from the flu, an argument with a family member, being late for an appointment, or a scary incident such as a near-miss while driving. It seems that, if anything, we are more easily aroused (at least mentally) as we get older, which can interfere with our ability to learn and remember. Before reading about techniques to reduce anxiety and arousal, you might stop reading now and take some time to identify particular circumstances that make you anxious. Then as you continue reading, think about how you might use the following techniques so that you can alleviate memory problems.

Overcoming the Effects of High Anxiety

One obvious approach to overcoming the memory problems associated with anxiety is to lower your anxiety level in some way. Medicines are available to treat anxiety, and you should consult your physician if you are interested in this approach. Under most circumstances, however, you should be able to reduce anxiety in the following ways.

- Do aerobic exercise, which has been shown not only to have great benefits for the fitness of your heart and lungs but also to reduce depression and anxiety. Exercise may improve concentration as well.[5]
- Learn relaxation techniques. You should consult your physician or a clinical psychologist for specific procedures. Relaxation techniques can lower your body's arousal reaction to

stressful and anxiety-provoking situations. This in turn should improve your ability to learn and remember in these situations.[6]

■ For chronic anxiety (as opposed to episodes that occur now and then), a cognitive therapy group can be helpful. These groups can offer new ways of dealing with anxiety and provide group support for handling worries. With the group, you might identify things you have no control over so that they can be removed from your worry list. The group can offer ideas for solving problems that create worry throughout the day. With the help of the group, daily preoccupation with worry can be lessened, and improvements in memory are likely to follow.[7]

The other approach is to overlearn the material in preparation for situations that will create stress. Practice, practice, practice is the rule.

■ If you are nervous about making an upcoming speech or talk, prepare yourself by practicing the talk repeatedly. The authors of this book customarily practice giving convention talks to each other a couple of hours before the actual talk. This strengthens the ideas in memory and helps ensure that they will be retrieved even under stress.

■ Try to anticipate those memory situations that might be somewhat difficult and somewhat arousing. For example, if you are bringing new friends to a party where a lot of old friends will be present, it would be helpful to practice retrieving the names of the new and old friends in preparation for the introductions you will surely make. Remember: what seems foremost in your mind when you are relaxed may not be as easy to retrieve when you are anxious.

Depression, Illness, and Memory

Like anxiety, illness and depression can deplete mental resources needed for attending to and remembering things.

Depression

Depressive symptoms tend to occur at a higher rate in older people and to be especially prevalent among those who have serious health problems or who are very frail. Indeed, some surveys report depressive symptoms in anywhere from 30 to 65 percent of persons over 60. It should be noted, however, that in that population the level of clinical depression considered serious enough to require treatment is much lower (about 4 to 7 percent). Older adults often suffer temporary depressive episodes resulting from the emotional losses and physical ailments that typically accompany aging. Research shows that depression negatively affects memory for several reasons. First, motivation may be dampened, so the person does not try to remember things. The person does not care as much about trying to remember the fine points of a newspaper editorial, the time of an interesting television program, or the name of a new book that friends are reading. And, as indicated in Chapters 2 and 6, active learning is critical for good memory. Second, depression may create thoughts that interfere with attention and concentration. For example, while listening to a talk or reading a book, thoughts of sadness or despair are likely to occupy part of your working memory resources, leaving fewer resources available for processing the talk or book. The result is that memory will suffer, particularly on complex or very difficult tasks (which require more processing resources).[8]

Whatever you can do to diminish your depression should enhance your memory. Exercise, for example, has been shown to be helpful in relieving depression. If you feel that your symptoms are more than temporary, see a mental health professional, your physician, or both to discuss possible options. Counseling, medication, or both are recommended to help ongoing depression. During periods of depression, if you can force yourself to use good processing strategies (e.g., organize the material you are learning, and think deeply about the material; see Chapter 6), this will improve memory.

Physical Illness

Physical illness and other biological disturbances—especially diseases that involve the brain—can contribute to memory problems. Sometimes brain areas responsible for memory have been damaged. This can be caused by well-known degenerative nerve diseases like Parkinson's as well as strokes and head traumas. After a stroke or head trauma, memory may improve with time but may not completely recover.[9]

What may not be so obvious is that illness in general can cause memory problems. Fever, infection, circulatory problems, heart disease, dehydration, anemia, low blood sugar, and recovery from surgery can create some degree of memory loss. These physical problems can produce a foggy state of mind and can impair concentration. Illness or surgery can deprive a person of sleep or reduce energy levels, thereby reducing concentration ability. Serious infections can produce confusion. Cloudy thinking, confusion, and decreased concentration can impair memory. Some people may become preoccupied with their illnesses, and this preoccupation can decrease the mental resources necessary for attending to and remembering a wide variety of information.

These memory problems are typically not permanent, but they still may be cause for concern because they may signal an undetected physical ailment. Detecting and successfully treating the illness will usually eliminate memory problems. Heart bypass surgery may represent an exception to the statement that illness-related memory problems will be eliminated after recovery. A recent study reported that the cognitive and memory decline that can result from bypass surgery is present even five years after surgery in 40 percent of individuals. Whether these memory problems are directly associated with the surgery or with other circulatory and health problems that occur after surgery is not known at this time.[10]

During periods of illness or after surgery, you may have to force yourself to use effective processing strategies (described in Chapters 6, 7, and 8) or to rely more on external aids in order to remember things more easily and accurately.

Table 11.1 Drugs Reported to Impair Concentration and/or Memory

Drugs	Some of the Associated Prescription Labels
acyclovir	Zovirax
anticonvulsants	Dilantin
antihistamines	Benadryl, Dramamine, Chlor-trimeton, Teldrin, Claritin, many others
anti-parkinsonism drugs	Carbex, Eldepryl, Novo-Selegiline
barbiturates	Amytal, Butisol, Nembutal, Seconal
benzodiazepines	Valium, Librium, Ativan
isoniazid	antituberculosis drugs
monoamine oxidase (MAO) inhibitor drugs	Marplan, Nardil, Parnate
phenytoin	Dilantin
primidone	Myidone
scopolamine	Kinesed

Medication and Memory

Older adults take a lot of prescription medications. The World Health Organization estimates that 50 percent of all prescription drugs are taken by older adults and that about a third of older adults consume three or more prescription drugs daily. These medications influence biological processes in the body, and some can influence memory. Table 11.1 lists the prescription drugs that are thought to have some influence on memory, and Table 11.2 lists those that can create confusion and disorientation. If you are taking any of the drugs listed in these tables and you are experiencing memory difficulties, you may want to talk to your doctor about alternative treatments.[11]

Table 11.2 Drugs Reported to Cause Confusion, Delirium, or Disorientation

acetazolamide	dantrolene	meprobamate
acyclovir	digitalis	methyldopa
amantadine	digitoxin	metoclopramide
aminophylline	digoxin	narcotic pain relievers
amphetamines	disulfiram	(analgesics)
amphotericin B	diuretics	NSAIDs
anticholinergics	ethchlorvynol	para-aminosalicylic acid
antidepressants	ethinamate	phenelzine
antihistamines	fenfluramine	phenothiazines
antipsychotics	fluoroquinolone	phenytoin
atropinelike drugs	antibiotics	piperazine
barbiturates	glutethimide	primadone
benzodiazepines	histamine H_2-receptor	propranolol
beta-adrenergic blockers	antagonists	quinidine
(some)	interferons	reserpine
bromides	isoniazid	scopolamine
carbamazepine	lamotrigine	tacrine
chloroquine	levodopa	theophylline
cimetidine	lidocaine	tricyclic antidepressants
clonidine	lipsomal amphotericin B	zolpidem
cortisonelike drugs	lisinopril	
cycloserine	melatonin	

Summary

Research clearly shows that emotional and arousal states can influence memory. Memory is most effective at moderate levels of arousal and in neutral emotional states (as opposed to depressed states). If you tend to be anxious, you should discuss this problem with your physician and consider developing an exercise routine, learn relaxation techniques, or both. Exercise is also useful for attenuating depressive symptoms. It is also helpful to overlearn materials so that you will be able to retrieve them even when you are stressed. Finally, be aware that illness can interfere with memory and also that various medications are thought to interfere with memory. If you are taking a medication that seems to be impairing your memory, you may want to consult with your physician about remedies that have fewer side effects on memory and general alertness.

CHAPTER TWELVE

Enhancing Memory with Nutritional Supplements and Vitamins

Recently, a middle-aged real estate salesman was remarking to me that his memory was failing. He was concerned that he was forgetting names of potential clients and forgetting details about these clients that would be helpful in his sales job. Upon finding out that I was a memory researcher, he confided that he was taking *Ginkgo biloba* to try to regain his memory. In fact, he was so eager to obtain positive effects that he was taking three times the recommended dose. Although he believed that ginkgo would help his memory, he was unsure. He knew that expectations sometimes lead people to believe there are improvements. He wondered whether there is scientific evidence that ginkgo might help his memory problems.

Many people are excited by the possibility that dietary supplements can enhance memory. This salesman had chosen ginkgo to help treat his memory problems. But it is very difficult today to discriminate fluff from substance when it comes to claims about various memory boosters and cures. Advertisements bombard us with particular vitamins, dietary supplements, and drugs, claiming that they can boost our memory abilities.

The other day on the radio I heard about a supplement that according to the salesperson would allow people of all ages to "soak up facts like a sponge." A television infomercial on this supplement claimed that it improves not only your concentration, learning, and memory but also your moods and your marriage! Such advertisements are often presented in a superficially compelling fashion. Very strong claims are made, followed by emotional testimonials from highly enthusiastic and satisfied users. Of course, testimonials are virtually useless in evaluating the effectiveness of any kind of treatment. And even if they are honest testimonials, the fact is that our subjective impressions of treatments are highly influenced by our expectations. Indeed, studies have shown that users rate placebos as highly effective in treating disorders even though they have absolutely no biological effects. The only proper way to evaluate the effectiveness of supplements is with scientifically controlled experiments that include proper control groups. This chapter will help you assess the claims that abound today for memory-improving supplements. You or some of your friends may be taking one or more of these supplements already. The question that all of us want answered is: "Do these supplements really work?"

What this chapter will do is introduce you to the particular nutrients that have generated widespread attention for enhancing memory. It's important, though, to have more than just a list of the nutrients and vitamins that people are pushing to help improve memory. The scientific evidence is too preliminary to allow unqualified and confident recommendations for any particular supplement. So, there is no definitive answer to the question of whether these supplements are effective in forestalling or treating memory problems. Still, some supplements may in fact be helpful in particular circumstances, and you may wish to consider these. To help you do so, this chapter will use nontechnical language to describe the scientific basis for the recommendations that are being suggested. After reading the chapter, you will be able to make a better-informed decision about the value of these recommendations. Before you make the decision to use these products, however, you should discuss your plans with your physician. Because of the possibility of side effects and interactions with other drugs you are taking, it is best for you to take even nonprescription supplements and drugs under the supervision of a physician.

The absence of convincing scientific evidence does not in general prevent individuals and companies from promoting the effectiveness of nonprescription nutritional supplements. Huge profits are to be made from sales of these products. Ginkgo alone attracted $240 million in sales in 1997.[1] Unfortunately, when there is a profit to be made, individuals may make claims based on very little evidence. Some may truly believe in the effectiveness of a certain supplement. While not intending to deceive, they may present very confident recommendations that are based on overly optimistic or superficial evaluation of the evidence. Others may intentionally exaggerate. What's the harm in this? Well, some of these nutritional supplements can be quite expensive, with several products currently costing over $50 monthly to meet the recommended dosage. Also, some of the supplements may have side effects. We may be willing to tolerate expensive supplements or side effects for a desired positive effect, but it makes little sense to spend money or experience negative side effects if the supplement does not produce the improvement in memory that you desire.

To help you decide if purportedly memory-enhancing dietary supplements and certain drugs might be useful, this chapter presents three kinds of information:

1. The reasons that lead scientists to expect "brain-specific" nutrients to help memory
2. The scientific tests that have been conducted and the research findings
3. What doctors and geriatricians are advising for their patients

Accurately determining the effects of a drug or supplement on memory requires a particular research design, a design that is the "gold standard" for scientific studies. Briefly, this design involves giving any supplement of interest to one group of individuals and giving a placebo pill that contains no active agent to a control group of individuals. Also, neither the researchers nor the participants know who is being given the placebo and who is being given the real supplement (a "double-blind" design). It is not unusual to see some improvement in a placebo group, possibly because of expectations that the pill should do some good. For scientists to find proof that whatever supplement is of interest has a "real" benefit, the group given the supplement must perform better than the group given the placebo control. Studies that do not use a placebo control cannot prove a specific benefit for any particular supplement. For this reason, only those research studies that have used a placebo-controlled, double-blind design are considered here.

"Brain-Specific" Nutrients, Drugs, and Memory

The brain stores our memories through networks of cells (neurons) that communicate with each other. If the neurons themselves die or function less effectively, then memory loss may occur. Also, if the communication between the neurons becomes slowed or muddled, then memory loss may occur. As noted in Chapter 1, scientists believe that with age, deterioration occurs on both fronts. Neurons seem to shrink or die as the brain ages. One recent study suggests that an average individual loses about two to three grams of brain mass each year.[2] Also, the remaining neurons begin to work less well.

A little background on how neurons communicate with each other will help you understand the possible effects of "brain-specific" nutrients. Neurons communicate by chemicals known as neurotransmitters, and aging and brain disease may cause a decrease in the production of neurotransmitters. One neurotransmitter called acetylcholine seems heavily involved in the networks of neurons associated with memory, and aging may depress the availability of acetylcholine.[3] Also, with age or brain-related disease, amyloid protein and fatty substances can build up in the brain and interfere with the chemical messages carried by neurotransmitters. With disruption of neurotransmitters, neuron networks cannot effectively maintain communication and memory suffers.

The theory is that memory decline might be avoided by slowing down neuron loss, other brain tissue loss, and depletion of memory-related neurotransmitters. Because good nutrition is vital for maintaining healthy cells, one sensible recommendation is to eat a well-balanced diet for good mental health.[4] We might be able to do even better, however. The theory supposes that some nutrients might be especially useful in arresting the loss of neural cell functioning as we age. The idea is that there are "brain-specific" nutrients that are important specifically for maintaining the activity of neurons or even for helping restore function to neurons that have stopped working. These brain-specific nutrients include *Ginkgo biloba,* phosphatidylserine, choline-related nutrients thought to be involved in producing acetylcholine, vinpocetine, acetyl-L-carnitine, and vitamin E. The first five nutrients listed are those typically found in products marketed to enhance brain and memory functioning. In fact, these five nutrients have recently been combined in a single product called Memory 2000 (produced by Natural Balance).

There are also some hormones and drugs that may specifically aid neuron functioning or protect against the depletion of specific neurotransmitters. Some of these hormones may have more serious side effects and the drug is not directly available in the United States; some of these agents are presented at the end of the chapter.

Ginkgo Biloba

Ginkgo biloba (or simply "ginkgo") is a concentrated extract from the *Ginkgo biloba* tree, a leafy ornamental tree originating in eastern China. Traditional healers have used ginkgo for many years to improve mental alertness, and it is readily available commercially as a dietary supplement. It is the single most popular brain-specific nutrient in terms of sales.

Ginkgo has several potential effects that would be expected to help maintain neural functioning. As we age, tissue-damaging chemicals (free radicals) become more prevalent, which may be responsible for some age-related loss of neurons. Some suggest that ginkgo neutralizes these chemicals so that they cannot damage cell tissue (known as an antioxidant effect). Damaged neurons can release substances that are toxic to nearby neurons, and ginkgo has been shown to decrease the release of these substances from damaged neurons (in rats). Either of these effects could help aging neurons stay healthy. Ginkgo has also been found to increase the production of acetylcholine (a neurotransmitter) and the sensitivity of neurons to acetylcholine in memory areas of the brain in aging rats. This is thought to help neurons communicate more effectively, thereby potentially preventing memory loss when neurotransmitter production begins to decline with age. Ginkgo also appears to help blood circulation. Thus, ginkgo seems to have basic effects on brain tissue that could potentially translate into improved memory and other mental functions.[5]

Several "gold-standard" published research studies have tested the effects of ginkgo on memory performance. They have found that ginkgo produced improvement on tests measuring memory and cognitive processes. These findings, though encouraging, do not mean that ginkgo will help everybody. In one study the improvement in attention and memory was found in just over a third of the participants in the study. This number must be compared with 18 percent of participants who showed improvement after being given the placebo only. Ginkgo, then, had positive effects on roughly one-fifth of the participants. In a second study, using an Alzheimer's Disease Assessment Scale (see Chapter 13), ginkgo was effective in an even lower proportion of patients. The participants in both studies were groups of patients with significant memory problems caused by mild to moderate Alzheimer's disease or stroke-related dementia (dementia is a term used to describe memory loss and impairment in concentration and thinking that result from diseases of the brain or brain structure dysfunction). In the second study almost two-thirds of the patients did not complete the study. If all the subjects had completed the study perhaps the effects would have "washed out." Overall, the improvement in the cognitive function scores was small.[6]

Will ginkgo help improve memory in normal middle-aged adults with no sign of memory-impairing diseases? One exciting experiment just completed at several sites in Sweden and Great Britain suggests that it might. Adults between the ages of 38 and 67 were given either a compound of ginkgo and ginseng or a placebo pill. The treatment lasted for twelve weeks, with memory testing occurring before the treatment, during the treatment period, and two weeks after the treatment was discontinued. After just four weeks of treatment, the ginkgo/ginseng–treated group showed significantly more improvement on the memory tests than did the placebo group. Further, this improvement due to ginkgo/ginseng was still present two weeks after the treatment had been discontinued. Understandably, the researchers were excited by these findings, as it "represents one of the first substantial demonstrations of improvements to the memory of healthy middle-age" adults.[7]

A closer look at the results of this recent study raises some flags, however. On memory-test days, testing was repeated at various times throughout the day. The curious thing is that when testing was at 7:30 a.m., there was little or no difference in memory improvement between the ginkgo/ginseng and the placebo groups. For most of the memory tests, at the end of treatment the placebo group actually showed slightly more improvement (but not significantly so) than the ginkgo/ginseng group showed at 7:30. When testing was at 2:30 p.m., ginkgo/ginseng produced the most pronounced memory benefit, showing on average a 7.5 percent improvement in memory. These unexplained differences in ginkgo/ginseng effects across testing times raise interesting questions. Are the benefits limited to times of day that are not optimal for adult cognitive functioning (see Chapter 4)? Perhaps repeated testing of lists of items throughout the day produces interference on later testing, and maybe ginkgo is especially helpful for memory situations with heavy interference. It is not even clear if ginkgo alone can benefit memory in healthy middle-aged adults or if ginseng is needed as well. The current research provides no answers to these questions. What is certain is that the scientific support for the memory benefits of ginkgo is tantalizing but preliminary.

No severe side effects of ginkgo were reported in these studies. One side effect in a study that used ginkgo to treat patients with multiple sclerosis was hiccups! In a few isolated case reports, prolonged bleeding has been noted.[8]

In the United Kingdom, for the past twenty years ginkgo has

been prescribed to help treat patients who have memory problems caused by reduced blood circulation in the brain. In Germany, the German Federal Health Authority approved ginkgo for treatment of dementia. In the United States, some centers that specialize in brain longevity and Alzheimer's prevention advocate a diet that includes ginkgo as one of several brain-specific nutrients. Ginkgo is sold in strengths of 40 to 60 milligrams. The research reports used dosages of 120 to 160 mg total, divided into one, two, or three doses per day. There has been no reported increase in benefits when doses have been increased to as much as 240 mg. These dosages should be kept in mind when considering the so-called brain boosters on the market. These boosters may include ginkgo, but at much smaller levels. The effects of ginkgo may not appear until about four to six weeks after taking it.

In summary, the scorecard on ginkgo is *cautiously* favorable. Studies sponsored by the National Institute of Health are under way to investigate whether ginkgo can help prevent memory problems in older adults without dementia. Ginkgo is creating tremendous interest, so be alert for more information about it in the next five years.

Phosphatidylserine

In recent years, phosphatidylserine (PS) has created excitement as a potential "brain-specific" nutrient to help older adults improve declining memory.[9] It is a naturally occurring substance that is taken into our body in our normal diet. PS is considered a brain-specific nutrient because it is most predominant in brain cells. Like ginkgo, it can be purchased as an over-the-counter supplement in many grocery stores and drugstores. PS is marketed as a substance for brain health and to promote memory functioning. How might it promote memory functioning?

Phosphatidylserine is thought to be especially vital to the neuronal membrane. The membrane of the neuron is particularly important for the communication between neurons. You'll recall that networks of communicating neurons store memories. Some of the neuron membrane contains receptors responsible for receiving the neurotransmitter message from other neurons. Other parts of the neuron membrane allow the neuron to pass the message from one end of the neuron to the other. This process is a truly fascinating one, in which the cell membrane essentially transmits an electrical current from one end of itself to the other.

A problem is that as we age, the neuronal membrane changes somewhat in its composition. The membrane starts to lose receptors. Another problem is that the receptors that are left begin to lose their capacity to receive messages. When many neurons become less able to relay messages, the neuron networks that store memories will fail and memory will decline.

Phosphatidylserine seems to help the neuronal membrane resist these age-related changes in its composition, possibly even to revitalize itself so that the aging neuron can perhaps reverse some of those changes. Research with aging animals has shown that PS actually stimulates new receptor growth on the membrane and makes existing receptor membrane more responsive. For instance, in one study with older mice, PS restored the sensitivity of their receptors to levels seen in young mice. PS also increased the number of receptors almost to the levels present in young mice. In addition, PS seems to help the neuron membrane to maintain its charged state so that it can transmit its electrical message. Finally, this nutrient may be important for maintaining the general structure and health of the neuron. Simply put, some theorize that supplements of PS allow neurons in the neuron networks to keep effectively communicating with one another so that existing memories can be retained and new memories formed. To do this, as we age we need to supplement the brain with much more PS than we get through our normal diets.[10]

Several well-controlled (gold-standard) studies have examined the effects of PS on memory performance in older humans. In these studies, typically, older adults between 50 and 85 years are given a 300-mg dose of PS, divided into three daily doses of 100 mg each, for a period ranging from twelve to twenty-four weeks. Other older adults are given a placebo pill with no active ingredients. These are the control participants against whom the PS-treated participants are compared. A simple summary of the results is that PS produces some increase in the memory performance of the PS group relative to the control group. This finding has been reported for older adults who meet the criteria for probable Alzheimer's disease and for older adult patients who are characterized as having symptoms of memory impairment. A positive effect of PS on memory has also been reported for "normal" older adults—adults over the age of 50 who did not exhibit any history or existence of brain dysfunction, neurological disorder, or use of drugs that could produce cognitive deterioration. These are adults who show the usual memory loss associated with normal aging.[11]

This summary is impressive and has been used as evidence to recommend PS to help boost memory. Indeed some proponents of PS report that "Those who took PS demonstrated a 30 percent improvement in cognitive function, including memory, learning, and recalling names, faces, and numbers."[12] But summaries can be tricky and sometimes a bit misleading. You need the whole story to get an accurate picture of the effectiveness of PS.

To get the whole story, you need to have a few more details about the results in the population of normal older adults who participated in this study. They were tested at three, six, nine, and twelve weeks after beginning the twelve-week treatment. They were tested on five primary memory tests: learning of name-face associations, delayed recall of the name-face associations, memory for faces, telephone number recall, and recall of misplaced objects. The controls and PS-treated adults were compared on each of these tests at each of the test intervals, for a total of twenty comparisons. Of the twenty comparisons, only six showed an advantage for the PS treated adults. In a sense, one might term this a 30 percent improvement in that 30 percent of the comparisons showed an advantage. It is more significant, however, that four of these differences occurred on tests given during the first half of the treatment. By the end of the twelve-week treatment, these differences no longer remained. Further, these differences were slight in that they represented about a one-point improvement over a score of just over 9. Thus for most of the comparisons the improvement was just about 10 percent, and the improvement due to PS was very transient. The only advantage produced by PS that remained at the end of the treatment was for face memory: participants given PS scored an average of 15.54 on the face memory test compared to an average score of 12.98 for the placebo control.

The researchers then examined the subgroup of participants who were at the bottom of the group in terms of initial memory performance. For these participants, at the conclusion of the treatment there were benefits of PS relative to the control for all the primary memory measures as well as for paragraph recall. Again, the most striking improvement was on the face memory test. In several other well-conducted research studies as well, older adults who were particularly forgetful relative to their peers showed some memory improvement after several months of PS treatment. This result is encouraging. The rest of the story is less exciting. The improvement in PS-treated adults relative to the placebo control is typically quite modest. For instance, in one study, at the end of six months of treatment the PS-treated group had an average total recall for word lists of 63 percent versus 60 percent for the placebo group.[13]

It's doubtful, though perhaps possible, that users of PS could tell any practical difference in their everyday memory use with a 3 percent gain in recall accuracy. One study of Alzheimer's patients (who had not progressed to middle and later stages) did examine observations of both psychiatrists and family members of the patients who were treated with either PS or a placebo.[14] The results were mixed. A psychiatrist noted improvement (on recalling details of everyday events) after twelve weeks of PS treatment. The family members did not. The researchers noted that any effect of PS appears to be subtle. Of course this is an average—some folks might see more benefit, some less.

Another way to gauge the degree of improvement would be to consider how many of the forgetful older adults showed improvement for PS relative to how they performed before the PS was administered (of course any placebo effect would need to be factored out). Unfortunately, we do not know the full story because in these studies the researchers did not report the needed numbers. We are not told the percentage of either the PS-treated adults or the placebo controls who showed improvements from baseline memory testing (prior to the experiment) to posttreatment testing (at the conclusion of the experiment).

Studies have reported no adverse side effects from the PS treatment. Researchers report that PS is well tolerated. In one study, many of the participants were patients on medication. PS did not interact negatively with any of the pharmaceutical drugs that these patients were taking. However, patients taking antipsychotics, antidepressants, barbiturates, methyl-dopa, reserpine, and bromocriptine were excluded from the study. Thus, there is no evaluation of possible interactions of PS with all potential pharmaceuticals taken by adults.

PS has purportedly been in use in Italy for over twenty years. A handful of proponents suggest that "PS is effective in delaying and usually reversing age-associated memory impairment." They also claim that millions of people are taking PS regularly throughout the United States and in the rest of the world. The typical dosage in research studies is 100 mg taken three times daily. Most of the studies used PS extracted from cows, but PS purchased over the counter is now commonly derived from soy. It is relatively expensive, with a month's supply (400 mg per day, recommended by the manufacturer) typically costing over $75. Some memory disorder treatment centers suggest the use of PS in conjunction with other brain-specific nutrients like ginkgo. Reflecting this suggestion, ginkgo and PS are combined in some products (NeuroPS). Many physicians are not aware of the use of PS as a nutritional supplement to treat memory problems.[15]

In summary, as with ginkgo there is reason to be cautiously optimistic about the benefits of PS for memory. PS produces effects in the mammalian brain that enhance brain functioning and thus possibly memory. The proven memory benefits for PS are in older adults with above-average memory impairment. Older adults with normal memory decline have shown only modest benefits from taking PS, benefits that did not extend to all the memory tests used in the research. The effects on adults showing normal memory decline are arguably not large enough to support the published claim that PS is the foundation for a "memory cure." One concern is that the modest increases shown on the memory test scores do not necessarily translate into noticeable differences in memory functioning. In the plus column, PS scores well in terms of no reported negative side effects or interactions with pharmaceuticals. Thus, there may be no harm in trying PS.

Choline

Choline is used to produce acetylcholine. Areas of the brain have neurons that depend on this neurotransmitter. Also, impairments that devastate memory like Alzheimer's disease largely wipe out the acetylcholine-rich neurons. Choline is found in a number of safe chemical compounds, including phosphatidylcholine (PC for short) and citicholine. PC, the primary dietary source of choline, is a central substance in the neuronal membrane. Both sources of choline can be purchased as nutritional supplements, with lecithin being a major source of PC. Some manufacturers have even boosted their foods with PC (by adding lecithin). In appropriate dosages, these nutrients can find their way into the cells, embuing them with more of the nutrient.[16]

The theory is that more acetylcholine can be produced if the brain has more of the ingredient (choline) needed to make acetylcholine. With diminishing neurons resulting from disease or age, the theory is that the remaining neurons function more effectively if more acetylcholine is available for transmitting messages. This line of reasoning has produced great interest in the possibility that choline supplements might improve memory.

The research investigating PC versus that investigating citicholine is not directly comparable, but at this point the sparse evidence favors citicholine. PC has been tested extensively for its effectiveness in treating Alzheimer's disease. One scholarly review of this research reported that the results were uniformly negative. In only a single report (out of more than twenty) was there evidence for memory improvement in a subset of patients with Alzheimer's. One unpublished study found that PC significantly enhanced the speed of learning nonsense syllables, but primarily in older adults who learned more slowly than their peers. Thus, the research does not strongly support the idea that PC supplements boost memory in older adults, at least those with probable Alzheimer's disease.[17]

A gold-standard study that administered 1,000 mg per day of citicholine for ninety days also did not find memory improvement in normal adults ranging in age from 50 to 85. But, a higher dose of 2,000 mg per day given to just those older adults with poor memory produced striking benefits to memory. Memory was tested by having people recall an unfamiliar story, measured by the number of ideas recalled. With the placebo, about nine of the ideas from the story were recalled. With citicholine, recall improved to about fourteen ideas, a gain of more than 50 percent. Though encouraging, this study was very limited. Only one memory measure was used, and only twenty-seven subjects were tested. These subjects had worse memory than their peers, and most were over 70 years of age.[18]

The evidence supporting memory benefits for choline-like substances is minimal, and not all choline supplements appear to produce positive memory effects. At the present time, citicholine seems to offer the most promising choline treatment, with the memory benefit limited to older adults with more than usual memory decline. It must be emphasized that the research with citicholine is very sparse. Nevertheless, a variety of choline substances are still included as one ingredient in some supplements advertised to substantially boost mental alertness and cognitive functioning. It may well be that choline supplement alone does not translate into more available acetylcholine. The choline must first be absorbed by the neuron, which requires an energy-dependent transport process. Interestingly, this process can by enhanced by ginkgo, perhaps suggesting that the "memory cocktail" approach that combines several of the "brain-specific" nutrients mentioned in this chapter might be on the right track. PC and citicholine are well tolerated, having infrequent, minor side effects.[19]

Vinpocetine

Vinpocetine is an extract from the periwinkle plant. It was introduced in clinical practice in Hungary about twenty years ago. In one journal article, a physician indicated that he now recommends vinpocetine as "the most important part" of a "brain-friendly" nutritional supplement.[20] Vinpocetine is sold alone as a supplement to "help improve memory and concentration" and is a featured ingredient in the product BrainPower. Advertisements claim that vinpocetine "has been shown to recharge your mind and memory," and that it is "recommended by pharmacists."

Vinpocetine seems to increase blood flow and circulation in the brain. It may also increase the transport and uptake of glucose to the neurons. More glucose should help neuronal functioning. Finally, vinpocetine may increase the acetylcholine neurotransmitter, a neurotransmitter especially important in memory regions of the brain.

The thinking is that both increased blood flow and improved delivery of glucose to neurons should be especially helpful to older adults who suffer from diminished oxygen supply to the brain caused by decreased blood flow (ischemia). Diminished oxygen can damage or kill neurons, and if the damage is extensive enough memory loss can follow. Studies have shown that vinpocetine can reduce the loss of neurons due to ischemia in memory regions of the brain. If the reduction in loss is great enough, then it could be the case that memory impairment would be slowed or avoided.

Two gold-standard studies investigated treatment with vinpocetine in older adults who had memory problems associated with brain dysfunction (either circulation problems in the brain or mild to moderate dementia-related brain disease). In both studies, the groups given vinpocetine showed more improvement than the placebo groups on tests measuring attention, concentration, and memory. The size of this improvement ranged from moderate to very modest. Patients taking vinpocetine for thirteen weeks improved three points (17.4 to 20.5) on the Mini–Mental State Questionnaire (described in Chapter 13). The patients taking the placebo showed no improvement. The effects were less strong in a more recent study. Both the low-dose and high-dose vinpocetine groups scored four points better on the test after taking the vinpocetine than before the vinpocetine. The important piece of information is that the placebo group gained three points (all patients had to score at least nine points on the test before the study began). Those who took vinpocetine for sixteen weeks showed only a one-point gain in memory and concentration performance over those who took an inactive pill.[21]

It is worthwhile mentioning that the results were more promising in terms of global improvement in the illness of these dementia patients. In a global improvement rating, in one study 21 percent of the patients given vinpocetine were classified as "strongly improved." Only 7 percent of the patients given the placebo pill were classified as strongly improved. The other study showed positive effects of vinpocetine that were just as strong when rated on global improvement.[22]

In these studies the side effects reported with vinpocetine were not any more extreme than those reported with the placebo pill. However, vinpocetine probably should not be taken with blood thinners (anticoagulant medicine).

The smallest dosage used in the studies was 30 mg a day (taken in dosages of 10 mg three times a day) for the first thirty days, dropping to 15 mg a day for the last sixty days. The highest dosage was 60 mg a day (taken in dosages of 20 mg three times a day), but this dosage did not produce significantly more benefit than a consistent dose of 30 mg a day. Some of the products sold in stores are in 5-mg doses, with the manufacturer recommending three doses per day. Based on the dosages used in the research, this dosage may be too low to provide a benefit of vinpocetine.

Because of its positive effects on blood circulation and metabolism processes in the brain and because of the placebo-controlled research just described, vinpocetine has been identified as a potential supplement for older adults with chronic brain circulation problems and dementia, and it has been shown to be effective with some of these older adults. The research evidence supporting a memory benefit for vinpocetine is somewhat less strong than for PS. Statistically significant improvements have been found in a few studies, but the effects are modest at best and memory performance was not extensively tested.

Acetyl-L-carnitine

Acetyl-L-carnitine (ALC) is an amino acid that is included in some "brain power" supplements sold in health food stores and advertised on radio and in magazines. In studies with rats, ALC has been found to have several effects that support the claim that it can help brain functioning and memory. It enhances the release of the neurotransmitter acetylcholine and the sensitivity of receptor sites to acetylcholine in memory areas of the brain, and it decreases deterioration of the parts of the neuron involved in communicating with other neurons. ALC also facilitates energy production within the neuron. If we look beyond brain activity to observable behavior, long-term ALC administration in rats increases longevity, improves spatial learning, and improves long-term memory performance. The evidence for benefits in humans, however, is not as conclusive.[23]

One gold-standard study has examined a one-year treatment of ALC in patients with Alzheimer's disease.[24] These patients had been diagnosed as having the disease for at least six months. The study used one of the most comprehensive sets of tests of any of the studies that have looked at the effects of nutritional supplements. After the year of treatment, on a number of measures the group given ALC showed less decline than did the group given the placebo pill. A key point, though, is that many of these differences were not significant. The most consistent effect was that ALC-treated patients were rated as deteriorating less on performance of everyday activities and habits, as well as in personality and interests. For objective memory and cognitive measures, treatment with ALC did not show consistent benefits. For long-term memory of individual words, ALC did significantly reduce the memory loss produced by the disease. But, patients given ALC did not show significantly less deterioration than did patients given the placebo for verbal comprehension, ability to copy geometric forms, retention of the structure of word meanings, memory of stories, or long-term memory of spatial information. The researchers suggest that perhaps for less impaired patients, more benefits would be found. At this point, though, we simply do not know if this is the case.

ALC is typically well tolerated at normal dosages (1 to 2 grams). One possible side effect is increased restlessness and overactivity. For this reason, ALC should be taken long before bedtime to avoid agitation during sleeping hours.

The available evidence is sparse, but does suggest that a year-long treatment of 2 g of ALC daily can slow the behavioral deterioration associated with Alzheimer's disease. The effects on memory are generally not significant. It remains to be seen whether memory benefits for ALC would be found for aging adults without brain disease.

Vitamin E

Vitamin E is an antioxidant. As mentioned in the section on ginkgo, antioxidants neutralize certain toxic chemicals (free radicals) that become more prevalent with age. The theory is that by neutralizing chemicals that kill neurons, vitamin E may slow memory decline that results from age or brain diseases.

The largest and best study on vitamin E investigated patients with moderate Alzheimer's disease.[25] A dose of 2,000 IUs (international units) per day of vitamin E delayed by about nine months the progression of the disease to certain landmarks. Patients on vitamin E did not require nursing home placement and did not lose daily living skills as rapidly as did patients given the placebo. Unfortunately, vitamin E did not halt the speed of memory decline.

Vitamin E is considered reasonably safe and it has recently been shown to delay some major signs of decline in Alzheimer's patients. For these reasons, physicians generally do not hesitate to recommend vitamin E to patients with Alzheimer's disease. Note that the 2,000-IU dosage needed to achieve the positive effects is within the range used in attempts to treat some patients with cancer and with Parkinson's disease (800 to 2,000 IUs are typically used). However, this dosage is considerably higher than the 30-IU guideline for normal consumption (percent daily value) set by the Food and Drug Administration, as well as dosages in the range of 400 IUs recommended by some nutritionists. Given the devastation of Alzheimer's disease, it is probably reasonable to sidestep these guidelines in the case of Alzheimer's disease (of course, you should consult your physician before taking megadoses of any supplement). The FDA has not approved the use of vitamin E for treatment of Alzheimer's. This is because vitamin E has not been shown to slow cognitive and memory declines. Also, there is no evidence that vitamin E helps prevent serious brain disease or the memory decline that comes with aging.

Estrogen and Related Hormones

Menopause is accompanied by reduced estrogen levels, and post-menopausal women sometimes report difficulties with memory and concentration. Also, women are twice as likely as men to be affected by Alzheimer's disease. Accordingly, there has been much interest in the possibility that estrogen therapy after menopause (and hysterectomy) may improve memory and cognitive functioning and that it may provide some protective effects against brain degenerative diseases such as Alzheimer's. Some studies (not using the gold-standard placebo control) have found that memory and cognitive performance are modestly better in women on estrogen therapy than in those not using estrogen, but other studies have found no improvement. Some large-scale studies (one with a sample of over three thousand women) show that estrogen users had lower incidence of Alzheimer's disease than did nonusers. In these studies, estrogen use was associated with a one-third to two-thirds reduction in risk of Alzheimer's disease, with the greatest benefit occurring for women who had used estrogen for the longest period of time. These studies are considered as only suggestive because women who use estrogen can differ in a number of ways from those who do not use estrogen. However, nonhuman animal experiments suggest that estrogen treatment protects against brain damage caused by insufficient blood flow to the brain (e.g., stroke) and to damage produced by beta-amyloid protein (the abnormal protein associated with Alzheimer's disease). Thus, there are reasons to expect that estrogen treatment in women may provide protection against brain decline associated with memory loss.[26]

In several gold-standard experiments, postmenopausal women (or women in whom estrogen reduction resulted from surgery such as hysterectomy) were randomly assigned to estrogen or placebo treatment. These studies showed a positive benefit of estrogen that was limited to memory of verbal information (short stories and paired associated word lists). Estrogen had no significant effect on memory of visual information or of working (short-term) memory tasks. As yet, no gold-standard (placebo-controlled) studies have been conducted to show whether estrogen protects against the onset of Alzheimer's disease. And the association between estrogen and some cancers may discourage estrogen treatment. For more detailed information, you can refer to *Hormone Therapy and the Brain* (2000), by Victor Henderson, a researcher at the University of Southern California.[27]

Another hormone that has gained attention as a possible treatment for age-related declines in memory is dehydroepiandrosterone (DHEA). This hormone is secreted by the adrenal cortex. DHEA may facilitate neural functioning in brain areas responsible for memory. It may also have indirect effects on memory as a potential building block for estrogen (as well as testosterone) and as an agent that alleviates depression. As we age, however, DHEA concentrations significantly decrease. Thus, it may be that DHEA hormone treatments will help improve memory in older adults in general, and in postmenopausal women in particular. Two placebo-controlled studies, one with elderly men and women and one with postmenopausal women, did find that a two- to four-week daily oral dose of 50 mg of DHEA significantly improved memory. These results must be considered preliminary. The memory tests were limited to recall of pictures and recognition of word lists. Furthermore, DHEA improved word recognition only when the presentation of the words for study was quite fast (less than a second per word). The potential advantage of DHEA is that in long-term hormone replacement (twelve months), there was no evidence of body changes that tend to signal possible endometrial cancer, as with estrogen replacement therapy.[28]

Piracetam

Piracetam is a drug that was developed in the 1960s to improve cognitive functions like memory and learning. It is sold under several names (Nootropil, Pirroxil) in Europe and Mexico, and used as well in Asia and South America. Piracetam is not easily available in the United States, as it is not approved by the FDA. Those in the United States obtain piracetam for personal use from Europe or Mexico. Piracetam appears to have a number of effects on the brain that could potentially facilitate memory. These effects include improved metabolic processes in the neuron, maintenance of the neuron components, and facilitation of neurotransmitters. It has been reported that piracetam improves memory in aging mice, with the effects most prominent in animals with brain dysfunction.[29]

Three gold-standard studies have examined the effects of piracetam either alone or in combination with lecithin (a source of choline) on Alzheimer's patients. On an array of memory tests there was little evidence that piracetam (either with or without lecithin) produced benefits. One interesting study was conducted with 135 adults age 55 and older who had visited a general practitioner for isolated memory problems but who had no signs of depression or dementia.

In one popular book on "brain fitness," it is suggested that this study produced "dramatic results" in relieving age-associated memory impairment. Memory was tested with recall of a word list both at the start of the experiment and at the end of a three-month treatment period. Low- and high-dose levels of piracetam were compared to a placebo control. All these groups received some memory strategy training as well. The degree of improvement in recall performance was measured from the start of the experiment to the end. The result does appear impressive: the high-dose piracetam group showed a 35.5 percent improvement, the low-dose group showed slightly less improvement, and the placebo group showed much less (12.5 percent) improvement. But there's a potential problem in interpreting this result. By chance the placebo group performed better at the start of the experiment than did the piracetam groups. By the end of the experiment the performance of the three groups was indistinguishable. It is possible that had the placebo group's recall at the start of the experiment been as low as that of the piracetam groups' recall, the placebo group could have improved as much (e.g., perhaps the memory training produced the gains in memory to the level shown at the end of the experiment). Indeed, on another recall test used in the experiment, the performance at the beginning of the experiment was equivalent across the groups, and for this test there was no effect of either piracetam dose. From this analysis of the gold-standard research with humans, it seems that there is reason for the FDA's current skepticism about the memory benefits of piracetam.[30]

Additional Information

Those who would like a more detailed review of the scientific evidence on the memory benefits of the supplements mentioned in this chapter can access two important and comprehensive review articles in a prominent journal published by the American Psychological Society. The articles are "Ginkgo Biloba: A Cognitive Enhancer?" by P. E. Gold, L. Cahill, and G. L. Wenk and "'Brain-Specific Nutrients': A Memory Cure?" by M. A. McDaniel, S. F., Maier, and G. O. Einstein. Both articles are in the May 2002 issue (volume 3) of *Psychological Science in the Public Interest,* published by the American Psychological Society. Summaries of these articles can also be found in the April 2003 issue (volume 288) of *Scientific American.*

CHAPTER THIRTEEN

Alzheimer's Disease

THE SIGNALS AND WHAT YOU CAN DO ABOUT IT

I attended his eighty-second birthday celebration at the Ronald Reagan Presidential Library in Simi Valley, along with several hundred other guests, including Margaret Thatcher, and we all froze when he toasted her twice, at length, and in exactly the same words. There was nothing we could do but give her two standing ovations, and not look too closely at Nancy Reagan's stricken face, while Dutch stood obliviously smiling.

—Edmund Morris, *Dutch: A Memoir of Ronald Reagan*

I t's horrifying to imagine having a memory lapse this severe—especially in front of hundreds of people. All of us have mistakenly repeated a dose of medication, perhaps lost our glasses several times in one day, or repeated a story to a friend several hours later. Immediately repeating a detailed and long toast, however, does signal a fairly profound memory problem, and behaviors like this along with other symptoms could certainly be an indication of Alzheimer's disease. One question that many of us have is whether our own memory failures or those of our loved ones are attributable to normal aging or to something more serious. The first part of this chapter tackles this pressing question. In answering this question, it is helpful to understand the general characteristics of the disease and how it is diagnosed. Another important question is whether or not there are preventative measures for Alzheimer's disease. A reasonable answer to this question requires consideration of the effects of Alzheimer's on the brain and a review of the theories concerning the causes of the disease. The second part of the chapter clarifies these fundamental issues and discusses possible preventative measures. The end of the chapter presents useful information and resources for those who take care of Alzheimer's patients.

Prevalence

Alzheimer's disease may well be the most dreaded disease of this new century. Early on, it was believed that Alzheimer's was relatively rare and affected only a very small segment of the population. More recent estimates of the prevalence of the disease are much higher. This is due in part to the increased recognition among physicians of the widespread occurrence of Alzheimer's among older adults, and to the discarding of outdated terms like "senile dementia." The increased diagnosis of Alzheimer's disease also has a lot to do with the fact that we are living longer these days. Indeed, life expectancy at the beginning of the twenty-first century is thirty years longer than it was at the beginning of the twentieth century. It's humbling to realize that many of us would not have survived to our present age if we had been born a hundred years ago.

Although Alzheimer's disease occurs occasionally at younger ages (early-onset Alzheimer's), it is a disease that is closely related to advancing age. Estimates of the prevalence of Alzheimer's disease are somewhat variable, because it is difficult to diagnose with certainty and because not all older adults who experience cognitive decline seek treatment. Nonetheless, the strikingly clear trend is that the probability of contracting Alzheimer's disease increases steadily with age. Katzman and Kawas's estimates, shown below, reveal that the probability of contracting Alzheimer's disease doubles every five-year period after the age of 65.[1]

Age Range	Percentage of the Population
65–70	2%
71–75	4%
76–80	8%
81–85	16%
Over 85	Some estimates are as high as 45%

It has been estimated that by the year 2050, 70 million Americans will be 65 and older, with about 19 million of these over the age of 85. According to current estimates from the Alzheimer's organization (*www.alz.org*), by then as many as 14 million Americans may be diagnosed with this dread disease. Considering the great pain this disease causes victims and caregivers alike, as well as the economic impact of round-the-clock care for patients, you can understand why Alzheimer's disease has become an important national health care issue and a scientific funding priority in the United States.

Terminology

Before exploring the various facets of Alzheimer's disease, it is worthwhile to distinguish among the various terms used to refer to the cognitive changes associated with aging. "Dementia" is a diagnostic term for an acquired brain disorder that causes substantial and significant impairment in cognitive functioning (e.g., memory, language, mental calculations, visual and spatial skills, abstract reasoning, and judgment). Someone with dementia might have problems remembering the details from a conversation thirty minutes earlier, finding words when speaking, comprehending two- and three-step commands, remembering directions while driving home, balancing the checkbook, completing a simple home repair job (a job that would have been no problem before the dementia), and experiencing lapses in judgment such as leaving a 2-year-old grandchild alone in the car for thirty minutes on a hot day. In the past, when dementia was associated with older age, it was often labeled "senile dementia." This term is rarely used these days as people prefer to use more specific labels. "Alzheimer's disease," a subcategory of dementia, is the most common cause of dementia in adults over the age of 65. However, there are many other causes of dementia, including one or multiple strokes (the second most common cause of dementia in older adults), tumors, traumatic brain injury, and infections.[2]

The term "senescence" refers to the normal effects of aging (sometimes the normal effects of aging on memory are called "age-associated memory impairment"). As described in Chapter 2 and elsewhere, normal aging affects memory and other cognitive processes, yet the symptoms are much less severe than those that define dementia. Nearly everyone who is lucky enough to live to a ripe old age will experience senescence and will have to cope with irritating, but not debilitating, reductions in cognitive powers. In summary, then, the normal effects of aging are referred to as "senescence"; Alzheimer's disease is a pathological condition and *not* the normal outcome of aging.

Symptoms

One feature of Alzheimer's disease is that the cognitive deterioration does not occur suddenly. The onset is often characterized as "insidious," in contrast to the abrupt development of major cognitive symptoms, which would indicate other causes like a stroke. Although the initial stages of Alzheimer's disease are mild, it is a progressive disease, and those with the disease gradually develop more pronounced symptoms that are impossible to ignore. The disease eventually produces severe impairments in memory, reasoning, language, and the ability to carry out even simple tasks. People with Alzheimer's disease can live for up to twenty years, but the more typical duration is eight to ten years.[3]

Table 13.1 lists the seven stages that Reisberg, Ferris, DeLeon,

Table 13.1 The Stages of Alzheimer's Disease

Stage of Cognitive Decline	Characteristics
1. Normal adult	No functional decline
2. Normal older adult	This stage is characterized by personal awareness of some functional decline such as forgetting where familiar objects are placed or temporarily forgetting familiar names.
3. Early	Noticeable deficits in demanding job situations. Difficulty in finding words and names, and little retention after reading a passage. Person may get lost while traveling. Difficulty in retrieving names becomes noticeable to people who know this person well.
4. Moderate	Decreased knowledge of recent events in their own lives, difficulty with complex tasks like managing personal finances. Can still distinguish familiar people from strangers.
5. Moderately severe	Can no longer survive without assistance. Difficulty recalling one's address or the names of grandchildren. No difficulty in eating or taking care of bathroom functions but may require assistance in choosing proper attire. Some disorientation in terms of knowing the current date and location.
6. Severe	Needs assistance in dressing, bathing, and toileting. May have urinary and fecal incontinence. May occasionally forget name of spouse. Person is largely unaware of recent events and life experiences. Personality and emotional changes (delusions, ob-

(*continued*)

Table 13.1 Continued

Stage of Cognitive Decline	Characteristics
	sessions, anxiety, agitation) tend to occur during this stage.
7. Very severe	Nearly all verbal abilities are lost and frequently there is no speech. Progressive loss of ability to walk, sit up, and hold head up. Brain seems no longer able to tell the body what to do.

Source: Adapted from B. Reisberg, S. H. Ferris, M. J. DeLeon, and T. Cook, "The Global Deterioration Scale for Assessment of Primary Degenerative Dementia," *American Journal of Psychiatry* 139 (1982): 1136–1139.

and Crook use to describe the cognitive and physical declines associated with Alzheimer's impairment.[4] You should note that in the earlier stages there is no or only slight cognitive decline. Because most older adults experience stage 2 symptoms, these are considered symptoms of normal aging. In fact, it is impossible at this point to distinguish the incipient stages of Alzheimer's disease from normal aging. For those with the disease, however, the symptoms will become increasingly severe and noticeable to family and friends. Whereas memory loss tends to be the first cognitive function that is noticed, the effects of Alzheimer's disease eventually extend into other areas such as language, judgment, thinking, and personality, causing progressive deterioration. For example, the progressive loss in language ability starts with problems in expressing thoughts and finding words, develops into problems in comprehension, and frequently culminates in mutism (producing no speech, only grunts). In the final stages of Alzheimer's disease, the person often loses all memory, language, and mental control over behavior (e.g., urinary and fecal incontinence, loss of the ability to walk). In the end, the Alzheimer's patient is typically bedridden and requires total supervision. Most eventually die from pneumonia.

Diana McGowin was diagnosed with Alzheimer's disease at the age of 52. The earliest signs of Alzheimer's disease are indistinguishable from normal aging. At some point, however, the cognitive lapses become alarming to the person as well as to relatives and friends. Consider Diana McGowin's unnerving description of one of her earliest realizations that something was dreadfully wrong.

The telephone rang, . . . It was my husband, asking me to prepare a lunch and deliver it to him at his work-place. He would only have a thirty-minute lunch break; not enough time to get to a restaurant. As I drove to Jack's office, I noticed a strip shopping center, new to me. It was strange I had not noticed this mall previously. I traveled this route frequently. I passed the street leading to the off-site, and drove several miles down the road before realizing my error. No doubt the new shopping center had thrown my judgment off, I mused, and turned around to retrace my steps. Near the driveway leading to my husband's office, I observed a fire station which was also new to me. That would be a good landmark to guide me to the company entrance in the future.

Jack saw my car approaching and came out of his building to greet me. Accepting the lunch with thanks, he leaned against the car. "Jack, when did they build that new strip shopping center on Kirkman Road? Funny, but I don't remember it being built, and it is already open for business." Jack frowned thoughtfully, than shook his head. I continued, "Oh well, I'm glad to see the new fire station near your entrance. It will give me a good landmark." Jack laughed and again shook his head. "Diane, that station has always been here," he chided. "Even before my building was built!"

I suddenly became irate. I started the car and began to pull away from Jack, who leaped from his position leaning against the vehicle. "Whoa! What's your rush?" I braked, staring before me in confusion. What was the exit? "Jack," I asked shakily, "How do I get out of here?" Jack now roared with laughter, "Diane, shape up!

Figure 13.1 Excerpts from Diana McGowin's autobiography.

You certainly have something on your mind! 'New' shopping center, 'new' fire stations, and now you can't find your way out of a parking lot!" I fought tears of frustration as I shouted at Jack, "Don't laugh at me! Just tell me how to get out of this place!" Jack bowed ceremoniously and pointed ahead of my car.

Memory losses in Alzheimer's patients are often painful. They elicit shame and attempts to cover up the losses.

As I entered the corridor, a well-dressed young man was turning the corner. "Hey, Diane! Good to see you! How have you been?" He greeted me with a smile. Oh God, not another one! I felt I was on a trip to never-never land. This time, I attempted to bluff my way through the small talk with this young stranger. As we walked along together, he asked me how long I had worked for this firm. I hesitated, then replied I had been with them for about three years. The lad nodded approvingly, and said he was there to interview for a job as a messenger or courier. Could I help him?

I threw in the towel, and smiled resignedly to him. "Please forgive me. I know that I know you, but it is just one of those days! I simply can't bring your name to mind. I will be happy to put in a word for you, if you could write down your name and other relevant details."

"I don't get it," he muttered.

"Your name?" I did not waver.

"Diane, I'm your cousin Rich," he said slowly.

Tears began to surface in my eyes and I embraced my cousin, whispering, "I was just trying to keep anyone from overhearing that one of my relatives is applying. Of course I'll put in a good recommendation with the personnel department. Absolutely!"

In the later stages of the disease, Diana found comfort in people who recognized her problems and came to her aid.

Becoming hopelessly lost [although she was living at home, she was in the hospital for her father's surgery], I finally whispered to a kind-looking nurse that I was an Alzheimer's patient, and requested that she give me simply drawn directions to the waiting room. She wrote down the direction and then escorted me to the elevator. As I entered the elevator with many others, I noticed a distinguished man in a navy blue suit board the elevator beside me. As he entered, he somehow deleted all the other floor destinations and, much to my relief, he pushed the button to my floor. As we exited, he asked to see the room number and directions the nurse had placed into my perspiring palm. I was astounded. How did he know I had such instructions? After reading the note tightly gripped in my fist, he escorted me to a nurse's station, and asked the staff to assist me. I do not know who this man was, but suspect he was a physician who had overheard me whisper to the directing nurse.

Such individuals are the unsung but appreciated saviors of the Alzheimer's patient.

To give you some sense of how these cognitive declines affect day-to-day living and one's sense of self, Figure 13.1 presents some poignant passages from Diana McGowin's book *Living in the Labyrinth.*[5] McGowin wrote this book after being diagnosed with early-onset Alzheimer's disease at the age of 52. In this book, she courageously and vividly describes her journey into confusion and darkness.

Diagnosis

Ronald Reagan's older daughter, Maureen Reagan, remembered the early symptoms of her father's illness and how they led to his diagnosis:

No actor ever forgets a role, so I should have realized something was wrong. It was late in 1993 and we were having dinner with my father. We were discussing a 1950s film he made, "Prisoner of War." For years he had told me about the

gruesome tortures inflicted on American prisoners by the
North Koreans. But now he seemed to be hearing me tell the
stories for the first time. Finally he looked at me and said,
"Mermie, I have no recollection of making that movie."

That was my "click of awareness." Another six months
went by before Dad complained to his doctor of feeling dis-
oriented in unfamiliar surroundings, like hotel rooms. It was
in the fall of 1994, at the Mayo Clinic, that my father was diagnosed with Alzheimer's disease.[6]

The world learned of Alzheimer's disease in 1907 when a German physician, Alois Alzheimer, reported the autopsy results of a 51-
year-old female patient. She was a person who had had severe dementia, and upon postmortem examination, Dr. Alzheimer detected the
massive neuronal loss as well as abnormal conditions now known as
"amyloid plaques" and "neurofibrillary tangles."

When cognitive problems are noticed, it is important to get a diagnosis as early as possible. The physician will want to assess a patient
for the presence of dementia, and, if it is present, determine whether
Alzheimer's disease is likely to be the cause. Dementia can have many
possible causes—for example, vitamin deficiencies, reactions to medication, strokes, tumors, infections, long-term abuse of alcohol, diseases like Huntington's or Pick's disease. Because some of these causes
are treatable, it is important to make an early diagnosis. Early diagnosis of Alzheimer's disease is also important because the medications
that are currently available tend to be most effective in the early and
moderate stages. Early diagnosis also enables the patient and family
to better prepare for the future.

Alzheimer's disease is difficult to diagnose, mainly because the
earliest symptoms are indistinguishable from the symptoms of normal aging. Also, the symptoms of Alzheimer's are similar to those
caused by other diseases and problems (e.g., vitamin deficiencies, tumors, strokes, depression). Thus, for the present at least, Alzheimer's
disease is an "exclusionary disease." That is, a diagnosis of "probable
Alzheimer's disease" is given when the behavioral symptoms of progressive losses in cognitive functioning occur and when these cannot

be medically attributed to other causes. Confirmation of Alzheimer's disease can be done only by examining the brain tissue directly and looking for the telltale signs of neuronal loss, neurofibrillary tangles, and amyloid plaques. Because of the danger involved in examining brain tissue while the patient is alive, this type of analysis is nearly always done during an autopsy. It is reassuring to know that clinical testing procedures have improved to the point where the diagnosis of Alzheimer's disease is accurate (i.e., confirmed by an autopsy) in about 90 percent of the cases.[7]

Figure 13.2 lists the criteria of the American Psychiatric Association for the diagnosis of Alzheimer's-type dementia.[8] As you will see, diagnosing Alzheimer's disease requires that the memory and other cognitive problems show a "gradual onset," "progressive deterioration," and cognitive problems that are severe enough to interfere with daily life.

Diagnostic Procedures

When you suspect that someone has Alzheimer's disease, you should consult a physician for a clinical diagnosis. The assessment is likely to involve conducting (1) a complete medical history, (2) a mental status examination, (3) laboratory tests (such as blood work) and neuroimaging tests, and (4) neuropsychological and other examinations. Follow-up examinations are also very important. Making the diagnosis is a complex process that involves considering all these sources of information.

Once again, it is important to realize that severe cognitive impairment in older adults can have myriad causes. Although Alzheimer's disease is the leading cause of dementia in older adults, problems in cognitive functioning are often due to depression. Distinguishing dementia from depression is a crucial task of the physician because both can cause confusion, impaired concentration, and problems remembering and paying attention. Dementia-like symptoms can also be due to delirium (also called "acute confusional state"), which is a transient change in a person's cognitive and emotional state and may last for days or weeks. Delirium is often caused

A. The development of multiple cognitive deficits manifested by both:

1. Memory impairment (impaired ability to learn new information or to recall previously learned information)
2. One (or more) of the following cognitive disturbances:
   a. aphasia (language disturbance)
   b. apraxia (impaired ability to carry out motor activities despite intact motor function)
   c. agnosia (failure to recognize or identify objects despite intact sensory function)
   d. disturbance in executive functioning (i.e., planning, organizing, sequencing, abstracting)

B. The cognitive deficits in Criteria A1 and A2 each cause significant impairment in social or occupational functioning and represent a significant decline from a previous level of functioning.

C. The course is characterized by gradual onset and continuing cognitive decline.

D. The cognitive deficits in Criteria A1 and A2 are not due to any of the following:

1. Other central nervous system conditions that cause progressive deficits in memory and cognition (e.g., cerebrovascular disease, Parkinson's disease, Huntington's disease, subdural hematoma, normal-pressure hydrocephalus, brain tumor)
2. Systematic conditions that are known to cause dementia (e.g., hypothyroidism, vitamin B12 or folic acid deficiency, niacin deficiency, hypercalcemia, neurosyphilis, HIV infection)
3. Substance-induced conditions

E. The deficits do not occur exclusively during the course of a delirium.

F. The disturbance is not better accounted for by another Axis I disorder (e.g., Major Depressive Disorder, Schizophrenic).

Figure 13.2 Diagnostic criteria for dementia of the Alzheimer's type. *Source:* American Psychiatric Association, *Diagnostic and Statistical Manual of Mental Disorders* (4th edition, text revision) (Washington, D.C.: American Psychiatric Press, 2000).

by factors like drug intoxication and metabolic disorders (such as kidney failure), and it is important to diagnose and treat these disorders quickly.[9] If the physician determines that a patient has dementia, then there is the task of distinguishing among the many possible causes of it, some of which are treatable. The task of the physician is a complex one and goes well beyond determining whether there is cognitive impairment.

Medical History

It is important to determine the person's past and present physical health status and level of mental functioning. The physician is likely to interview the patient as well as family and/or friends in order to learn about family history, the symptoms the person is currently displaying, how these are interfering with normal activities and daily living, the degree to which they are changing over time, and the speed with which they are changing.

Mental Status Examinations

When dementia is suspected, the physician is likely to administer a mental status examination. These are fairly brief and quantifiable tests that help assess the severity of the cognitive problems. They are extremely valuable because previous scores on these tests have been collected among very large samples. Thus, a patient's score can be compared with those that are typical for a given age group and educational background. As you can imagine, however, there are some problems in interpreting the results from these examinations. One problem is that it is important to identify the changes in cognitive functioning in recent years. Remember: the progressive deterioration of cognitive abilities is an important sign of Alzheimer's disease. Given that patients are probably taking these tests for the first time, there are no comparison data for each particular individual. Thus, people who are experiencing the beginning stages of dementia and who have functioned at very high levels throughout their lives may still do very well on these exams. Another problem is that many older adults are uncomfortable when their mental status is being examined, and the scores are very sensitive to variables like anxiety (see Chapter 11). In light of these problems, it is very useful to consider multiple sources of information in developing a diagnosis.

To give you a good idea of the types of problems that warrant concern for dementia, two often-used tests of dementia are described below. These tests are *not* for you to use in order to evaluate people yourself; rather, this information can help you determine whether someone should see a physician.

- *Mini–Mental State Examination.* This is the most popular screening device for examining the cognitive functioning of older adults.[10] It can be administered in less than ten minutes, and it measures, among other things, general awareness of the present context (like knowing the month and the year and what town you are in at the moment), attention, memory for three objects that have just been presented, the ability to name familiar and simple objects (like a pencil), and the ability to read and follow directions. It is important to note that one must interpret the errors on this test in relation to the person's prior level of functioning. Overall, realize that this test assesses what most people would consider to be fairly simple cognitive abilities. Keep in mind that occasional memory problems such as not remembering someone's name or forgetting a conversation you had with someone a couple of weeks ago should not be taken as evidence of Alzheimer's disease.
- *The 7-Minute Screen for Diagnosing Alzheimer's Disease.* This is a reliable test that holds some promise for quickly distinguishing between normal aging and dementia.[11] The four parts of this test are summarized in Figure 13.3. It tests for general awareness of present circumstances, profound difficulties in embedding new information in memory (with repeated presentations and with cueing), and the ability to retrieve from memory basic information like food items and the image of a clock.

Part 1: Orientation

This section evaluates the person's basic awareness of current circumstances. Specifically, the person is asked to identify the current time, date, day of the week, month, and year. As you might expect, errors in knowing the month and year are considered more serious than forgetting the other items.

Part 2: Memory

This part tests the ability to learn and remember new events. The examiner displays a card like the one below and asks the person to identify and name the "tool" on the page. The answer is "screwdriver" and the examiner identifies it if the person cannot find it or makes a mistake. This is done for all four items. Next, the picture card is removed, and the examiner cues memory for each of the items by presenting the category names "tool," "musical instrument," "article of clothing," and "vehicle." If a mistake is made, the picture card is presented a second time, the items are again identified and then cued. This procedure is repeated for four different cards (a total of 16 items).

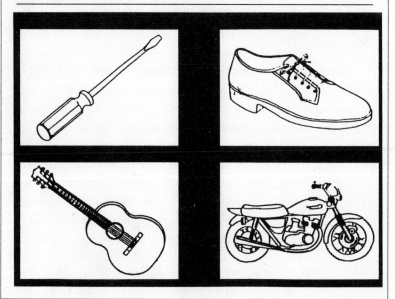

Figure 13.3 continued on next page

After a short distraction period, the person is asked to first recall as many items as possible without any cues and then is asked to recall the items given the category cues (e.g., "I showed you a picture of a tool; what was it?") This is scored by the total number of items that a person can recall (out of 16) with or without cueing. Although this sounds fairly difficult, you must remember that the pictures are presented, identified, cued, and represented if needed. Also, at recall, the cues are again presented. Thus, recall tends to be fairly high. In one of Solomon and Pendlebury's studies, the mean recall for a group of normal older adults (average age was 77.5) was 15.9. By contrast, the mean recall of a group of Alzheimer's patients (average age was 77.6) was 6.8.

Part 3: Clock Drawing

For this section, the person is given a blank sheet of paper and asked to draw the face of a clock and to include all the numbers. Next, the patient is asked to draw in the hands to a particular time. The drawing is scored for accuracy in terms of including all the numbers, getting them in the correct order and the correct position, and drawing the hands in the correct positions.

Part 4: Verbal Fluency

This section tests the person's ability (fluency) at retrieving information from long-term memory. It's a simple test in which the patient is given a category name and then asked to say as many items from that category as quickly as possible. The patient is given one minute to come up with the items. For example, if given the category "foods," the person would start naming items from that category like "pizza," "bread," "corn," "tomato," "banana," and so on. Solomon and Pendlebury reported that their sample of normal older adults was able to name over twice as many items as their Alzheimer's group in the one-minute period.

Figure 13.3 "The 7-Minute Screen" for diagnosing Alzheimer's disease. *Source:* Adapted from P. R. Solomon and W. W. Pendlebury, "Recognition of Alzheimer's Disease: The 7 Minute Screen," *Family Medicine* 30 (1998): 265–271.

Laboratory and Neuroimaging Tests

These tests are very useful for helping physicians identify the source of problems. Laboratory evaluations in the form of blood and urine tests are useful for determining whether other factors such as infections, hypothyroidism, or nutritional deficiencies are causing the dementia, and also whether the patient is genetically at risk for Alzheimer's disease. Neuroimaging tests, like magnetic resonance imaging (MRI), allow trained observers to see the physical structures of the brain with remarkable clarity, and these can be very useful for eliminating other causes of dementia. For example, tumors and strokes can be identified through neuroimaging.

At present, laboratory tests and neuroimaging techniques are used mainly to rule out causes of dementia other than Alzheimer's. However, the future holds good promise for using these kinds of tests to positively identify the presence of Alzheimer's disease in its early stages. It may eventually be possible to detect the presence of chemical markers of Alzheimer's in cerebrospinal fluid, blood, or urine samples. Also, a good deal of research is under way to examine the usefulness of MRI for early detection of atrophy in brain structures (like the hippocampus) that are particularly affected by Alzheimer's disease.[12]

Neuropsychological and Other Tests

A battery of standardized neuropsychological tests enables the physician to assess performance across many cognitive functions (e.g., language, memory, reasoning, visual and spatial skills) and to more specifically determine which of these have been most affected. These tests are useful for distinguishing between normal aging and early dementia and for differentiating among the possible causes of dementia. For instance, those with Alzheimer's disease are likely to show disturbances on two or more functions, whereas those with more localized diseases in the brain are likely to show a more limited set of disturbances. Psychiatric and psychological tests are also useful for examining the role of depression in producing dementia-like symptoms.

Normal Aging or Alzheimer's Disease?

We hear a lot these days about Alzheimer's disease, and nearly all of us
have family members and/or friends with this disorder. It is natural,
then, that when we have memory lapses and perhaps sense some decline in our own memory ability, we start to worry about whether or
not we are experiencing the beginning stages of Alzheimer's. If this is
the case for you, rest assured that in the great majority of cases, these
are signs of normal aging and not Alzheimer's disease. The types of
forgetfulness that most of us experience as we get older—such as forgetting the plot of a movie we saw several months ago, not being able
to remember very much about a newspaper article we read this morning, or temporarily forgetting the name of a good friend—are much
more likely to be signs of normal aging than of Alzheimer's disease.
Indeed, these memory failures happen to young people too, and they
reflect other factors like inattention and distraction—factors that can
affect older people as well. If you refer to the items in Figure 13.3, you
will see that it is more severe deficits like the inability to draw a clock
or profound problems in getting new information into and out of
memory that lead to a diagnosis of Alzheimer's-type dementia. In
trying to evaluate whether or not someone has Alzheimer's disease,
you should keep these criteria in mind, as well as the Alzheimer's Association's ten warning signs of Alzheimer's disease, shown in Figure
13.4.[13]

To provide some idea of how people's fears about memory loss
stack up against the actual prevalence of Alzheimer's disease, the authors recently asked faculty and staff in one university to provide their
age and respond to the following question: "Have you ever had the
thought (with some degree of seriousness) that you might have Alzheimer's disease?" From over 280 responses, the results were tabulated
and are displayed, by age category, below.

Age Category	Percentage Concerned
30–39	10.1
40–49	31.3
50–59	37.3
60–79	36.0

1. Memory loss. One of the most common early signs of dementia is forgetting recently learned information. While it's normal to forget appointments, names, or telephone numbers, those with dementia will forget such things more often and not remember them later.

2. Difficulty performing familiar tasks. People with dementia often find it hard to complete everyday tasks that are so familiar we usually do not think about how to do them. A person with Alzheimer's may not know the steps for preparing a meal, using a household appliance, or participating in a lifelong hobby.

3. Problems with language. Everyone has trouble finding the right word sometimes, but a person with Alzheimer's disease often forgets simple words or substitutes unusual words, making his or her speech or writing hard to understand. If a person with Alzheimer's is unable to find his or her toothbrush, for example, the individual may ask for "that thing for my mouth."

4. Disorientation to time and place. It's normal to forget the day of the week or where you're going. But people with Alzheimer's disease can become lost on their own street, forget where they are and how they got there, and not know how to get back home.

5. Poor or decreased judgment. No one has perfect judgment all of the time. Those with Alzheimer's may dress without regard to the weather, wearing several shirts or blouses on a warm day or very little clothing in cold weather. Individuals with dementia often show poor judgment about money, giving away large amounts of money to telemarketers or paying for home repairs or products they don't need.

6. Problems with abstract thinking. Balancing a checkbook may be hard when the task is more complicated than usual. Someone with Alzheimer's disease could forget completely what the numbers are and what needs to be done with them.

7. Misplacing things. Anyone can temporarily misplace a wallet or key. A person with Alzheimer's disease may put things in unusual places: an iron in the freezer or a wristwatch in the sugar bowl.

Figure 13.4 Ten warning signs of Alzheimer's disease. *Source:* Alzheimer's Association Web site (2003): *www://alz.org/AboutAD/10Signs.htm.*

8. Changes in mood or behavior. Everyone can become sad or moody from time to time. Someone with Alzheimer's disease can show rapid mood swings—from calm to tears to anger—for no apparent reason.

9. Changes in personality. People's personalities ordinarily change somewhat with age. But a person with Alzheimer's disease can change a lot, becoming extremely confused, suspicious, fearful, or dependent on a family member.

10. Loss of initiative. It's normal to tire of housework, business activities, or social obligations at times. The person with Alzheimer's disease may become very passive, sitting in front of the television for hours, sleeping more than usual, or not wanting to do usual activities.

Because these are self-reported impressions, they should be interpreted with some degree of caution. Nonetheless, the results include a couple of interesting features. One is that the subjective impression of memory problems increases threefold from the decade of the 30s to the decade of the 40s. This probably reflects the fact that many begin to notice memory losses in their early 40s. The other is that the actual incidence of Alzheimer's disease is much lower than is the concern that one might have the disorder. Thus, while almost a third of the people in their 40s have thought that they might have Alzheimer's disease, much less than 1 percent of the population in that age range actually have it. In a recent study, 60- to 78-year-old individuals complaining of memory problems were tested for dementia 3.5 years later. Only 9 percent of these had dementia, and these results are consistent with the authors' conclusion that memory concerns far outweigh the actual prevalence of dementia.[14]

The relief that we experience in knowing that Alzheimer's disease strikes a relatively small proportion of the population should be balanced with a realistic appraisal of our cognitive functioning. If you see that someone has the warning signs, if you think he or she would have difficulty on the mental status exams presented in this chapter, and/or if you notice a progressive deterioration in cognitive abilities, then it would be worthwhile to check it out. Remember that early diagnosis is important and that some forms of dementia are treatable.

How Does Alzheimer's Disease Affect the Brain?

Although aging affects all brains that are fortunate enough to make it into older adulthood, the age and rate of change vary greatly from individual to individual. Some of these changes are caused by normal aging, whereas others are the result of pathological conditions like Alzheimer's disease. As mentioned earlier in this chapter, Alois Alzheimer discovered *amyloid plaques, neurofibrillary tangles, and neuronal cell loss* in the brain of his severely demented patient. To this day, these are seen as the identifying neuropathological characteristics of Alzheimer's disease. Although these are present in nonpathological or normal brains, they are especially prevalent in the brains of those with Alzheimer's.

Amyloid plaques are deposits of amyloid protein. It is not completely understood how amyloid plaques develop, but the basic idea is that they are the result of beta-amyloid protein fragments that are cleaved from a larger protein called amyloid precursor protein (APP). The purpose of APP in the brain is not clear. The beta-amyloid fragments accumulate and harden into plaque. In Alzheimer's patients, these plaques develop in very large numbers in certain regions of the brain, and because they are toxic they damage the surrounding neurons. So, it is fairly accurate to think about amyloid plaques as areas of hardened plaques surrounded by clumps of dead neurons. As described in Chapter 1, neurons are specialized cells in the body that conduct and process information. We think and remember what we do because of our neurons, and thus large losses of neurons compromise our cognitive abilities.[15]

Another identifying feature of Alzheimer's disease is neurofibrillary tangles. Normal neurons contain filaments that run down the length of the neuron and give the cell support. These filaments also act as "railroad tracks" for transporting nutrients within the cell. When neurofibrillary tangles develop, these filaments become twisted and the system of transportation within the neuron breaks down. The result is that the affected neurons can no longer communicate effectively and eventually many of them die. The prevalence of these tangles has been shown to correlate with the severity of cognitive dysfunction in patients with Alzheimer's disease. While counting neurofibrillary tangles in the hippocampus (a brain structure thought to be very important for the storage and retrieval of memories), researchers have found tangles in 6 percent of the neurons from normal brains, 43 percent of the neurons from those with "mild" Alzheimer's disease, and 71 percent of the neurons from those in the later stages of Alzheimer's disease.[16] Another result of Alzheimer's disease is that there is a substantial reduction in a number of neurotransmitters, especially acetylcholine. As described in Chapter 12, acetylcholine is the primary neurotransmitter (a chemical messenger that allows neurons to communicate with other neurons) for several brain structures that are critically involved in learning and memory. Research has shown that there is a marked reduction in acetylcholine, as well as in the number of neurons that synthesize acetylcholine, in the brains of people with Alzheimer's. There is also a reduced presence of choline acetyltransferase, an enzyme involved in the synthesis of acetylcholine, and an increased presence of butyrylcholinesterase, an enzyme that breaks down acetylcholine. The drugs currently used to treat patients with Alzheimer's disease are effective to the extent that they are able to increase the levels of acetylcholine in the synapses of the brain. This process is described in more detail in the section on treatment.[17]

Causes

One of the most commonly asked questions about Alzheimer's disease is: "What role does genetics play in contracting this disease?" Often, this question comes from someone whose mother or father has Alzheimer's disease. It turns out that some types of the disease do tend to run in families and are passed on from generation to generation. Others, however, do not. A key determinant seems to be whether the Alzheimer's disease is early-onset or not. Early-onset Alzheimer's disease occurs before the age of 65. This type of Alzheimer's is particularly pernicious, progressing rapidly. Fortunately, early-onset Alzheimer's disease is much rarer than the late-onset form of the disease.

Early Onset

About 10 percent of the cases of Alzheimer's disease occur before the age of 65, and about 50 percent of these are thought to be due to defective genes on chromosomes 21, 14, and 1. It is interesting to note that persons with Down's syndrome, who have three copies of chromosome 21, almost always show brain pathology similar to that of patients who have developed Alzheimer's disease by the age of 30. According to the "Progress Report on Alzheimer's Disease 1999," by the National Institute on Aging, if either of your parents has passed on any one of these defective genes to you, you have a fifty percent chance of developing early-onset Alzheimer's disease. Although the science is somewhat speculative at this point, some believe that these gene mutations lead to the production of more beta amyloid and/or the production of a more sinister version of beta amyloid (i.e., one that is "stickier" and accumulates more readily), which in turn leads to more plaques and more dead neurons.[18]

Late Onset

The role of genetics is much less clear and direct in patients with late-onset Alzheimer's disease. It has been found that persons with a certain form of gene (an allele) on chromosome 19 have increased risk for late-onset Alzheimer's disease. It is thought that a certain version of this gene (Apolipoprotein E-4, or Apo E-4) causes the brain to produce a protein that binds to amyloid, and this contributes to the process of creating amyloid plaques. Those who inherit this gene from one parent have twice the risk of developing Alzheimer's disease, and those who inherit this gene from both parents are at even greater risk. Inheriting this gene, however, does not ensure that you will develop the disease. By the same token, not having this gene does not guarantee that you will not get the disease. What the presence of the gene probably means is that you have an increased predisposition toward contracting Alzheimer's disease. Those who inherit this particular gene and in addition are exposed to precipitating or activating factors are the ones who are more likely to get the disease. Interestingly, those with another version of this gene (Apo E-2) on chromosome 19 seem to have a lower-than-average risk for developing the disease.[19]

The importance of nongenetic factors in producing Alzheimer's disease is made clear in the results of a study conducted on identical twins in Finland.[20] The researchers found that if one member of the twin pair developed Alzheimer's disease, the probability was about 50 percent that the other member also developed the disease. In other words, given the exact same genetic makeup, 50 percent of the time when one member of the pair had Alzheimer's disease, the other member did not. Moreover, even when both members of the pair developed Alzheimer's, there was often a gap of several years or more before the second member was diagnosed with the disease. Clearly, then, nongenetic factors also play a large role in the development of this disease. Some of these factors are considered below.

Possible Risk and Preventative Factors

What are some of the risk and precipitating factors for Alzheimer's disease? Before this question is addressed, one qualification is necessary. The research thus far enables us to identify factors associated with reduced or increased risk of Alzheimer's disease, but it does not allow us to unequivocally identify the causes. This is due to the fact that most studies to date have examined the relation between uses of a treatment and Alzheimer's disease under natural conditions in which very little control existed. For example, assume that we discover that people who take vitamin X have a reduced risk for Alzheimer's disease; does that mean that vitamin X is the causative agent in reducing risk for Alzheimer's disease? Not necessarily. It could be, but it could also be that people who take vitamin X also exercise regularly, and thus it may be exercise that reduces the risk of Alzheimer's disease. Better and more carefully controlled studies (ones in which vitamin X is likely to be the only factor that differs among the groups) are currently being conducted, and these hold great promise for identifying the preventative factors with a greater degree of probability.

Age

As indicated in the beginning of this chapter, the prevalence of Alzheimer's disease doubles every five years after the age of 65.[21]

Oxidative Processes

One of the risk factors for Alzheimer's disease is thought to be the oxidative processes in neurons. Through normal metabolic processes, free radicals are released in neurons. The release of too many free radicals can injure or destroy neurons. It is thought that vitamin E (and possibly other free radical scavengers like the plant extract *Ginkgo biloba*) can help safeguard neurons against the destructive effects of free radicals. Studies have shown that taking vitamin E slowed down the progression of the disease in Alzheimer's patients, and several studies are currently under way to examine the extent to which free radical scavengers can delay or prevent the disease (see Chapter 12 for more details on vitamin E and *Ginkgo biloba*).[22]

Mini-Strokes

Multiple small strokes in combination with Alzheimer's disease can exacerbate dementia. Strokes or brain infarctions occur when there is a blockage in the arteries of the brain. When this occurs, neurons that receive their blood supply from these blocked cerebral arteries die. Research suggests that mini-strokes in some regions of the brain, in combination with certain levels of neuronal plaques and tangles seen in Alzheimer's disease, can cause dementia. In some cases neither the mini-strokes alone nor the plaques and tangles alone are sufficient to cause dementia. However, in aggregation, the neuronal destruction caused by these two factors may be sufficient to push the damage beyond some hypothetical threshold and produce dementia. Actually, as discussed in the section on brain reserve capacity, the loss of neurons means fewer remaining functioning neurons, and Alzheimer's disease may be related more to the number of neurons that are still functioning than to the number that have been damaged. So, lifestyle changes and medications that reduce the risk of having a stroke should also reduce the probability of developing Alzheimer's disease.[23]

Brain Inflammation and Anti-Inflammatory Agents

Another risk factor for developing Alzheimer's is inflammation of the brain. Brain inflammation occurs more frequently in older people and is thought to be harmful to neurons by causing amyloid plaques. This was initially noticed when it was found that people suffering from severe arthritis have lower rates of Alzheimer's disease. More recent studies have shown that frequent use of anti-inflammatory medication is associated with decreased risk for Alzheimer's disease. For example, in a large-scale examination of older adults in the Baltimore Longitudinal Study (which monitored older people over a thirty-eight-year period), researchers found that people who regularly took anti-inflammatory drugs for at least two years were 30 to 60 percent less likely to develop Alzheimer's disease.[24]

Head Trauma

There is some evidence that a history of head injury increases one's risk for Alzheimer's disease.[25] It is thought that head injuries can increase the production of amyloid plaques in those who have the Apo E-4 gene. Head injuries can also disrupt transmission of information between neurons. So, use your seat belt and wear a helmet when riding your bicycle.

Brain Size, Intelligence, and Education

Growing evidence shows that having a larger brain size, higher intelligence, and a higher level of education reduces the risk for Alzheimer's disease. The mechanism for these relationships may be increased brain reserve capacity, described in a later section.[26]

Active Lifestyle

There is increasingly clear evidence that people with cognitively active lifestyles and/or jobs have a reduced risk of Alzheimer's disease. A large-scale study that compared 193 Alzheimer's patients (diagnosed with either "possible" or "probable" Alzheimer's disease) with 358 healthy older adults (comprising mainly friends and neighbors of the Alzheimer's patients) suggests that activity levels at mid-life predict the onset of Alzheimer's disease.[27] The average age of the participants was around 72, and the researchers assessed their levels of passive (e.g., watching TV, listening to music, attending social clubs, attending church), intellectual (e.g., reading a book, doing crossword puzzles, painting, writing letters, playing board games, playing a musical instrument), and physical (e.g., gardening, jogging, playing racquet sports) activities many years earlier—during early adulthood (20s and 30s) and during middle adulthood (40s and 50s). They found that the Alzheimer's patients had significantly fewer activities of all types in their early and middle adulthood. Thus, high activity levels appear to protect people against the development of Alzheimer's disease. Importantly, the largest difference between the groups was in intellectual activities: a reduction in intellectual activities from early to middle adulthood was associated with an increased probability of Alzheimer's disease.

Wilson and colleagues came to the same conclusion in their study of 801 older people (Catholic nuns, priests, and brothers) who did not have Alzheimer's disease. The researchers followed these people for an average of 4.5 years, over which approximately 14 percent of the participants developed Alzheimer's disease. Interestingly, at the start of the study the researchers measured participants' levels of cognitive activity in their everyday lives. Cognitive activity scores ranged from 1.57 to 4.71 (the average score was 3.57) and reflected participation in activities like reading, visiting museums, and playing puzzle games. The results showed that an increase of one point on the cognitive activity score was associated with a 33 percent decrease in the probability of developing Alzheimer's disease over the 4.5-year period. It is important to note that one point on this scale reflects a rather large change in cognitive activity, as it would move someone from an average score to nearly the highest score. The one-point advantage in cognitive activity was also associated with substantially smaller declines in working memory ability and perceptual speed. These results are consistent with those presented in Chapter 9 showing that intellectual activities may help buffer individuals from age-associated cognitive declines. So, the lesson here is to stay active—especially intellectually active.[28]

One explanation of this association between cognitive activity and reduced risk of Alzheimer's disease is that cognitive activity leads to the development of richer neuronal connections. This interpretation is supported by research with adult animals showing that exposure to new complex environments leads to the development of new neurons and new connections among them. The beneficial effects of cognitive activity therefore may be to make these neural networks less susceptible to the advancing disease process associated with Alzheimer's disease. With richer neural connections, the idea is that it would take a longer amount of time for disease to damage the system.[29]

Although very promising in terms of identifying participation in activities as a protective factor against Alzheimer's disease, some of these studies need to be qualified with a word of caution. Which is the cause and which is the effect?

Estrogen and Estrogen Replacement Therapy

Estrogen is the female sex hormone, and there is some evidence that it plays a role in decreasing the risk for Alzheimer's disease. Excitement surrounding this as a drug treatment that can prevent or delay the onset of Alzheimer's first developed when researchers discovered that women who were taking estrogen after menopause were less likely to develop Alzheimer's disease. For example, Tang and colleagues found that women who were *not* taking estrogen replacement therapy were about three times more likely to develop Alzheimer's disease than women who were (8.4 percent versus 2.7 percent). The thinking is that estrogen helps develop growth in neurons that use acetylcholine (these neurons in the brain tend to be very heavily involved in memory processes) and that this somehow protects these neurons from damage. It has also been proposed that estrogen prevents the formation of amyloid plaques and may promote connections among neurons in the brain, a process that is thought to be important for learning and memory. Note, however, that a recent study showed that fifteen months of estrogen replacement therapy had no noticeable effect on the cognitive functioning of women with mild to moderate Alzheimer's disease. Despite this negative finding, a substantial amount of human and animal research has shown benefits of estrogen replacement therapy on cognitive functioning, and further research is needed to understand who can benefit from this therapy. For example, estrogen therapy may protect women who are cognitively healthy but not women who have developed dementia.[30] Some of the initial excitement about estrogen replacement therapy has diminished because of recent research showing that estrogen replacement therapy is associated with an increased risk of cancer (see Chapter 12).

Statins

A recent surprise is that popular cholesterol-lowering drugs known as statins (brand names such as Lipitor and Zocor) may prevent or delay Alzheimer's disease. Two studies published in 2000 compared the records of tens of thousands of people who had taken statins to treat heart disease with tens of thousands of people who had no history of taking statins. Those taking statins showed 30 to 40 percent fewer incidences of memory-deteriorating brain disease (dementia, including Alzheimer's). This suggestive finding has stimulated much additional research, including a large 3-year placebo-controlled experiment that is underway in Europe to study whether statins can prevent mental decline. This study is known as the Prospective Study of Pravastatin in the Elderly at Risk (PROSPER). There are currently several suggested mechanisms by which statins have their effects, including the reduction of amyloid plaques, the reduction of inflammation in the brain, and improved blood flow to the brain.[31]

What Should You Do?

There is cause for optimism in finding treatments that prevent or delay Alzheimer's, and those described above are good candidates. Given the low cost involved and the minimal side effects for some of the preventative factors (e.g., anti-oxidants and anti-inflammatory medications), you should consult your physician concerning the use of these treatments. Also, keep tabs on the latest developments in drug and other treatments by consulting the Alzheimer's Disease Forum Web site (*www.alzforum.org*) as well as the other sites listed at the end of this chapter.

Brain Reserve Capacity

The microscope analysis of her brain tissue . . . left little doubt that Alzheimer's disease had spread far and wide. Tangles had cluttered her hippocampus and her neocortex, all the way up to the frontal lobe. Her neocortex had an abundance of plaques as well. Markesbery ranked her as a Braak stage VI, indicating the most severe presence of Alzheimer's pathology.

"I suppose you're now going to tell me that she was mentally intact," he joked as he finished his report. By then, he had grown accustomed to the occasional disconnect between his pathology findings and Riley's cognitive records.

All eyes turned to Riley. "Yes," Riley said. "She was mentally intact. She had normal scores for each one of our mental and physical tests."

Riley then told us that Sister Bernadette, who had a master's degree, had taught elementary school for twenty-one years and high school for another seven. She had taken the nun study tests when she was eighty-one, eighty-three, and eighty-four years old. On each exam she scored high, showing no mental deterioration at all, not even a hint. In a particularly impressive video taped exchange done with each exam, Sister Bernadette—without looking at a clock or a watch—stated the time within four minutes of the actual time.

"Maybe this has something to do with it," one of the technicians offered. "Look at the initial MRI scan. It shows an unusual amount of gray matter." As it turned out, Sister Bernadette had more gray matter—formed by the cell bodies of neurons in the neocortex—than 90 percent of the other sisters we'd studied.

Sister Bernadette represented an extreme example: Despite an abundance of plaques and tangles in her neocortex, the function of that brain region seemed to be incredibly preserved. It was as if her neocortex was resistant to destruction for some reason. Sister Bernadette appears to have been what we, and others, have come to call an "escapee." Death had intervened before her symptoms had time to surface.[32]

How might we explain this finding that massive levels of plaques and tangles in the brain are not always accompanied by dementia? An interesting emerging perspective is that one's susceptibility to dementia in general and Alzheimer's disease in particular is influenced by one's *brain reserve capacity.* This is a phrase some use to explain how aging can produce dementia and why some people seem to be more vulnerable to it than others.[33] The basic idea is that a certain number of neurons are needed to carry on fairly normal cognitive functioning. When sufficient brain damage occurs such that the number of normally functioning brain cells falls below this threshold level, then signs of dementia will appear. Thus, those who start off with more neurons and greater connections among them can experience greater neuronal loss before developing dementia. Conversely, those who start off with fewer neurons and fewer connections among them are especially prone to dementia because it will take less cell loss to fall below that critical or threshold level needed to maintain normal cognitive functioning.

These points can be illustrated with the results of a study by Katzman and colleagues.[34] They performed autopsies on the brains of 137 people who had been living in a nursing home. When alive, these people had been assessed for their cognitive processes and on this basis were categorized as either high or low functioning. As expected, when the researchers counted amyloid plaques and neurofibrillary tangles in the brains of these two groups, they found substantial numbers of plaques and tangles in the low-functioning group. What was very surprising, however, was that they also found high levels of plaques and tangles in the brains of the high-functioning group. Indeed, neuronal damage in the high-functioning group was about 80 percent of what it was in the low-functioning group. An important additional finding was that the high-functioning group had larger brains and more neurons than the low-functioning group. These results suggest that the high group had good levels of cognitive functioning, not only because they suffered less neuronal damage but also because they started off with more brain reserve capacity—that is, larger brains containing more neurons.

This view is consistent with the results of neuroimaging studies of patients who are at genetic risk for Alzheimer's disease. These studies suggest that changes in the brain precede the symptoms of Alzheimer's disease by several years. So, there is quite a bit of brain loss before the critical threshold is reached and cognitive and behavioral symptoms emerge. This pattern is true of other degenerative diseases of the brain. For example, in Parkinson's disease, it is now thought that as many as 80 percent of the neurons in the substantia nigra die before the symptoms appear.[35]

According to this view, other factors like cell loss being equal, people who start off with less brain capacity are more susceptible to Alzheimer's disease. In case you are wondering about your own brain capacity, some researchers believe that the size of the brain you inherit, scores on intelligence tests, and educational levels are positively related to brain reserve capacity. Support for this thinking comes from the research described above as well as a large-scale study of 678 nuns conducted by Snowdon. Many years ago (1931 to 1943), when the nuns were young (around 22 or so), all of them were required to write an autobiography. In more recent years, when the nuns were much older and participating in the study, they were given a variety of cognitive tests. Interestingly, the researchers found that the grammatical complexity and the density of ideas in their autobiographies (as measured by the number of ideas produced per ten words) was highly related to the existence of symptoms of dementia fifty to sixty years later. Thus, early ability seems highly predictive of lower susceptibility to Alzheimer's disease. Examples of their writing, the first sentences from Sister Helen (who had the lowest score) and Sister Emma (who had the highest score), are presented below:[36]

Sister Helen (lowest score for idea density and grammatical complexity)
I was born in Eau Claire, Wis., on May 24, 1913 and was baptized in St. James Church.

Sister Emma (highest score for idea density and grammatical complexity)
It was about a half hour before midnight between February twenty-eighth and twenty-ninth of the leap year nineteen-hundred-twelve when I began to live and to die as the third child of my mother, whose maiden name is Hilda Hoffman, and my father, Otto Schmitt.

Another possibly important factor, however, is the mental activity that you engage in throughout your life. So, it may be that the more mentally active you are now and throughout your life, the more reserve capacity you create. This theory is somewhat speculative at this point, but it is consistent with very recent work showing that new connections and reinstated neuronal functioning can occur in older mammals that maintain a rich, stimulating environment. One recent study showed that mice exposed to three hours of enriched environmental experiences each day substantially improved their learning and memory capacity. These effects showed up not only on tests of learning and memory but also in microscopic examinations of their brains. Mice who had the exposure to the enriched environments had richer neuronal connections in the hippocampus (a brain area that is very important for learning and memory).[37]

Thus, the emerging pattern is that neuronal cell loss can cause Alzheimer's disease, with greater loss typically resulting in more severe dementia. However, different individuals may wind up with different levels of cognitive functioning even if they suffer equal degrees of cell loss. Those who have more brain reserve capacity seem to be less susceptible to the cognitively debilitating effects of aging and neuronal damage.

Treatment

As mentioned earlier in the chapter, there is at present no cure for Alzheimer's disease. The medications that do exist help control the symptoms for some people, and their effects are temporary. They do not reverse or even stop the advancement of the disease, but they have been shown to slow its progression.

This rather pessimistic state may change in a few years. Alzheimer's disease is receiving a great deal of funding these days, and as our research efforts rapidly expand so does our understanding. For example, Elan Corporation presented extremely promising results in 1999 suggesting that administration of a beta-amyloid vaccine generated antibodies that protected the mouse brain from the deposit of amyloid and even cleared existing amyloid plaques. Unfortunately, recent trials with humans have shown that the vaccine is toxic to the brain in some cases, and Elan has stopped these clinical trials. Nonetheless, new trials are being conducted with other vaccines, and it is possible that refinements of this general approach will lead to the development of a safe immunization procedure that not only prevents the disease but also reverses its effects once someone has it.[38]

Although many promising new research directions are emerging, today's Alzheimer's drugs only slow the pace of the disease and do not change its course. The Food and Drug Administration has approved four medications for treating memory disorders caused by Alzheimer's disease, with at least several others reportedly close to approval. These drugs are tacrine (Cognex®), donepezil (Aricept®), rivastigmine (Exelon®), and galantamine hydrobromide (Reminyl®). All of these help control the symptoms of the disease through their effects on neurons in the brain that produce acetylcholine. As described earlier, acetylcholine is a neurotransmitter found in several regions of the brain that are critically involved in forming memories, and researchers have found decreased levels of this neurotransmitter in the brains of patients with Alzheimer's disease.

To understand the function of these medications, it is necessary to briefly review how neurons work and communicate with one another. Neurotransmitters are chemical substances that allow one neuron to communicate with another. Transmission within a neuron is electrical in nature, and when that electrical signal reaches the end of the neuron, it leads to the release of a chemical substance (neurotransmitter) that travels across the gap (called a synapse) between the neurons. If this neurotransmitter is present in sufficient concentration at the synapse, it affects the next neuron (e.g., it could cause the next neuron to initiate an electrical signal). The neurotransmitter tends to have short-lived effects (unless the first neuron continues to fire) because enzymes in the synapse between the neurons destroy or deactivate the neurotransmitter. The enzyme that destroys the lingering acetylcholine is called cholinesterase.

The four approved drugs (tacrine, donepezil, rivastigmine, and galantamine hydrobromide) work by blocking cholinesterase, and this gives the small amounts of acetylcholine that are released in the synapses of Alzheimer's patients extra time to affect the next neuron—with the result being that the neuron is more likely to transmit a message to the next neuron. Although these drugs can be very helpful, they do have limitations. They tend to help only some people and only for a limited time (from a month to two years), and they tend to be effective only in patients with less severe to moderate symptoms.[39] Typically, a physician will give a patient one of these medications on a two- to six-month trial basis and, depending on the degree (if any) of improvement, decide to continue or discontinue treatment.

Tacrine, which was approved by the Food and Drug Administration in 1993, is not commonly used anymore, as it can produce liver and gastrointestinal problems. Donepezil (approved in 1996), rivastigmine (approved in 2000), and galantamine (approved in 2001 and derived from the bulbs of daffodils) produce less severe effects than tacrine and can provide modest improvements in cognitive functioning in Alzheimer's patients. Although tests of cognitive functioning and caregivers' assessments suggest that some patients show little or no noticeable improvements with these drugs, many show temporary stabilization of behavioral and cognitive symptoms and even improvements in memory and thinking. Indeed, long-term evaluations suggest that taking these drugs significantly slows down cognitive losses and behavioral disturbances such that they delay the placement of patients into nursing homes. In a recent study, Alzheimer's patients who were and were not treated with cholinesterase inhibitors were examined three years after an initial evaluation. Whereas only 6 percent of the those taking the cholinesterase inhibitors were admitted to nursing homes over that period, this figure was 40 percent in a matched group of untreated patients. When they are effective, these drugs can significantly improve the person's cognitive abilities, and even though the effects will be transient they can be very helpful and comforting.[40] The next several years may bring FDA approval for several new promising drugs, now in the experimental stage. Until then, there are limits to the extent to which current medications can control the cognitive symptoms and declines associated with Alzheimer's disease. It is important to keep in mind that Alzheimer's patients are likely to also need a variety of drug treatments to control other symptoms that often accompany this disease—like aggression, delusion, and depression—and that interactions among these drugs may create problems. Consult your physician for more details.

An Effective Memory Strategy

As should be clear by now, people with Alzheimer's disease have fundamental difficulties storing new information in memory. This can be enormously frustrating not only for the patients but also for caregivers, who often have to answer the same questions over and over again, constantly remind patients of what they are supposed to do, and so on. The frustration is often compounded because memory techniques like those described in Chapter 6 tend to be ineffective for those with Alzheimer's. There is a technique, however, that is effective in helping people with Alzheimer's disease remember things over long periods of time. This technique capitalizes on the basic finding that practice at retrieving information is often more effective in improving memory than is additional practice in studying information.[41]

This technique, developed by Camp and colleagues and called "spaced-retrieval training," has been shown to be effective in persons with Alzheimer's disease who have mild to moderate cognitive deficits.[42] The basic idea is to get patients to retrieve a thought over and over again after progressively longer delays. Let's say, for example, that you live with your husband, who has Alzheimer's disease, and you want him to remember to check a calendar in the morning in order to figure out his chores for the day. With spaced-retrieval training, you would initially tell him that he should "Check the calendar in the morning." Then, you would wait twenty seconds and then ask him "What are you supposed to do in the morning?" With such a short delay, he should be able to remember nearly all the information. Then, you gradually increase the length of the delay by twenty-second intervals, asking him each time to tell you what he is to do in the morning. If he ever forgets, you then decrease the interval by twenty seconds. So, assuming that he correctly remembers each time, you would ask the question after twenty seconds, then forty, then sixty, then eighty , and so on. If he forgets at the sixty-second delay, then the sequence of delays would be twenty seconds, forty seconds, sixty seconds, forty seconds, sixty seconds, eighty seconds, and so on.

Camp and colleagues used this exact procedure with people who had mild to moderate dementia. Over thirty- to forty-five-minute training sessions per day, they used spaced-retrieval training to teach participants to remember to look at their calendars in the morning. These researchers assumed good long-term memory for this idea if the participants could answer what it was that they were supposed to do when queried every day for two consecutive weeks. Sixty-one percent of the participants reached this criterion after two weeks of training, and another 26 percent reached it after three to six weeks of training (for a total of 87 percent!). Moreover, with some additional training (again using spaced retrieval), 75 percent of these participants could effectively use their memory to actually check the calendar and perform the chores.

As you can imagine this technique can be used in a variety of ways to help learning and memory. For example, you could use it to help someone with dementia learn or relearn someone's name. You could also use it to help someone remember where he or she is. As you can see in the real-life testimonial below, it has been used successfully by a caregiver to help his mother (who had Alzheimer's disease) remember where she was going.[43]

I drive my mother to the Alzheimer's center each weekday. Since we live on the north shore [of Lake Pontchartrain] and the center is on the south shore, this is a long drive [about 35 miles total, one way]. All the way to the center my mom would keep asking "Where are we going?" I'd tell her "We're going to the school" [that was the name the family used to refer to the center]. Then she'd ask again, and again, and again. It used to drive me crazy. Well, after your talk I decided to try the thing you were talking about. So, the next day when we got into the car I said "Mom, we're going to the school now." Then I waited a few seconds and asked her "Where are we going?" and she answered. "You said we were going to the school." Then I waited a couple of minutes and asked her "Where are we going?" She looked at me like I was a little crazy and said "We're going to school!" Then I waited a few more minutes and asked "Where are we going?" Mom seemed a little mad, but said "We're going to school, like you said." That was the last I brought up the subject, but you

know, she never asked me that question the whole trip. Now
I ask her when we get in the car, she answers, and that's that.
I just thought you'd like to know that it actually works.

Advice for Caretakers

If the Alzheimer's patient will be living at home, it will help to give
some attention to modifying the house so that it can be as safe and
supportive as possible. If not, decisions about the kind and level of
care will have to be addressed. The family is likely to have a lot of
questions. Rather than starting from scratch, it would be useful for
you to contact the local chapter of the Alzheimer's Association as
quickly as possible. You can locate your local chapter through the Internet or by calling the toll-free number listed in the Resources section below. The Alzheimer's Association chapters have a wealth of information, including information about educational programs that
can help you understand the issues at each stage of the disease, advice
for home safety (e.g., install grab bars in the bath), and support
groups and services. Some chapters even provide chat groups for discussing issues of concern. It would also be very helpful to read Mace
and Rabins's book *The 36-Hour Day* (listed in the Resources section
at the end of this chapter), which is a guide for understanding how to
live with and care for people at all stages of Alzheimer's disease.[44]

At some point in the progression of the disease, the patient will
need nearly constant supervision. Studies have shown that the demands of round-the-clock care by family members, many of whom
are older themselves, take their toll. The caretakers tend to be the hid-
den victims of Alzheimer's disease, and very often their burden results
in high levels of stress (in around 80 percent of cases) and psychological problems like depression (in as many as 50 percent of cases).[45]
For these reasons, it is highly recommended that caregivers seek regular breaks for themselves. These breaks will necessitate the temporary
institutionalization of the patient, day care, or home nursing help—
strategies that are all enormously important for the mental health of
the caregivers.

Eventually, changes in personality as well as disturbing and disruptive behaviors make it extremely difficult for caregivers to manage the patient independently. In addition to incontinence, wandering away from home during the day and night, and memory disturbances, it is not uncommon to see increasing levels of anxiety, depression, irritability, aggressiveness including physical violence, verbal abuse, and suspiciousness.[46] Your physician may be able to prescribe medications to help control some of these symptoms. When the disruptive behaviors get to the point that they cannot be tolerated or managed at home, caregivers should seriously consider institutionalizing the patient. The local chapter of your Alzheimer's Association should be helpful in making decisions of this sort.

The Future

Although realities facing Alzheimer's victims are grim, this chapter ends on a realistically optimistic note. With the increased prevalence of Alzheimer's and the realization of the costs of the disease (both financial and emotional), research has become a funding priority in this country and in others. Indeed, research is now being conducted at a feverish pace, and our understanding of the disease is progressing accordingly. The past two decades of research have produced a remarkable foundation of knowledge upon which cures are likely to be developed. Each year, we are getting better and firmer evidence concerning possible preventative factors like brain reserve capacity, antioxidants, statins, and anti-inflammatory medications. We are also developing a better understanding of the genetic and biochemical elements underlying Alzheimer's disease, and current research suggests that we are on the precipice of developing more reliable methods of diagnosing the disease at earlier stages. In one way or another this disease touches nearly all of our lives, and we are fortunate to live in a time when our hopes for understanding and controlling this disease are likely to be realized.

Resources

The good news about Alzheimer's disease is that its prevalence has led to the publication of a tremendous amount of information that is invaluable for patients, family members, and caregivers. These sources provide news and advice ranging from the latest research on the disease to very practical information about how to help the patient with dental care and how to get in touch with local support groups. Much of this information is available on the World Wide Web, which allows for rapid updating and thus the most current information. We encourage you to take advantage of these resources.

- Administration on Aging
  Web site: *www.aoa.dhhs.gov*
     This is a government agency Web site. Among other things, it has a resource directory and information on local care and services for older people. The phone number of the "Eldercare Locator" is (800) 677-1116.
- Alzheimer's Association
  Web site: *www.alz.org*
  Phone number: (800) 272-3900
  E-mail: *info@alz.org*
     This site provides a wealth of information about the disease, tips and resources for caring for patients, medical issues related to diagnosis and treatment, legal and financial issues, and current research in the field. It also enables you to find the local chapter of the Alzheimer's Association nearest you. The local chapters are very helpful in finding out about support services in your area.
- Alzheimer's Disease Education and Referral Center (a public service center of the National Institute on Aging)
  Web site: *www.alzheimers.org*
  Phone number: (800) 438-4380
  E-mail: *adear@alzheimers.org*
     This site contains up-to-date information about Alzheimer's disease. Through it, you can print a copy of the current annual "Progress Report on Alzheimer's Disease," which pre-

sents an overview of the disease and summarizes the latest (even ongoing) research.

■ Alzheimer's Research Forum
Web site: *www.alzforum.org/members/index.html*

This is a forum for researchers in the area of Alzheimer's disease and is therefore a great site for keeping up with the latest scientific findings. Its features include descriptions of promising new studies, summaries (abstracts) of recent articles on Alzheimer's disease, and interviews with major researchers in the field.

■ Doctor's Guide to Alzheimer's Disease Information and Resources
Web site: *www.pslgroup.com/alzheimer.htm*

This site contains recent news and medical information about Alzheimer's disease.

■ *Living in the Labyrinth: A Personal Journey through Alzheimer's Disease,* by Diana McGowin (New York: Delacorte Press, 1993)

Diana McGowin presents her poignant story of living with Alzheimer's disease. Diagnosed with the disease at the age of 52, she courageously takes the reader through the day-to-day horrors (as well as some joys) as she copes with a disease that progressively robs her of her cognitive abilities. This book gives the reader insight into her emotional state and sensitizes her audience to the trials of living with this disease. Through her experiences and advice for caregivers, she helps people understand how to treat (and not to treat) someone with Alzheimer's disease.

■ National Institute on Aging
Web site: *www.NIHSeniorHealth.gov*

This site was developed by the National Institute on Aging. The goal was to present useful and scientifically based health information concerning older adults. Moreover, the site is very friendly to older populations. For example, you can ask for a larger font size when reading the text, you can have the text read aloud by your computer, and the site uses video and illustrations to make its points. In addition to sections on "Alzheimer's Disease" and "Caring for Someone with Alzheimer's," the site covers the topics of "Hearing Loss," "Exercise for Older Adults," "Arthritis," "Lung Cancer," and others.

■ *The 36-Hour Day: A Family Guide to Caring for Persons with Alzheimer's Disease, Related Dementing Illnesses, and Memory Loss in Later Life,* by Nancy Mace and Peter Rabins (Baltimore: Johns Hopkins University Press, 2001)

Chapter titles include: Getting Medical Help for the Impaired Person; Characteristic Problems of Dementia; Problems in Independent Living; Problems Arising in Daily Care; Medical Problems; Problems of Mood; Getting Outside Help; How Caring for an Impaired Person Affects You; Caring for You, For Children and Teenagers; Financial and Legal Issues; and Nursing Homes and Other Arrangements. This book provides specific and useful information that will help you understand Alzheimer's disease, its progression, the day-to-day problems that arise, and how to care for someone who has it.

Notes

Chapter One. Thanks for the Memories

1. Alzheimer's Association, *www.alz.org* (May 2001).
2. J. M. Rybash, P. A. Roodin, and W. J. Hoyer, *Adult Development and Aging,* 3rd edition (Madison, Wisc.: Brown and Benchmark, 1995).
3. A. D. Smith and J. L. Earles, "Memory Changes in Normal Aging," in *Cognitive Changes in Adulthood and Aging,* ed. T. Hess and F. Blanchard-Fields (New York: McGraw-Hill, 1996), 192–220; T. A. Salthouse, *Adult Cognition: An Experimental Psychology of Human Aging* (New York: Springer-Verlag, 1982).
4. R. S. Wilson et al., "Individual Differences in Rates of Change in Cognitive Abilities of Older Persons, *Psychology and Aging* 17 (2002): 179–193.
5. D. S. Woodruff-Pak, *The Neuropsychology of Aging* (Malden, Mass.: Blackwell, 1997); I. Wilkelgren, "For the Cortex, Neuron Loss May Be Less Than Thought," *Science* 273 (1996): 48–50; N. Raz, "Aging of the Brain and Its Impact on Cognitive Performance: Integration of Structural and Functional Findings," in *The Handbook of Aging and Cognition,* ed. F. I. M. Craik and T. A. Salthouse (Hillsdale, N.J.: Erlbaum, 2000), 1–90.
6. Woodruff-Pak, *The Neuropsychology of Aging;* D. J. Selkoe, "Aging Brain, Aging Mind," *Scientific American* 267 (1997): 134–143; Raz, "Aging of the Brain."
7. Rybash, Roodin, and Hoyer, *Adult Development and Aging;* Woodruff-Pak, *The Neuropsychology of Aging;* Raz, "Aging of the Brain"; R. L. West, "An Application of Prefrontal Cortex Function Theory to Cognitive Aging," *Psychological Bulletin* 120 (1996): 272–292.
8. Raz, "Aging of the Brain"; A. Smith and O. Sugar, "Development of Above Normal

Language and Intelligence 21 Years After Left Hemispherectomy," *Neurology* 25 (1975): 813–818; E. Gould, A. J. Reeves, M. S. Graziano, and C. G. Gross, "Neurogenesis in the Neocortex of Adult Primates," *Science* 286 (1999): 548–552.

9. B. Levy and E. Langer, "Aging Free from Negative Stereotypes: Successful Memory in China and among the American Deaf," *Journal of Personality and Social Psychology* 66 (1994): 989–997.

10. Ibid.

11. C. Yoon, L. Hasher, F. Feinberg, T. A. Rahal, and G. Winocur, "Cross-Cultural Differences in Memory: The Role of Culture-Based Stereotypes about Aging," *Psychology and Aging* 15 (2000): 694–704; T. A. Rahal, L. Hasher, and S. J. Colcombe, "Instructional Manipulations and Age Differences in Memory: Now You See Them, Now You Don't," *Psychology and Aging* 16 (2001): 697–706.

Chapter Two. Overview of Memory Systems and Processes

1. R. C. Atkinson and R. M. Shiffrin, "Human Memory: A Proposed System and Its Control Processes," in *The Psychology of Learning and Motivation: Advances in Research and Theory,* ed. W. K. Spence and J. T. Spence (Vol. 2) (New York: Academic Press, 1968), 89–195.

2. G. C. Gilmore, T. M. Allan, and F. L. Royer, "Iconic Memory and Aging," *Journal of Gerontology* 41 (1986): 183–190; D. H. Kausler, *Learning and Memory in Normal Aging* (San Diego: Academic Press, 1994).

3. Gilmore, Allan, and Royer, "Iconic Memory and Aging"; Kausler, *Learning and Memory in Normal Aging;* D. H. Kausler and D. M. Kleim, "Age Differences in Processing Relevant versus Irrelevant Stimuli in Multiple Item Recognition Learning," *Journal of Gerontology* 33 (1978): 87–93.

4. L. Hasher and R. T. Zacks, "Working Memory, Comprehension, and Aging: A Review and a New View," in *The Psychology of Learning and Motivation,* ed. G. Bower (New York: Academic Press, 1994), 193–225; R. T. Zacks, and L. Hasher, "Directed Ignoring: Inhibitory Regulation of Working Memory," in *Inhibitory Processes in Attention, Memory, and Language,* ed. D. Dagenbach and T. H. Carr (San Diego: Academic Press, 1994), 241–264.

5. G. O. Einstein and M. A. McDaniel, "Aging and Mind Wandering: Reduced Inhibition in Older Adults," *Experimental Aging Research* 23 (1997): 343–354; L. M. Giambra, "Task Unrelated-Thought Frequency as a Function of Age: A Laboratory Study," *Psychology and Aging* 4 (1989): 136–143.

6. T. A. Salthouse and R. L. Babcock, "Decomposing Adult Age Differences in Working Memory," *Developmental Psychology* 27 (1991): 763–776; D. C. Park, G. Lautenschlager, T. Hedden, N. S. Davidson, A. D. Smith, and P. K. Smith, "Models of Visuospatial and Verbal Memory Across the Adult Life Span," *Psychology and Aging* 17 (2002): 299–320.

7. R. W. Engle, S. W. Tuholski, J. E. Laughlin, and A. R. A. Conway, "Working Mem-

ory, Short-Term Memory and General Fluid Intelligence: A Latent Variable Approach," *Journal of Experimental Psychology: General* 288 (1999): 309–331.

8. T. A. Salthouse, *Theoretical Perspectives on Cognitive Aging* (Hillsdale, N.J.: Erlbaum, 1991); T. A. Salthouse and R. L. Babcock, "Decomposing Adult Age Differences in Working Memory," *Developmental Psychology,* 27 (1991): 763–776; D. C. Park et al., "Models of Visuospatial and Verbal Memory Across the Adult Life Span," *Psychology and Aging* 17 (2002): 299–320.

9. A. E. Schonfield and B. A. Robertson, "Memory Storage and Aging," *Canadian Journal of Psychology* 20 (1966): 228–236; F. I. M. Craik, "A Functional Account of Age Differences in Memory," in *Human Memory and Cognitive Capabilities: Mechanisms and Performances,* ed. F. Klix and H. Hangendorf (Amsterdam: Elsevier, 1986), 409–422.

10. Ibid.

Chapter Three. Forgetting and Distorting Are Normal

1. D. G. Payne, and J. M. Blackwell, "Truth in Memory: Caveat Emptor," in *Truth in Memory,* ed. S. J. Lynn, and K. M. McConkey (New York: Guilford, 1998), 32–61.

2. Ibid.

3. S. J. Lynn and D. G. Payne, "Memory as the Theater of the Past: The Psychology of False Memories," *Current Directions in Psychological Science* 6 (1997): 55.

4. T. A. Salthouse, *Adult Cognition: An Experimental Psychology of Human Aging* (New York: Springer-Verlag, 1982).

5. R. S. Nickerson and M. J. Adams, "Long-Term Memory for a Common Object," *Cognitive Psychology,* 11 (1979): 287–307.

6. D. J. Simons and D. T. Levin, "Failure to Detect Changes to People During a Real-World Interaction," *Psychonomic Bulletin & Review* 5 (1998): 644–649.

7. P. A. Tun, A. Wingfield, M. J. Rosen, and L. Blanchard, "Response Latencies for False Memories: Gist-Based Processes in Normal Aging," *Psychology and Aging* 13 (1998): 230–241.

8. H. L. Roediger and K. B. McDermott, "Creating False Memories: Remembering Words Not Presented in Lists," *Journal of Experimental Psychology: Learning, Memory, and Cognition* 21 (1995): 803–814.

9. P. Baggett, "Memory for Explicit and Implicit Information in Picture Stories," *Journal of Verbal Learning and Verbal Behavior* 14 (1975): 538–548.

10. W. Brewer and J. C. Treyens, "Role of Schemata in Memory for Places," *Cognitive Psychology* 13 (1981): 207–230.

11. A. Wingfield, "Speech Perception and the Comprehension of Spoken Language in Adult Aging," in *Cognitive Aging: A Primer,* ed. D. Park and N. Schwarz (Philadelphia: Taylor & Francis, 2000).

12. D. M. Burke and L. L. Light, "Memory and Aging: The Role of Retrieval Processes," *Psychological Bulletin* 90 (1981): 513–546.

13. J. S. McIntyre and F. I. M. Craik, "Age Differences in Memory for Item and Source Information," *Canadian Journal of Psychology* 41 (1987): 175–192; J. M. Jennings and L. L. Jacoby, "An Opposition Procedure for Detecting Age-Related Deficits in Recollection: Telling Effects of Repetition," *Psychology and Aging* 12 (1997): 352–361; Wingfield, "Speech Perception"; Burke and Light, "Memory and Aging."

14. M. Naveh-Benjamin and F. I. M. Craik, "Memory for Context and Its Use in Item Memory: Comparison of Younger and Older Persons," *Psychology and Aging* 10 (1995): 284–293.

15. R. F. Belli, "Influences of Misleading Post-Event Information: Misinformation, Interference, and Acceptance," *Journal of Experimental Psychology: General* 118 (1989): 72–85.

16. M. S. Zaragoza and K. J. Mitchell, "Repeated Exposure to Suggestion and the Creation of False Memories," *Psychological Science* 7 (1996): 294–300; National Institute of Justice, "Eyewitness Evidence: A Guide for Law Enforcement," U.S. Department of Justice, Office of Justice Programs. *http://www.ojp.usdoj.gov/nij* (1999).

17. Tun et al., "Response Latencies for False Memories"; Simons and Levin, "Failure to Detect Changes to People During a Real-World Interaction"; M. K. Johnson, S. Hashtroudi, and D. S. Lindsay, "Source Monitoring," *Psychological Bulletin* 114 (1993): 3–28; D. A. Balota et al., "Veridical and False Memories in Healthy Older Adults and in Dementia of the Alzheimer's Type," *Cognitive Neuropsychology* 16 (1999): 361–384.

18. E. Loftus and K. Ketcham, *The Myth of Repressed Memories: False Memories and Allegations of Childhood Sexual Abuse* (New York: St. Martin's Press, 1994).

19. Ibid.

20. Ibid.

21. Loftus and Ketcham, *The Myth of Repressed Memories;* S. J. Ceci, "Cognitive and Social Factors in Children's Testimony," Master Lecture at the American Psychological Association Convention (1993); S. J. Ceci and N. Bruck, *Jeopardy in the Courtroom: A Scientific Analysis of Children's Testimony* (Washington, D.C.: American Psychological Association, 1995); B. L. Cuttler and S. D. Penrod, "Forensically Relevant Moderators of the Relation between Eye-Witness Identification Accuracy and Confidence," *Journal of Applied Psychology* 74 (1989): 650–652; G. Wells and G. N. Murray, "Eye-Witness Confidence," in *Eye-Witness Testimony: Psychological Perspectives,* ed. G. L. Wells and E. F. Loftus (New York: Cambridge University Press, 1984).

22. U. Neisser and N. Harsch, "Phantom Flashbulbs: False Recollections of Hearing the News about 'Challenger'," in *Affect and Accuracy in Recall: Studies of "Flashbulb" Memories,* ed. E. Winograd and U. Neisser (New York: Cambridge University Press, 1992).

23. H. Schmolck, E. A. Buffalo, and L. R. Squire, "Memory Distortions Develop Over Time: Recollections of the O. J. Simpson Trial Verdict after 15 and 32 Months," *Psychological Science* 11 (2000): 39–45; Neisser and Harsch, "Phantom Flashbulbs."

24. D. L. Schachter, *The Seven Sins of Memory* (Boston: Houghton Mifflin, 2001).

Chapter Four. Working Memory and Avoiding Distractions

1. M. L. Turner and R. W. Engle, "Is Working Memory Task Dependent?" *Journal of Memory and Language* 28 (1989): 127–154.

2. R. W. Engle, S. W. Tuholski, J. E. Laughlin, and A. R. A. Conway, "Working Memory, Short-Term Memory and General Fluid Intelligence: A Latent Variable Approach," *Journal of Experimental Psychology: General* 288 (1999): 309–331; V. J. Shute, "Who Is Likely to Acquire Programming Skills?" *Journal of Educational Computing Research* 7 (1991): 1–24.

3. T. A. Salthouse, D. R. Mitchell, E. Skovronek, and R. L. Babcock, "Effects of Adult Age and Working Memory on Reasoning and Spatial Abilities," *Journal of Experimental Psychology: Learning, Memory, and Cognition* 15 (1989): 507–516.

4. N. Schwarz and B. Knauper, "Cognition, Aging, and Self-Reports," in *Cognitive Aging: A Primer*, ed. D. Park and N. Schwarz (Philadelphia: Psychology Press, 2000): 233–252.

5. M. Kleigel, M. Martin, and M. A. McDaniel, *Age and Individual Differences in Planning: Older Adults Are Not Necessarily Worse*, poster presented at the Cognitive Aging Conference, Atlanta, Georgia (April 2000).

6. L. Hasher and R. T. Zacks, "Working Memory, Comprehension, and Aging: A Review and a New View," in *The Psychology of Learning and Motivation*, ed. G. Bower (New York: Academic Press, 1988), 193–225; R. T. Zacks and L. Hasher, "Directed Ignoring: Inhibitory Regulation of Working Memory," in *Inhibitory Processes in Attention, Memory, and Language*, ed. D. Dagenbach and T. H. Carr (San Diego: Academic Press, 1994), 241–264.

7. Schwarz and Knauper, "Cognition, Aging, and Self-Reports"; Kleigel, Martin, and McDaniel, *Age and Individual Differences in Planning;* Hasher and Zacks, "Working Memory, Comprehension, and Aging"; Zacks and Hasher, "Directed Ignoring"; L. Hasher, E. R. Stoltzfus, R. T. Zacks, and B. Rypma, "Age and Inhibition," *Journal of Experimental Psychology: Learning, Memory, and Cognition* 17 (1991): 163–169.

8. S. L. Connelly, L. Hasher, and R. T. Zacks, "Aging and Reading: The Impact of Distraction," *Psychology and Aging* 6 (1991): 533–541.

9. C. P. May, "Synchrony Effects in Cognition: The Costs and a Benefit," *Psychonomic Bulletin and Review* 6 (1999): 142–147; S. A. Mednick, "The Associative Basis of the Creative Process," *Psychological Review*, 69 (1962): 220–232.

10. G. O. Einstein, J. L. Earles, and H. M. Collins, "Gaze Aversion: Spared Inhibition for Visual Distraction in Older Adults," *Journal of Gerontology: Psychological Sciences* 57B (2002): 1–9.

11. K. Z. H. Li, U. Lindenberger, A. M. Freund, and P. B. Baltes, "Walking While Memorizing: Age-Related Differences in Compensatory Behavior," *Psychological Science* 12 (2001): 230–237.

12. J. Horne and O. Ostberg, "Individual Differences in Human Circadian Rhythms," *Biological Psychology* 5 (1977): 179–190.

13. C. P. May and L. Hasher, "Synchrony Effects," *Journal of Experimental Psychology: Human Perception and Performance* 24 (1998): 363–379; C. Yoon, C. P. May, and L. Hasher, "Aging, Circadian Arousal Patterns, and Cognition," in *Cognitive Aging: A Primer,* ed. D. Park and N. Schwarz (Philadelphia: Psychology Press, 2000), 233–252; Horne and Ostberg, "Individual Differences in Human Circadian Rhythms."

14. C. P. May, L. Hasher, and E. R. Stoltzfus, "Optimal Time of Day and the Magnitude of Age Differences in Memory," *Psychological Science* 4 (1993): 326–330.

15. May, "Synchrony Effects in Cognition"; Yoon, May, and Hasher, "Aging, Circadian Arousal Patterns, and Cognition."

16. May and Hasher, "Synchrony Effects."

17. R. M. Reitan, "The Validity of the Trail Making Test as an Indicator of Organic Brain Damage," *Perceptual and Motor Skills* 8 (1958): 271–276; May and Hasher, "Synchrony Effects."

18. L. Ryan, C. Hatfield, and M. Hofstetter, "Caffeine Reduces Time-of-Day Effects on Memory Performance in Older Adults," *Psychological Science* 13 (2002): 68–71.

Chapter Five. Most Memories Are There

1. H. P. Bahrick, P. C. Bahrick, and R. P. Wittlinger, "Fifty Years of Memories for Names and Faces: A Cross-Sectional Approach," *Journal of Experimental Psychology: General* 104 (1975): 54–75.

2. F. I. M. Craik, "A Functional Account of Age Differences in Memory," in *Human Memory and Cognitive Capabilities: Mechanisms and Performances,* ed. F. Klix and H. Hagendorf (Amsterdam: Elsevier, 1986), 409–422.

3. R. A. Bjork, "When Forgetting Enables Learning: Implications for Theory and Practice," paper presented at the Western Psychological Association Rocky Mountain Psychological Association Joint Convention, Albuquerque, New Mexico (April 1998).

4. T. Mäntyä, "Optimizing Cue Effectiveness: Recall of 500 and 600 Incidentally Learned Words," *Journal of Experimental Psychology: Learning, Memory, and Cognition* 12 (1986): 66–71.

5. F. I. M. Craik and J. McDowd, "Age Differences in Recall and Recognition," *Journal of Experimental Psychology: Learning, Memory, and Cognition* 13 (1987): 474–479.

6. E. Tulving and D. M. Thomson, "Encoding Specificity and Retrieval Processes in Episodic Memory," *Psychological Review,* 80 (1973): 352–373.

7. S. M. Smith, "Remembering In and Out of Context," *Journal of Experimental Psychology: Human Learning and Memory* 5 (1979): 460–471.

8. S. M. Smith, "Background Music and Context-Dependent Memory," *American Journal of Psychology* 5 (1985): 460–471; F. R. Schab, "Odors and the Remembrance of Things Past," *Journal of Experimental Psychology: Learning, Memory, and Cognition* 16 (1990): 648–655.

9. A. Searleman and D. Hermann, *Memory from a Broader Perspective* (New York: McGraw-Hill, 1994), 184–187.

10. K. E. Cherry, D. C. Park, D. A. Frieske, and R. L. Rowley, "The Effect of Verbal Elaborations on Memory in Younger and Older Adults," *Memory & Cognition* 21 (1993): 725–738.

11. R. Fisher, R. E. Geiselman, and M. Amador, "Field Test of the Cognitive Interview: Enhancing the Recollection of Actual Victims and Witnesses of Crime," *Journal of Applied Psychology* 74 (1989): 722–727; R. Fisher et al., "Enhancing Enhanced Eye-Witness Memory: Refining the Cognitive Interview," *Journal of Police Science and Administration* 15 (1987): 177–185. C. Dornburg and M. A. McDaniel, "The Cognitive Interview Enhances Long-term Free Recall of Older Adults: Associations with Frontal Functioning," manuscript submitted for publication.

12. M. A. McDaniel, B. Moore, and H. Whiteman, "Dynamic Changes in Hyperamnesia across Early and Late Tests: A Relational/Item-Specific Account," *Journal of Experimental Psychology: Learning, Memory, and Cognition* 24 (1998): 173–185.

Chapter Six. How to Learn and Remember Complex Material

1. F. I. M. Craik and M. J. Watkins, "The Role of Rehearsal in Short-Term Memory," *Journal of Verbal Learning and Verbal Behavior* 12 (1973): 598–607; D. Rundus, "Maintenance Rehearsal and Single-Level Processing," *Journal of Verbal Learning and Verbal Behavior* 16 (1977): 665–681.

2. A. P. Shimamura et al., "Memory and Cognitive Abilities in University Professors: Evidence for Successful Aging," *Psychological Science* 6 (1995): 271–277.

3. R. Kliegl, J. Smith, and P. B. Baltes, "Testing-the-Limits and the Study of Adult Age Differences in Cognitive Plasticity of a Mnemonic Skill," *Developmental Psychology* 25 (1989): 247–256.

4. J. D. Bransford and M. K. Johnson, "Contextual Prerequisites for Understanding: Some Investigations of Comprehension and Recall," *Journal of Verbal Learning and Verbal Behavior* 11 (1972): 717–726.

5. M. Pressley et al., "Elaborative Interrogation Facilitates Acquisition of Confusing Facts," *Journal of Educational Psychology* 80 (1988): 457–464.

6. M. A. McDaniel and M. E. Masson, "Long-Term Retention: When Incidental Semantic Processing Fails," *Journal of Experimental Psychology: Human Learning and Memory* 3 (1977): 270–281; G. O. Einstein et al., "Encoding and Recall of Texts: The Importance of Material Appropriate Processing," *Journal of Memory and Language* 29 (1990): 566–581; R. D. Hill, M. Storandt, and D. Simeone, "The Effects of Memory Skills Training and Incentives on Free Recall in Older Learners," *The Journals of Gerontology: Psychological Sciences* 45 (1990): 227–332.

7. M. A. McDaniel, G. O. Einstein, and T. Lollis, "Qualitative and Quantitative Considerations in Encoding Difficulty Effects," *Memory & Cognition* 16 (1988): 8–14.

8. K. A. Wollen, A. Weber, and D. H. Lowry, "Bizarreness versus Interaction of Mental Images as Determinants of Learning," *Cognitive Psychology* 2 (1972): 518–523; M. A. McDaniel et al., "The Bizarreness Effect: It's Not Surprising, It's Complex," *Journal of Experimental Psychology: Learning, Memory, and Cognition* 21 (1995): 422–435.

9. Pressley et al., "Elaborative Interrogation."

10. S. E. Wade et al., "Seduction of the Strategic Reader: Effects of Interest on Strategies and Recall," *Reading Research Quarterly* 28 (1993): 93–114.

11. Kliegl, Smith, and Baltes, "Testing-the-Limits."

12. F. I. M. Craik, "A Functional Account of Age Differences in Memory," in *Human Memory and Cognitive Capabilities: Mechanisms and Performances,* ed. F. Klix and H. Hagendorf (Amsterdam: Elsevier, 1986), 409–422.

13. M. A. McDaniel and M. E. J. Masson, "Altering Memory Representations Through Retrieval," *Journal of Experimental Psychology: Learning, Memory, and Cognition* 11 (1985): 370–384.

14. C. J. Camp et al., "Improving Prospective Memory Task Performance in Persons with Alzheimer's Disease," in *Prospective Memory: Theory and Applications,* ed. M. Brandimonte, G. O. Einstein, and M. A. McDaniel (Mahwah, N.J.: Erlbaum, 1996), 351–367.

15. W. H. Shafley, S. R. Otaka, and J. L. Bavaresco, "Context Effects: Classroom Tests and Context Independence," *Memory and Cognition* 5 (1985): 460–471.

16. S. M. Smith, "Remembering In and Out of Context," *Journal of Experimental Psychology: Human Learning and Memory* 5 (1979): 460–471.

17. A. Searleman and D. Hermann, *Memory from a Broader Perspective* (New York: McGraw-Hill, 1994); W. R. Balch, D. M. Myers, and C. Papotto, "Dimensions of Mood in Mood-Dependent Memory," *Journal of Experimental Psychology: Learning, Memory, and Cognition* 25 (1999): 70–83.

18. M. Csikszentmihalyi, *Finding Flow* (New York: Harper Collins, 1997).

Chapter Seven. Remembering Tough Things

1. R. Berg, M. Franzen, and D. Wedding, *Screening for Brain Impairment: A Manual for Mental Health Practice* (New York: Springer, 1987).

2. M. A. McDaniel and M. E. J. Masson, "Altering Memory Representation Through Retrieval," *Journal of Experimental Psychology: Learning, Memory, and Cognition* 11 (1985): 371–385.

3. T. Kjos, "You Can Learn Strategies to Boost Recall," *Tucson Globe* (March 19, 2001), A7.

4. D. L. McCarty, "Investigation of a Visual Imagery Mnemonic Device for Acquiring Name-Face Association," *Journal of Experimental Psychology: Human Learning and Memory* 6 (1980): 145–155.

5. J. Fogler and L. Stern, *Improving Your Memory* (Baltimore, Md.: Johns Hopkins University Press, 1994), 86.

6. A. Searleman and D. Hermann, *Memory from a Broader Perspective* (New York: McGraw-Hill, 1994).

7. M. A. McDaniel et al., "The Bizarreness Effect: It's Not Surprising, It's Complex," *Journal of Experimental Psychology: Learning, Memory, and Cognition* 21 (1995): 422–435; M. Pressley, J. Levin, and H. D. Delaney, "The Mnemonic Keyword Method," *Review of Educational Research* 52 (1982): 61–91.

8. K. A. Wollen, A. Weber, and D. H. Lowry, "Bizarreness versus Interaction of Mental Images as Determinants of Learning," *Cognitive Psychology* 3 (1972): 518–523.

9. M. R. Raugh and R. C. Atkinson, "A Mnemonic Method for Learning a Second-Language Vocabulary," *Journal of Educational Psychology* 67 (1975): 1–16; M. A. McDaniel and M. Pressley, "Putting the Keyword Method in Context," *Journal of Educational Psychology* 76 (1984): 598–609.

10. D. Rundus, "Maintenance Rehearsal and Single-Level Processing," *Journal of Verbal Learning and Verbal Behavior* 16 (1977): 665–681.

11. K. A. Ericsson, W. C. Chase, and S. F. Faloon, "Acquisition of a Memory Skill," *Science* 208 (1980): 1181–1182; K. A. Ericsson and I. A. Faivre, "What's Exceptional about Exceptional Abilities?" in *The Exceptional Brain: Neuropsychology of Talent and Special Abilities,* ed. L. K. Obler and D. Fein (New York: Guilford Press, 1988), 436–473.

12. J. Fogler and L. Stern, *Improving Your Memory* (Baltimore, Md.: Johns Hopkins University Press, 1994), 69.

13. M. K. Gardner, D. L. Stayer, D. J. Woltz, and R. D. Hill, "Cognitive Skill Acquisition, Maintenance, and Transfer in the Elderly," in *Cognitive Rehabilitation in Old Age,* ed. R. D. Hill, L. Backman, and A. S. Neely (New York: Oxford University Press, 2000), 42–60.

14. Ibid.

Chapter Eight. Remembering to Remember

1. M. A. McDaniel and G. O. Einstein, "Prospective Memory, Psychology of," in *Encyclopedia of the Social and Behavioral Sciences* (Amsterdam: Elsevier, 2001).

2. M. Kleigel, M. A. McDaniel, and G. O. Einstein, "Plan Formation, Retention, and Execution in Prospective Memory: A New Approach and Age-Related Effects," *Memory & Cognition* 28 (2000): 1041–1049; E. A. Maylor, "Age-Related Impairment in an Event-Based Prospective Memory Task," *Psychology and Aging* 11 (1996): 74–78; D. C. Park, C. Hertzog, D. P. Kidder, R. W. Morell, and C. B. Mayhorn, "Effect of Age on Event-Based and Time-based Prospective Memory," *Psychology and Aging* 12 (1997): 314–327.

3. E. Winograd, "Some Observations on Prospective Remembering," in *Practical As-*

pects of Memory (Vol. 1), ed. M. M. Gruneberg, P. M. Morris, and R. N. Sykes (Chichester, England: Wiley, 1988), 348–353; G. O. Einstein, M. A. McDaniel, M. Manzi, B. Cochran, and M. Baker, "Prospective Memory and Aging: Forgetting Intentions Over Short Delays," *Psychology and Aging,* 15 (2000): 617–683; M. A. McDaniel, G. O. Einstein, A. C. Stout, and Z. Morgan, "Aging and Maintaining Intentions Over Delays: Do It or Lose It," *Psychology and Aging,* 18 (2003): 823–835.

4. D. L. Schachter, *The Seven Sins of Memory: How the Mind Forgets and Remembers* (Boston: Houghton Mifflin, 2001).

5. I. Yaniv and D. E. Meyer, "Activation and Metacognition of Inaccessible Stored Information: Potential Bases for Incubation Effects in Problem Solving," *Journal of Experimental Psychology: Learning, Memory, and Cognition* 13 (1987): 187–205; D. Mathews, J. Poole, J. Wallace, E. Hall, and G. O. Einstein, "Remembering to Remember," paper presented at the Southeastern Psychological Association, New Orleans, Louisiana (March 1988).

6. P. M. Gollwitzer, "Implementation Intentions: Strong Effects of Simple Plans," *American Psychologist* 54 (1991): 493–503; S. Orbell, S. Hodgkins, and P. Sheeran, "Implementation Intentions and the Theory of Planned Behavior," *Personality and Social Psychology Bulletin* 23 (1997): 945–954.

7. Einstein, McDaniel, Manzi, Cochran, and Baker, "Prospective Memory and Aging: Forgetting Intentions Over Short Delays."

8. Ibid.

9. McDaniel et al., "Aging and Maintaining Intentions Over Delays: Do It or Lose It."

10. G. O. Einstein, M. A. McDaniel, R. E. Smith, and P. Shaw, "Habitual Prospective Memory and Aging: Remembering Intentions and Forgetting Actions," *Psychological Science* 9 (1998): 284–288; D. C. Park and D. P. Kidder, "Prospective Memory and Medication Adherence," in *Prospective Memory: Theory and Applications,* ed. M. Brandimonte, G. O. Einstein, and M. A. McDaniel (Mahwah, N.J.: Erlbaum, 1996), 369–390.

11. G. M. Ramuschkat, M. A. McDaniel, M. Kliegel, and G. O. Einstein, "Habitual Prospective Memory and Aging: Benefits of a Complex Motor Action," submitted for publication.

Chapter Nine. Mental Exercise and Memory

1. "To Be Old, Gifted, and Employed Is No Longer Rare," *New York Times.com* (January 14, 2001).

2. M. Hendricks, "I Forget," *Johns Hopkins Magazine* (September 1993): 29–34.

3. A. P. Shimamura et al., "Memory and Cognitive Abilities in University Professors," *Psychological Science* 6 (1995): 271–277.

4. Shimamura et al., "Memory and Cognitive Abilities"; H. Christensen and H. Henderson, "Is Age Kinder to the Initially More Able? A Study of Eminent Scientists and

Academics," *Psychological Medicine* 21 (1991): 935–946; D. Z. Hambrick, T. A. Salthouse, and E. J. Meinz, "Predictors of Crossword Puzzle Proficiency and Moderators of Age-Cognition Relations," *Journal of Experimental Psychology: General* 128 (1999): 131–164.

5. C. Schooler, M. S. Mulatu, and G. Oates, "The Continuing Effects of Substantively Complex Work on the Intellectual Functioning of Elder Workers," *Psychology and Aging* 14 (1999): 483–506; C. Schooler and M. S. Mulatu, "The Reciprocal Effects of Leisure Time Activities and Intellectual Functioning in Older People: A Longitudinal Analysis," *Psychology and Aging* 16 (2001): 466–482.

6. Schooler and Mulatu, "The Reciprocal Effects of Leisure Time."

7. D. F. Hultsch et al., "Use It or Lose It: Engaged Lifestyle as a Buffer of Cognitive Decline in Aging?" *Psychology and Aging* 14 (1999): 245–263.

8. Schooler and Mulatu, "The Reciprocal Effects of Leisure Time"; T. Y. Arbuckle, "The Role of Psychosocial Context, Age, and Intelligence in Memory Performance of Older Men," *Psychology and Aging* 7 (1992): 25–36; R. S. Wilson and D. A. Bennett, "Cognitive Activity and Risk of Alzheimer's Disease," *Current Directions in Psychological Science* 12 (2003): 87–90.

9. T. Salthouse, D. E. Berish, and J. D. Miles, "The Role of Cognitive Stimulation on the Relations Between Age and Cognitive Functioning," *Psychology and Aging* 17 (2002): 548–557.

10. Hultsch et al., "Use It or Lose It."

11. Christensen and Henderson, "Is Age Kinder to the Initially More Able?"; Salthouse et al., "The Role of Cognitive Stimulation."

12. R. Goldman, R. Klatz, and L. Berger, *Brain Fitness* (New York: Doubleday, 1999).

13. Hambrick et al., "Predictors of Crossword Puzzle Proficiency."

14. Schooler and Mulatu, "The Reciprocal Effects of Leisure Time"; T. A. Salthouse, *Theoretical Perspectives on Cognitive Aging* (Hillsdale, N.J.: Erlbaum, 1991).

Chapter Ten. Physical Exercise and Memory

1. National Institute on Aging, "Exercise: A Guide from the National Institute on Aging," *www.nih.gov/nia/health/agepages/exercise.htm* (2000); International Longevity Center, "Maintaining Healthy Lifestyles: A Lifetime of Choices" (International Longevity Center, 2000); Centers for Disease Control and Prevention, *U.S. Surgeon General's Report of Physical Activity and Health* (U.S. Department of Health and Human Services, 1996); American College of Sports Medicine, "ACSM Position Stand on Exercise and Physical Activity for Older Adults," *Medicine & Science in Sports & Exercise* 30 (1998): 992–1008.

2. A. F. Ferrini and R. L. Ferrini, *Health in the Later Years* (2nd edition) (Madison, Wisc.: Brown and Benchmark, 1993).

3. W. J. Hoyer, J. M. Rybash, and P. A. Roodin, *Adult Development and Aging* (4th edition) (Boston: McGraw-Hill, 1999).

4. J. M. Rybash, P. A. Roodin, and W. J. Hoyer, *Adult Development and Aging* (3rd edition) (Madison, Wisc.: Brown and Benchmark, 1995); Hoyer, Rybash, and Roodin, *Adult Development and Aging.*

5. Hoyer, Rybash, and Roodin, *Adult Development and Aging.*

6. National Institute on Aging, "Exercise: A Guide"; American College of Sports Medicine, "ACSM Position."

7. R. Dustman, R. Emmerson, and D. Shearer, "Physical Activity, Age, and Cognitive-Neuropsychological Function," *Journal of Aging and Physical Activity* 2 (1994): 143–181; F. Powell, "Physical Activity and Aging: What Can Happen to Your Body If You Remain Physically Active," in *Social Gerontology,* ed. D. Redburn and R. McNamara (Westport, Conn.: Auburn House, 1998); S. Powers and S. Dodd, *Total Fitness: Exercise, Nutrition, and Wellness* (2nd edition) (Boston: Allyn and Bacon, 1999); K. A. Ericsson, "Peak Performance and Age: An Examination of Peak Performance in Sports," in *Successful Aging: Perspective from the Behavioral Sciences,* ed. P. Baltes and M. Baltes (1990).

8. American College of Sports Medicine, "ACSM Position"; D. C. Neiman, *Fitness and Sports Medicine: A Health-Related Approach* (Palo Alto, Calif.: Bull Publishing, 1995).

9. National Institute on Aging, *Exercise Can Boost Cardiac Fitness in Conditioned and Out-of-Shape Older People* (Washington, D.C.: National Institutes of Health, August 2, 1996).

10. American College of Sports Medicine, "ACSM Position."

11. American College of Sports Medicine, "ACSM Position"; Ferrini and Ferrini, *Health in the Later Years.*

12. American College of Sports Medicine, "ACSM Position"; W. W. Campbell, M. C. Crim, G. E. Dallai, V. R. Young, and W. J. Evans, "Increased Protein Requirements in the Elderly: New Data and Retrospective Reassessments," *American Journal of Clinical Nutrition* 60 (1994): 167–175.

13. H. G. Koenig and D. G. Blazer, "Epidemiology of Geriatric Affective Disorders," in *Clinics in Geriatric Medicine,* ed. G. S. Alexopoulos (Philadelphia: Saunders, 1992): 235–252; T. C. Camacho, R. E. Roberts, N. B. Lazarus, G. A. Kaplan, and R. D. Cohen, "Physical Activity and Depression: Evidence from the Alameda County Study," *American Journal of Epidemiology* 134 (1991): 220–230; American College of Sports Medicine, "ACSM Position."

14. American College of Sports Medicine, "ACSM Position."

15. S. H. Boutcher and D. M. Landers, "The Effects of Vigorous Exercise on Anxiety, Heart Rate, and Alpha Activity of Runners and Nonrunners," *Psychophysiology* 25 (1988): 696–702; A. F. Kramer et al., "Exercise, Aging and Cognition: Healthy Body, Healthy Mind?" in *Human Factors Interventions for the Health Care of Older Adults,* ed. A. D. Fisk and W. Rogers (Hillsdale, N.J.: Erlbaum, 2001); T. A. Jones, N. Hawrylak, A. Y. Klintsova, and W. T. Greenough, "Brain Damage, Behavior Rehabilitation Recovery, and Brain Plasticity," *Mental Retardation and Developmental*

Disabilities Research Review 4 (1998): 231–237; J. Greenough, "Brain Development: Is It Over at Age 3?" Colloquium presentation at the University of New Mexico, Albuquerque (October 2000).

16. Dustman, Emmerson, and Shearer, "Physical Activity"; Kramer et al., "Exercise, Aging and Cognition"; R. D. Hill, A. Wahlin, B. Winblad, and L. Backman, "The Role of Demographic and Life Style Variables in Utilizing Cognitive Support for Episodic Remembering among Very Old Adults," *Journal of Gerontology: Psychological Sciences* 50B (1995): 219–227; T. Abourezk and T. Toole, "Effect of Task Complexity on the Relationship Between Physical Fitness and Reaction Time in Older Women," *Journal of Aging and Physical Activity* 3 (1995): 251–260; D. J. Bunce, A. Barrowclough, and I. Morris, "The Moderating Influence of Physical Fitness on Age Gradients in Vigilance and Serial Choice Responding," *Psychology and Aging* 11 (1996): 671–682; L. Clarkson-Smith and A. A. Hartley, "Structural Equation Models of Relationships Between Exercise and Cognitive Abilities," *Psychology and Aging* 5 (1990): 437–446; L. Clarkson-Smith and A. A. Hartley, "Relationships Between Physical Exercise," *Psychology and Aging* 4 (1989): 183–189.

17. Hill et al., "The Role of Demographic and Life Style Variables."

18. Kramer et al., "Exercise, Aging and Cognition."

19. A. F. Kramer et al., "Aging, Fitness and Neurocognitive Function," *Nature* 400 (July 29, 1999): 418–419; R. L. West, "An Application of Prefrontal Cortex Function Theory of Cognitive Aging," *Psychological Bulletin* 120 (1996): 272–292.

20. Kramer et al., "Exercise, Aging and Cognition."

21. A. F. Kramer, "Healthy Body, Healthy Mind," invited talk at the Healthy Minds Symposium at the 109th Annual Convention of the American Psychological Association, San Francisco, Calif. (August 2001).

Chapter Eleven. Effects of Stress, Depression, Illness, and Medications on Memory

1. R. M. Yerkes and J. D. Dodson, "The Relation of Strength of Stimulus to Rapidity of Habit-Formation," *Journal of Comparative and Neurological Psychology* 18 (1908): 459–482.

2. M. M. Berkun, "Performance Decrement Under Physiological Stress," *Human Factors* 6 (1964): 21–30.

3. N. W. Eysenck and M. G. Calvo, "Anxiety and Performance: The Processing Efficiency Theory," *Cognition and Emotion* 6 (1992): 409–434; J. A. Easterbrook, "The Effect of Emotion on Cue Utilization and the Organization of Behavior," *The Journal of Psychological Review* 66 (1959): 183–201.

4. D. de Quervan, B. Roozendaal, R. Nitsch, J. McGaugh, and C. Hock, "Acute Cortisone Administration Impairs Retrieval of Long-Term Declarative Memory in Humans," *Nature and Neuroscience* 3 (2000): 313–314; S. J. Lupien, C. J. Gillin, and R. O. Hauger, "Working Memory Is More Sensitive Than Declarative Memory to the

Acute Effects of Corticosteroids: A Dose Response Study in Humans," *Behavioral Neuroscience* 113 (1999): 420–430.

5. V. C. Long and R. van Stabel, "Effects of Exercise Training on Anxiety: A Meta-analysis," *Journal of Applied Sports Psychology* 7 (1995): 167–189; R. E. Thayer, "Mood and Behavior (Smoking and Sugar Snacking) Following Moderate Exercise: A Partial Test of Self-Regulation Theory," *Personality and Individual Differences* (1993): 97–104.

6. J. A. Yesavage, "Relaxation and Memory Training in 39 Elderly Patients," *American Journal of Psychiatry* 141 (1984): 778–781.

7. J. Fogler and L. Stern, *Improving Your Memory* (Baltimore, Md.: Johns Hopkins University Press, 1994).

8. L. P. Dick and D. Gallagher-Thompson, "Late-Life Depression," in *Psychological Treatment of Older Adults: An Introduction Text,* ed. N. Hersen and V. V. vanHassalt (New York: Plenum Press, 1996), 181–208; A. La Rue, C. Dessonville, and L. F. Jarvik, "Aging and Mental Disorders," in *Handbook of the Psychology of Aging,* ed. J. E. Birren and K. W. Schaie (New York: Van Nostrand Reinhold, 1985), 664–702; W. J. Hoyer, J. M. Rybash, and P. A. Roodin, *Adult Development and Aging* (4th edition) (Boston: McGraw-Hill, 1999); H. C. Ellis and P. W. Ashbrook, "Resource Allocation Model: The Effects of Depressed Mood States on Memory," in *Affect, Cognition, and Social Behavior: New Evidence and Integrative Attempts,* ed. K. Fiedler and J. Forgus (Toronto: Hogrefe, 1988): 25–43; P. T. Hertel and S. S. Rude, "Depressive Deficits in Memory: Focusing Attention Improves Subsequent Recall," *Journal of Experimental Psychology: General* 120 (1991): 301–309.

9. M. W. Bondi, A. W. Kaszniak, K. A. Bayles, and K. T. Vance, "Contributions of Frontal System Dysfunction to Memory and Perceptual Abilities in Parkinson's Disease," *Neuropsychology* 7 (1993): 89–102; F. Benton and K. D. McDaniel, "Memory Disorders," in *Neurology in Clinical Practice* (Vol. II), ed. W. G. Bradley, R. B. Daroff, G. M. Fenichel, and C. D. Marsden (Butterworth-Heinemann, 1991), 1389–1406.

10. "Brain Power Lost After Operation," *Albuquerque Journal* (February 8, 2001).

11. World Health Organization, "Health Care in the Elderly: Report of the Technical Group on the Use of Medications by the Elderly," *Drugs* 22 (1981): 279–294; J. J. Rybacki and J. W. Long, *The Essential Guide to Prescription Drugs* (New York: Harper Perennial, 2000).

Chapter Twelve. Enhancing Memory with Nutritional Supplements and Vitamins

1. T. Drummond, "Elixirs for Your Memory," *Time* (September 13, 1999), 60–61.

2. R. E. Mrak et al., "Aging-Associated Changes in Human Brain," *Journal of Neuropathology and Experimental Neurology* 56 (1997): 1269–1275.

3. R. Schiffer, "Can Memory Loss Be Stopped?" *Journal of Longevity* 5 (1999): 24–26.

4. J. Fogler and L. Stern, *Improving Your Memory: How to Remember What You're Starting to Forget* (Baltimore, Md.: Johns Hopkins University Press, 1994).

5. W. C. LaFrance, Jr., et al., "The Use of Herbal Alternative Medicines in Neuropsychiatry," *Journal of Neuropsychiatry Clinical Neuroscience* 12 (1998): 177–192; J. Quinn and J. Kaye, "Treatment of Alzheimer's Disease," *Mediguide to Geriatric Neurology* 2 (1998): 1–8; J. Klein, S. S. Chatterjee, and K. Loffelholz, "Phospholipid Breakdown and Choline Release Under Hypoxic Conditions: Inhibition by Bilobuide, a Constituent of Ginkgo Biloba," *Brain Research* 755 (1997): 347–350; Z. Kristofikova, "In Vitro Effect of Ginkgo Biloba Extract (Egb761) on the Activity of Presynaptic Cholinergic Nerve Terminals in Rat Hippocampus," *Dementia and Geriatric Cognitive Disorders* 8 (1997): 43–48; K. A. Wesnes, T. Ward, A. McGinty, and O. Petrini, "The Memory Enhancing Effects of a Ginkgo Biloba/Panax Ginseng Combination in Healthy Middle-Aged Volunteers," *Psychopharmacology* 152 (2000): 353–361; Fogler and Stern, *Improving Your Memory.*

6. S. Kanowski et al., "Proof of Efficacy of the Ginkgo Biloba Special Extract Egb 761 in Outpatients Suffering from Mild to Moderate Primary Degenerative Dementia of the Alzheimer Type or Multi-Infarct Dementia," *Pharmacole Psychiatry* 29 (1996): 47–51; P. L. LeBars et al., "A Placebo-Controlled, Double-Blind, Randomized Trial of an Extract of Ginkgo Biloba for Dementia," *Journal of the American Medical Association* 278 (1997): 1327–1332.

7. Wesnes, Ward, McGinty, and Petrini, "The Memory Enhancing Effects."

8. LaFrance et al., "The Use of Herbal Alternative Medicines."

9. T. H. Crook III and B. Adderly, *The Memory Cure* (New York: Simon and Schuster, 1998).

10. S. A. Cohen and W. E. Müller, "Age-Related Alterations of NMDA Receptor Properties in the Mouse Forebrain: Partial Restoration by Chronic Phosphatidylserine Treatment," *Brain Research* 584 (1992): 174–180; J. K. Blusztajn et al., "Phospholipids in Cellular Survival and Growth," in *Lecithin: Technological, Biological, and Therapeutic Aspects,* ed. I. Hanin and G. B. Ansell (New York: Plenum Press, 1987), 85–94; G. Toffano, "The Therapeutic Value of Phosphatidylserine Effect in the Aging Brain," in *Lecithin: Technological, Biological, and Therapeutic Aspects,* ed. I. Hanin and G. B. Ansell (New York: Plenum Press, 1987), 85–94.

11. T. Cenacchi et al., "Cognitive Decline in the Elderly: A Double-Blind, Placebo-Controlled Multicenter Study on Efficacy of Phosphatidylserine Administration," *Aging Clinical Experimental Research* 5 (1992): 123–133; T. H. Crook et al., "Effects of Phosphatidylserine in Age-Associated Memory Impairment," *Neurology* 41 (1991): 644–649; T. H. Crook, W. Petrie, C. Wells, and D. C. Massari, "Effects of Phosphatidylserine in Alzheimer's Disease," *Psychopharmacology Bulletin* 28 (1992): 61–65.

12. Crook and Adderly, *The Memory Cure,* p. 82.

13. Crook et al., "Effects of Phosphatidylserine in Age-Associated Memory Impair-

ment"; Cenacchi et al., "Cognitive Decline in the Elderly"; Crook and Adderly, *The Memory Cure*.

14. Crook et al., "Effects of Phosphatidylserine in Alzheimer's Disease."

15. Crook and Adderly, *The Memory Cure;* D. S. Khalsa, "Integrated Medicine and Prevention and Reversal of Memory Loss," *Alternative Therapies in Health and Medicine,* 4 (1998): 38–43.

16. P. A. Spiers et al., "Citicholine Improves Verbal Memory in Aging," *Archives of Neurology* 53 (1996): 441–448; J. H. Growdon, "Use of Phosphatidylcholine in Brain Diseases: An Overview," in *Lecithin: Technological, Biological, and Therapeutic Aspects,* ed. I. Hanin and G. B. Ansell (New York: Plenum Press, 1987), 85–94.

17. Growdon, "Use of Phosphatidylcholine"; S. L. Ladd and S. S. Sommer, "*Phosphatidylcholine Enhances Short-Term Memory in Slow Learners,*" paper presented at the 95th Annual Meeting of the American Psychological Association, Boston, Mass. (August 1990).

18. Spiers et al., "Citicholine Improves Verbal Memory."

19. Spiers et al., "Citicholine Improves Verbal Memory"; P. E. Gold, L. Cahill, and G. L. Wenk, "*Gingko Biloba:* A Cognitive Enhancer?" *Psychological Science in the Public Interest* (2002): 2–11.

20. R. Schiffer, "Can Memory Loss Be Stopped?" *Journal of Longevity* 5 (1999): 24–26.

21. R. Balestreri, L. Fortuna, and F. Astengo, "A Double-Blind Placebo Controlled Evaluation of the Safety and Efficacy of Vinpocetine in the Treatment of Patients with Chronic Vascular Senile Cerebral Dysfunction," *Journal of the American Geriatric Society* 35 (1987): 425–430; I. Hindmarch et al., "Efficacy and Tolerance of Vinpocetine in Ambulant Patients Suffering From Mild to Moderate Organic Psychosyndromes," *International Clinical Psychopharmacology* 6 (1991): 31–43.

22. Balestreri et al., "A Double-Blind Placebo Controlled Evaluation"; Hindmarch et al., "Efficacy and Tolerance of Vinpocetine."

23. A. Imperato, M. T. Ramacci, and L. Angelucci, "Acetyl-L-Carnitine Enhances Acetylcholine Release in the Stratum and Hippocampus of Awake Freely Moving Rats," *Neuroscience Letters* 107 (1989): 251–255; L. Angelucci et al., "Nerve Growth Factor Binding in Aged Rats' CNS: Effect of Acetyl-L-Carnitine," *Journal of Neuroscience Research* 20 (1988): 491–496; A. L. Markowska et al., "Acetyl-L-Carnitine 1: Effects on Mortality, Pathology and Sensory-Motor Performance in Aging Rats," *Neurobiology of Aging* 11 (1990): 491–498; O. Ghirardi et al., "Long-Term Acetyl-L-Carnitine Preserves Spatial Learning in the Senescent Rat," *Progress in Neuropsychopharmacological and Biological Psychiatry* 13 (1989): 237–245; C. A. Barnes et al., "Acetyl-L-Carnitine 1: Effects on Learning and Memory Performance of Aged Rats in Simple and Complex Mazes," *Neurobiology of Aging* 11 (1990): 499–506.

24. A. Spagnoli, "Long-Term Acetyl-L-Carnitine Treatment in Alzheimer's Disease," *Neurology* 41 (1991): 1726–1732.

25. M. Juno et al., "A Controlled Trial of Selegiline, Alpha-Tocopherol, or Both as Treat-

ment for Alzheimer's Disease," *New England Journal of Medicine* 336 (1997): 1216–1222.

26. M. R. Foy, V. W. Henderson, T. W. Berger, and R. F. Thompson, "Estrogen and Neural Plasticity," *Current Directions in Psychological Science* 9 (2000): 148–152; M. M. Costa et al., "Estrogen Replacement Therapy and Cognitive Decline in Memory-Impaired Post-Menopausal Women," *Biological Psychiatry* 46 (1999): 182–188.

27. Foy, Henderson, Berger, and Thompson, "Estrogen and Neural Plasticity"; S. M. Philips and B. B. Sherwin, "Effects of Estrogen on Memory Function in Surgically Menopausal Women," *Psychoneuroendocrinology* 17 (1992): 485–495; V. W. Henderson, *Hormone Therapy and the Brain: A Clinical Perspective on the Role of Estrogen* (New York: Pantheon, 2000).

28. E. Hirshman et al., "The Effect of Dehydroepiandrosterone (DHEA) on Recognition Memory Decision Processes and Discrimination in Postmenopausal Women," *Psychonomic Bulletin and Review* 10 (2003): 125–134; O. T. Wolf et al., "Effects of a Two-Week Physiological Dehydroepiandrosterone Substitution on Cognitive Performance and Well-Being in Healthy Elderly Women and Men," *Journal of Clinical Endocrinology and Metabolism* 82 (1997): 2363.

29. M. A. McDaniel, S. F. Maier, and G. O. Einstein, "'Brain-Specific Nutrients': A Memory Cure?" *Psychological Science in the Public Interest* 3 (2002): 12–38.

30. L. Israel, M. Melac, D. Milinkevatch, and G. Dubos, "Drug Therapy and Memory Training Programs: A Double-Blind Randomized Trial of General Practice Patients with Age-Associated Memory Impairment," *International Psychogeriatrics* 6 (1994): 155–170; R. Goldman, R. Katz, and T. W. Berger, *Brain Fitness* (New York: Doubleday, 1999).

Chapter Thirteen. Alzheimer's Disease

Epigraph: E. Morris, *Dutch: A Memoir of Ronald Reagan* (New York: Random House, 1999).

1. R. Katzman and C. Kawas, "The Epidemiology of Dementia and Alzheimer's Disease," in *Alzheimer's Disease,* ed. R. D. Terry, R. Katzman, and K. L. Bick (New York: Raven, 1994), 105–122.

2. W. J. Hoyer, J. M. Rybash, and P. A. Roodin, *Adult Development and Aging* (4th edition) (Boston: McGraw-Hill, 1999).

3. National Institute on Aging, "Progress Report on Alzheimer's Disease 1999," National Institute on Aging (National Institutes of Health), *www.alzheimer's.org/pubs/prog99.htm* (1999).

4. B. Reisberg, S. H. Ferris, M. J. DeLeon, and T. Crook, "The Global Deterioration Scale for Assessment of Primary Degenerative Dementia," *American Journal of Psychiatry* 139 (1982): 1136–1139.

5. D. McGowin, *Living in the Labyrinth: A Personal Journey Through Alzheimer's Disease* (New York: Delacorte Press, 1993).

6. M. Reagan, "My Father's Battle with Alzheimer's," *Newsweek,* January 31, 2000, p. 55.

7. National Institute on Aging, "Progress Report on Alzheimer's Disease 1999."

8. American Psychiatric Association, *Diagnostic and Statistical Manual of Mental Disorders* (4th edition, text revision) (Washington, D.C.: American Psychiatric Press, 2000).

9. G. P. Lee and D. W. Loring, "Acute Confusional States in Toxic and Metabolic Disorders," in *Neuropsychology of Alzheimer's Disease and Other Dementias,* ed. R. W. Parks, R. F. Zec, and R. S. Wilson (New York: Oxford, 1993), 375–415.

10. M. F. Folstein, S. E. Folstein, and P. R. McHuch, "Mini-Mental State: A Practical Method for Grading the Cognitive State of Patients for the Clinician," *Journal of Psychiatric Research* 12(3) (1975): 189–198.

11. P. R. Soloman and W. W. Pendlebury, "Recognition of Alzheimer's Disease: The 7 Minute Screen," *Family Medicine* 30 (1998): 265–271.

12. R. J. Killiany et al., "Use of Structural Magnetic Resonance Imagery to Predict Who Will Get Alzheimer's Disease," *Annals of Neurology* 47 (2000): 430.

13. Alzheimer's Association Web site, "Treating Cognitive Symptoms," *www.alz.org* (2001).

14. T. Hanninen et al., "A Follow-Up Study of Age-Associated Memory Impairment: Neuropsychological Predictors of Dementia," *Journal of the American Geriatric Society* 43 (1995): 1007–1015.

15. J. L. Cummings, H. V. Vinters, G. M. Cole, and Z. S. Khachaturian, "Alzheimer's Disease: Etiologies, Pathophysiology, Cognitive Reserve, and Treatment Opportunities," *Neurology* 51 (1998): S2–S17; National Institute on Aging, "Progress Report on Alzheimer's Disease 2000," National Institute on Aging (National Institutes of Health), *www.alzheimer's.org/pubs/prog00.htm* (2000); D. Woodruff-Pak, *The Neuropsychology of Aging* (Oxford, UK: Blackwell, 1997).

16. Cummings et al., "Alzheimer's Disease"; National Institute on Aging, "Progress Report on Alzheimer's Disease 1999"; Woodruff-Pak, *The Neuropsychology of Aging.*

17. Cummings et al., "Alzheimer's Disease"; E. G. Zurad, "New Treatments for Alzheimer's Disease: A Review," *Drug Benefit Trends* 13 (2001): 27–40.

18. National Institute on Aging, "Progress Report on Alzheimer's Disease 1999"; Cummings et al., "Alzheimer's Disease."

19. Cummings et al., "Alzheimer's Disease"; National Institute on Aging, "Progress Report on Alzheimer's Disease 1999."

20. I. Raiha, J. Kaprio, M. Koskenvuo, T. Rajala, and L. Sourander, "Alzheimer's Disease in Finnish Twins," *Lancet* 347 (1996): 573–578.

21. Katzman and Kawas, "The Epidemiology of Dementia and Alzheimer's Disease."

22. National Institute on Aging, "Progress Report on Alzheimer's Disease 1999."

23. D. A. Snowdon et al., "Linguistic Ability in Early Life and Cognitive Function and Alzheimer's Disease in Late Life: Findings from the Nun Study," *Journal of the American Medical Association* 275 (1996): 528–532; National Institute on Aging, "Progress Report on Alzheimer's Disease 1999."

24. Cummings et al., "Alzheimer's Disease"; W. F. Stewart, C. Kawas, M. Corrada, and E. J. Metter, "Risk of Alzheimer's Disease and Duration of NSAID Use," *Neurology* 48 (1997): 626–632; J. Stevenson, "More Evidence Links NSAIDs, Estrogen with Reduced Alzheimer's Risk," *Journal of the American Medical Association* 275 (1996): 1389.

25. Cummings et al., "Alzheimer's Disease."

26. Cummings et al., "Alzheimer's Disease"; R. Katzman, "Education and the Prevalence of Alzheimer's Disease," *Neurology* 43 (1993): 13–20.

27. R. P. Friedland et al., "Patients with Alzheimer's Disease Have Reduced Activities in Midlife Compared with Healthy Control-Group Members," *Proceedings of the National Academy of Science* 98 (2001): 3440–3445.

28. R. S. Wilson et al., "Participation in Cognitively Stimulating Activities and Risk of Incident Alzheimer's Disease," *Journal of the American Medical Association*, 287 (2002): 742–748; D. F. Hultsch, C. Hertzog, B. J. Small, and R. A. Dixon, "Use It or Lose It: Engaged Lifestyle as a Buffer of Cognitive Decline in Aging," *Psychology and Aging* 14 (1999): 245–263.

29. R. S. Wilson and D. A. Bennett, "Cognitive Activity and Risk of Alzheimer's Disease," *Current Directions in Psychological Science* 12 (2003): 87–90.

30. M. Tang et al., "Effect of Estrogen During Menopause on Risk and Age at Onset of Alzheimer's Disease," *Lancet* 348 (1996): 429–432; C. Kawas et al., "Treating Alzheimer's Disease: Today and Tomorrow," *Patient Care* (1996): 62–83; M. R. Foy, V. W. Henderson, T. W. Berger, and R. F. Thompson, "Estrogen and Neural Plasticity," *Current Directions in Psychological Science* 9 (2000): 148–152; R. A. Mulnard et al., "Estrogen Replacement Therapy for Treatment of Mild to Moderate Alzheimer Disease: A Randomized Controlled Trial," *Journal of the American Medical Association* 283(8) (2000): 1007–1015.

31. J. Travis, "Statins Take on the Brain," *Science News* 159 (2001): 92–93.

32. D. Snowdon, *Aging with Grace: What the Nun Study Teaches Us About Leading Longer, Healthier, and More Meaningful Lives* (New York: Bantam, 2001), pp. 98–99.

33. P. Satz, "Brain Reserve Capacity on Symptom Onset After Brain Injury: A Formulation and Review of Evidence for Threshold Theory," *Neuropsychology* 7 (1993): 273–295.

34. R. Katzman et al., "Clinical Pathological and Neurochemical Changes in Dementia: A Subgroup with Preserved Mental Status and Numerous Neocortical Plaques," *Annals of Neurology* 23 (1988): 138–144.

35. Cummings et al., "Alzheimer's Disease"; J. W. Langston and C. M. Tanner, "Etiology of Parkinson's Disease," in *Handbook of Parkinson's Disease* (2nd edition), ed. W. C. Koller (New York: Marcel Dekker, 1992), 369–381.

36. R. Katzman, "Education and the Prevalence"; P. Satz, "Brain Reserve Capacity"; Cummings et al., "Alzheimer's Disease"; D. A. Snowdon et al., "Linguistic Ability in Early Life," *Journal of the American Medical Association* 275 (1996): 528–532; D. Snowdon, *Aging with Grace.*

37. Friedland et al., "Patients with Alzheimer's Disease,"; J. Greenough, "Brain Development: Is It Over at Age 3?" colloquium presentation at the University of New Mexico, Albuquerque, New Mexico (September 2000); C. Rampon, Y. P. Tang, J. Goodhouse, E. Shimizu, M. Kyin, J. Z. Tsien, "Enrichment Induces Structural Changes and Recovery from Nonspatial Memory Deficits in CA1 NMDAR1-Knockout Mice," *Nature Neuroscience* 3 (2000): 238–244.

38. D. Schenk et al., "Immunization with Amyloid-ß Attenuates Alzheimer-Disease-Like Pathology in the PDAPP Mouse," *Nature* 400(6740) (1999): 173–177; H. L. Weiner et al., "Nasal Administration of Amyloid-ß Peptide Decreases Cerebral Amyloid Burden in a Mouse Model of Alzheimer's Disease," *Annals of Neurology* 48(4) (2000): 567–579; D. Steinberg, "Testing Potential Alzheimer's Vaccines," *The Scientist* 16 (2002): 23–24.

39. Alzheimer's Association Web site, "Treating Cognitive Symptoms," *www.alz.org* (2001).

40. Alzheimer's Association Web site; E. R. Peskind, "Pharmacologic Approaches to Cognitive Deficits in Alzheimer's Disease," *The Journal of Clinical Psychiatry* 59(Suppl. 9) (1998): 22–27; M. W. Jann, "Rivastigmine, a New-Generation Cholinesterase Inhibitor for the Treatment of Alzheimer's Disease," *Pharmacotherapy* 20 (2000): 1–12; Alzheimer's Association Web site, "Treating Cognitive Symptoms," *www.alz.org* 2001.; O. L. Lopez et al., "Cholinesterase Inhibitor Treatment Alters the Natural History of Alzheimer's Disease," *Journal of Neurology, Neurosurgery, and Psychiatry* 72 (2002): 310–314.

41. C. J. Camp, J. W. Foss, A. B. Stevens, and A. M. O'Hanlon, "Improving Prospective Memory Task Performance in Persons with Alzheimer's Disease," in *Prospective Memory: Theory and Applications,* ed. M. Brandimonte, G. O. Einstein, and M. A. McDaniel (Mahwah, N.J.: Erlbaum, 1996), 351–368; M. A. McDaniel and M. E. J. Masson, "Altering Memory Representation Through Retrieval," *Journal of Experimental Psychology: Learning, Memory, & Cognition* 11 (1985): 371–385.

42. Camp, Foss, Stevens, and O'Hanlon, "Improving Prospective Memory Task Performance."

43. C. J. Camp, J. W. Foss, A. M. O'Hanlon, and A. B. Stevens, "Memory Interventions for Persons with Dementia," *Applied Cognitive Psychology* 10 (1996): 193–210.

44. S. H. Zarit, P. A. Todd, and J. M. Zarit, "Subjective Burden of Husbands and Wives as Caregivers: A Longitudinal Study," *The Gerontologist* 26 (1986): 260–266; N. L. Mace and P. V. Rabins, *The 36-Hour Day: A Family Guide to Caring for Persons with Alzheimer's Disease, Related Dementing Illnesses, and Memory Loss in Later Life* (Baltimore, Md.: Johns Hopkins University Press, 2001).

45. C. H. Hirsch, H. D. Davies, F. Boatwright, and G. Ochango, "Effects of a Nursing-Home Respite Admission on Veterans with Advanced Dementia," *The Gerontologist* 33 (1993): 523–528.

46. H. Tuokko, "Psychosocial Evaluation and Management of the Alzheimer's Patient," in *Neuropsychology of Alzheimer's Disease and Other Dementias,* ed. R. W. Parks, R. F. Zec, and R. S. Wilson (New York: Oxford, 1993), 565–588.

Index